An Introduction to Knowledge Engineering

An Introduction to Knowledge Engineering

Peter Smith

School of Computing and Information Systems
University of Sunderland

INTERNATIONAL THOMSON COMPUTER PRESS

I ⓣ P   An International Thomson Publishing Company

London • Bonn • Boston • Johannesburg • Madrid • Melbourne • Mexico City • New York • Paris
Singapore • Tokyo • Toronto • Albany, NY • Belmont, CA • Cincinnati, OH • Detroit, MI

An Introduction to Knowledge Engineering
Copyright © 1996 International Thomson Computer Press

I (T) P   A division of International Thomson Publishing Inc.
The ITP logo is a trademark under licence.

For more information, contact:

International Thomson Computer Press
Berkshire House
168–173 High Holborn
London WC1V 7AA
UK

International Thomson Computer Press
20 Park Plaza
Suite 1001
Boston, MA 02116
USA

Imprints of International Thomson Publishing

International Thomson Publishing GmbH
Königswinterer Straße 418
53227 Bonn
Germany

International Thomson Publishing Asia
221 Henderson Road #05-10
Henderson Building
Singapore

Thomas Nelson Australia
102 Dodds Street
South Melbourne, 3205
Victoria
Australia

International Thomson Publishing Japan
Hirakawacho Kyowa Building, 3F
2-2-1 Hirakawacho
Chiyoda-ku, 102 Tokyo
Japan

Nelson Canada
1120 Birchmount Road
Scarborough, Ontario
Canada M1K 5G4

International Thomson Editores
Campos Eliseos 385, Piso 7
Col. Polenco
11560 Mexico D.F. Mexico

International Thomson Publishing South Africa
PO Box 2459
Halfway House
1685 South Africa

International Thomson Publishing France
1, rue St. Georges
75009 Paris
France

British Library Cataloguing-in-Publication Data
A catalogue record for this book is available from the British Library

Library of Congress Cataloging-in-Publication Data
A catalog record for this book is available from the Library of Congress

First printed 1996
Typeset by Hodgson Williams Associates, Tunbridge Wells and Cambridge
Printed in the UK by The Alden Press, Oxford

ISBN 1-85032-277-5

Commissioning Editor Samantha Whittaker

Contents

Acknowledgements

I would like to express my sincere thanks to the following:

Special thanks to Colin Hardy, Ali Jawad, Dave Leonard and C Lin for providing the basis for the case study material.

British Gas plc for permission to use the forecasting case study.

Finn Gronskov and Prolog Development Center for material on ESTA.

Intelligent Environments for use of CRYSTAL material.

Paul Ross, Mark Lansbury, Dimitrios Markakis, Stephen Ng, Jason Kuo, Shi-Ming Huang, Xin Chen, Helen Edwards and Alan Gillies for their important contributions.

Dr Theodoulidis of UMIST for his invaluable comments and encouragement throughout the project; Dave Hatter for starting the ball rolling and Samantha Whittaker and Nikki Vaughan for seeing it through; Simon Kendal for providing useful comments and checking the draft.

And finally, but most importantly to Marie, Ashleigh, David and Laura for putting up with me while I sat in the corner for endless hours tapping away at a keyboard.

Peter Smith
1995

Preface

This book is about knowledge engineering; the development of knowledge-based systems (KBS).

KBS are complex pieces of software which attempt to encapsulate human knowledge within a computer system. They have much in common with traditional software products and suffer from the same difficulties and problems. In addition, however, the development of a KBS poses a new, and very different, set of challenges to the knowledge engineer.

It is the aim of this book to provide a practical introduction to the topic of knowledge engineering. This is achieved by covering all of the important aspects of the discipline in a practical manner.

Chapter 1 provides an introduction to the subject and answers the question 'What is knowledge engineering?'. Chapter 2 focuses upon the subject of KBS, while Chapter 3 explains the life cycle which must be followed when developing a KBS. Chapter 4 provides detailed coverage of knowledge acquisition, which is often seen as the most important stage in the knowledge-engineering process (and often described as a 'bottleneck'). Chapter 5 covers knowledge representation, while Chapter 6 presents KBS implementation in a programming language and two expert system shells. Chapter 7 presents a series of practical lessons and considerations. Finally Chapter 8 provides coverage of the management issues which are important in knowledge engineering.

A series of four practical case studies are introduced in Chapter 2. These are then referred to throughout the book, in order to maintain a practical bias. The four case studies include a quality-control system, a forecasting system, a monitoring system and an integrated system (which integrates KBS technology with traditional information systems). These case studies are based upon real KBS development projects in which the author has been involved.

Chapter 1

What is knowledge engineering?

OBJECTIVES

In this chapter you will learn:

- ❏ to distinguish between data, information and knowledge;
- ❏ what is meant by the term **engineer**;
- ❏ what is meant by the term **knowledge engineer**;
- ❏ to recognize the skills of a knowledge engineer;
- ❏ a little about knowledge engineering around the world.

1.1 Introduction

This book is about knowledge engineering. It is about the skills needed to perform a particular job, that of the knowledge engineer. But what do we mean by **knowledge engineering**?

The term knowledge engineering has emerged quite recently and is now commonly used to describe the process of knowledge-based-system (KBS) development in any field, whether it be in the public or the private sector, in commerce or in industry. In particular, the term is now taken to indicate a professional approach to the development of knowledge-based systems.

But what exactly do we mean when we use expressions like engineering, knowledge-based systems and knowledge engineering? And perhaps more importantly, what do people around the world really understand when we use the term 'knowledge engineer'? What skills, personality attributes and qualifications should a knowledge engineer have?

This chapter addresses the above questions and aims to give the reader a feel for the skills which can be expected of a knowledge engineer.

Concepts

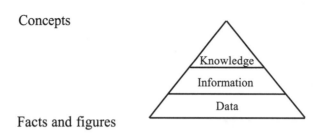

Facts and figures

Figure 1.1   *The knowledge triangle.*

1.2 Data, information, knowledge and KBS

The terms data, knowledge and information are often used interchangeably. This is because the differences between the three concepts can be difficult to explain. It is often difficult to distinguish the point at which data becomes information, and at which information becomes knowledge.

As we move from data to information and from information to knowledge, we are adding value at each stage. Information is of much more use than data, and knowledge is much more powerful and of more use than information. This can be shown by the knowledge triangle in Figure 1.1. As we move towards the apex of the triangle we are dealing with less tangible, but much more powerful, concepts.

Data refers to isolated facts such as individual measurements. Items of data have no meaning on their own; they do not signify anything and are useless unless placed in some sort of context. The following are pieces of data:

10
1.5672
mary
jones
red
1,000,000

Information also consists of symbols such as text or numbers, but this time there is some meaning associated with the symbols. Because of this added meaning, the information now has some use or value. The following are examples of information:

10°C
$1,000,000
Mary Jones, New Street, Birmingham, UK
the big red ball

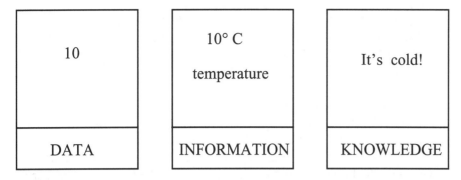

Figure 1.2 *Data, information and knowledge.*

Knowledge consists of symbols, the relationships between them and rules or procedures for manipulating them. It adds context to the information, providing greater meaning and is therefore of much greater use and value. New knowledge can be derived, or inferred, from the rules. Knowledge is dynamic and changes with time. Knowledge does not stand still; it is constantly being added to and develops as we discover new things.

Consider the following example (Figure 1.2). As a piece of data the number '10' does not convey very much. It is simply a number without any context. The item of information 'the temperature is 10°C' adds some meaning to the data. It is data collected and organized for a purpose.

The knowledge that 'if the temperature is 10°C it feels cold' is more significant. This tells us something that we know, perhaps through memory and experience. We could use this knowledge as the basis for making decisions about which clothes to wear, or whether to go out or not.

Knowledge is gained by experience. It signifies that the person who has the knowledge has a deep understanding of one or more concepts. Knowledge can be peculiar to a particular person. They may have accumulated that knowledge over time, and may not even be able to explain it. They simply feel that they 'know' something but find if difficult to express that knowledge in everyday words and phrases.

Because of its conceptual nature, it is not only difficult to express knowledge; it may also be difficult to write knowledge down in an English-like form. This, however, is the job of a knowledge engineer and the subject of this book.

A knowledge engineer is someone who has the complex task of:

- **Extracting knowledge from people** – this knowledge may be something that is second nature to them. They may not know how to express it. Even if they can express it and explain it to the knowledge engineer, they may not wish to do so, as they may fear that he/she is going to replace them with a computer system.

- **Representing it in some form** – having collected the knowledge it is then necessary to express it in terms of words, phrases, diagrams, etc. That is, some sort of model of the knowledge must be constructed by the knowledge engineer.
- **Including it in a computer program which makes use of that knowledge** – this program is the knowledge-based system, which has encapsulated within it human knowledge.
- **Validating the software system which has been produced** – this is making sure that the software does match the knowledge which has been put into it. That is, it is necessary to check that the system acts in the same way that the human would; that it is modelling the knowledge properly.

A KBS is a computer system which embodies knowledge about a specific problem domain and can thus be used to apply this knowledge to solve problems from that problem domain. A KBS has human knowledge in it, and that knowledge can then be used in the same way that a human would apply knowledge for problem solving. The knowledge may have come from one person or a group of people. It may also have been extracted from other knowledge sources, such as books and other documents.

Many KBS are often termed **expert systems**, as they behave in a similar manner to a human expert when solving a problem. In fact, the terms KBS and expert system are often used interchangeably. This isn't quite right, as there are many KBS which do contain **knowledge**, but are not really expert systems. That is, many systems which are called a KBS are software systems with some kind of knowledge built in, such as intelligent database systems. Expert systems, on the other hand, are systems which have been developed to apply expertise in order to solve problems.

The subject of KBS and the applications of KBS are discussed in full in the next chapter.

1.3 Engineering, software engineering and knowledge engineering

1.3.1 Engineering

Engineering is one of the world's oldest professions. Proof of this lies in the many and varied examples of civil engineering, some of which are quite spectacular. Some of the best known are the pyramids of ancient Egypt, the Taj Mahal, the Eiffel Tower and, in the UK, Buckingham Palace and Big Ben.

An engineer is a professional who makes a product of some form. The product which is made varies depending upon the particular branch of engineering. However, there are some common factors which apply to all branches of engineering, as shown in Table 1.1.

Table 1.1 *Attributes of an engineer.*

Engineers are professionals
Engineers have undergone training
Engineers apply quality control procedures
Engineers take pride in their work
Engineers are bound by a professional code of conduct
Engineers use methods
Engineers use tools
Engineers adhere to standards
Engineers adhere to rules, regulations and legal requirements
Engineers strive to do their best
Engineers constantly update their knowledge and skills
Engineers take account of human, financial, environmental and other constraints
Engineers plan and manage their projects

The oldest of the engineering disciplines is that of **civil engineering**, which was developed from techniques used in the ancient world and is concerned with the design, site preparation and construction of structures and facilities. Civil engineers design and build roads, houses and factories.

Traces of engineering go back as far as 2000 BC. However, the development of engineering as a well-defined profession dates back to the period 1747–1872, when in 1747 the first school of engineering, L'Ecole des Ponts et Chaussées (The School of Bridges and Highways), was formed in Paris.

Earlier than this practitioners of engineering were typically self-taught or trained by apprenticeship. No special methods or techniques were followed, and products would often fail to live up to expectations.

Some common engineering disciplines are:

- mechanical engineering
- communication engineering
- electrical engineering
- genetic engineering
- chemical engineering

1.3.2 Software engineering

Software engineering is the branch of computing which is closest to knowledge engineering. Indeed it could be said that knowledge engineering is simply a subset of software engineering as a KBS is, after all, a piece of software.

Over the last few decades the use of the term 'software engineering' has largely replaced the term 'programming' as the word which is used to describe someone who produces computer software. This is with the intention of implying a much more professional and rigorous approach to the craft of software production.

The expression 'software engineering' was first used in the 1960s in a conscious attempt to respond to the lack of discipline in programming. Up until that point, most programmers had relied on their intuition to solve programming problems. By this time, though, the larger scale and the growing complexity of software meant that a new approach was needed.

Managers, computer users and all sorts of people were demanding, and indeed expecting, a lot more from the computer. They had been given a taste of what the computer could do for them and wanted more. At the same time, the programmers and their bosses were becoming more imaginative and adventurous. Thus much larger and more complex pieces of software were being developed.

Large operating systems for the new generations of computers were being developed. However, no one really understood the best way to approach the development of such complex software products. Nor did they have any tools which could help them put together these pieces of software. As program size grew, so complexity increased and the need to manage that complexity increased. In the absence of appropriate tools and methods to manage complexity, the number of errors began to accelerate and the cost of fixing those errors, which is referred to as maintenance, increased out of control (Figure 1.3).

This was the point at which real problems began to arise:

- Software projects were taking a lot longer to finish than originally envisaged.
- Software was costing a lot more to develop than initially imagined.

Cost of Maintenance

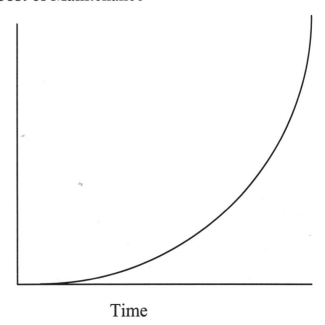

Time

Figure 1.3 *The software crisis.*

- Software was being delivered to the customer only to fail (i.e. produce incorrect results).
- Software projects were being abandoned because of disastrous failures.

In summary, software failures were costing an unacceptable amount of money and it was this which forced the software development community to rethink their working practices.

Let's turn away from the field of software development for a moment and consider parallels in civil engineering.

Consider a gang of labourers who have had no training in bricklaying, plumbing, electrical work or any of the activities needed to build a house. This gang of labourers have, however, managed to fumble their way through building a few small houses. The houses don't look great and may not be very comfortable – but at least they don't fall down and you can live in them. So the leader of the gang is confident that they can build houses and feels that the time is right to attempt a more ambitious project.

On Monday morning, without any warning, he informs the gang that they are going to build a skyscraper. The gang start piling bricks on top of each other, without any real thought about what they are doing. Soon they are running into real difficulties as the skyscraper begins to wobble about and ultimately it crashes to the ground!

This is, of course, an example of how not to go about constructing a building (or indeed anything else). A true engineer (because it is engineering that we discussing) would surely approach the problem in a much more systematic and professional manner. He/she would use methods, techniques, standards and tools to aid in the production process.

The type of disaster described above is, however, the very situation which had arisen in the software industry. A number of largely untrained (or, at the best, self-trained) programmers would attempt to throw together a very large and complex piece of software without following any rules or guidelines or attempting to apply any real methods. They would not plan out their work to any great extent, nor would they make any real estimate of the consequences of their actions. What is being described is, of course, a recipe for disaster – and that is exactly what happened in a large number of instances. It is this scenario that leads us to the emergence of the concept of software engineering.

So around the end of the 1960s, the term 'software engineering' was proposed as a direct result of the software crisis, and seen as the only way of avoiding further disasters in the long term. The idea behind software engineering is really quite simple. Software is an artefact, a product, which is constructed just as you might construct a plane, a car, a skyscraper, a bridge or a washing machine.

Software is, of course, much less tangible than most products. You cannot hit software with a hammer, nor can you measure it with a ruler or microm-eter or adjust it with a screwdriver. Nevertheless, it is still a product; an item which people make. The idea behind software engineering is then that software should be engineered, in as professional a manner as a civil engineer might construct a bridge or a motor engineer might construct a car.

Software engineering may be defined as 'the application of traditional engineering approaches to the development of software.'

In particular, software engineering implies the use of tools, techniques and methods for the production of quality software. That is, software engineers must approach the construction of their product, software, in a professional manner. Their work should, therefore, involve adherence to standards, quality control procedures and professional practices. Software production should be carefully managed from the highest level, and each software engineer should be clear of their own responsibilities, and take pride in their work.

All of this is, of course, a very fine ideal. At the time that these ideas were proposed they certainly seemed a long way from reality. Everyone agreed that it would be wonderful if software engineers could adhere to such practices; few people had the vision to imagine how this might be achieved.

It was difficult (and still is) to imagine or predict the answer to the following questions:

- How do you measure the quality of software?
- How can you provide tools to aid in software construction?
- How can you plan complex software projects?
- How can you devise methods to aid in software design?

The past two decades has seen much research effort go into answering the above important questions from the field of software engineering. We have undoubtedly come a long way in that period and a lot of methods, tools and techniques have arisen.

Some of these methods and tools are now in wide usage in business and commerce; others are still very much at the research stage. One thing is, however, without question – software development has been raised from what was a somewhat haphazard cottage industry into a professional discipline. Whether it is worthy of the title 'software engineering' is still a matter for some debate, but the term is now in common usage.

The concept of professionalism is at the very heart of software engineering. In the UK, members of computing's professional body, the British Computer Society (BCS), can now apply for chartered engineer status, which signifies their recognition as a professional engineer. The BCS is the 'society for information systems engineering', signifying the importance of taking a professional engineering approach to the design of information systems.

Some people, including traditional engineers in other disciplines, would, however, argue that computing is still too immature a discipline to warrant being termed 'engineering' and that there are still too few methods, tools, techniques and quality assurance procedures being applied in industry and commerce.

The software engineering movement, then, can be described as an attempt to impose a disciplined, engineering approach to the production of computer software. Implicit in the use of the word 'engineering' is the idea of a rigorous, professional, methodical and structured approach to software development. Engineers use formal theories and apply tried and tested tools and methodologies to aid them in their work: software engineering gave voice to a desire to see these conditions replicated in the world of programming.

The goals of software engineering can additionally be summed up in the assertion that the end product, i.e. the software, should be reliable, efficient, usable, economical and maintainable.

1.3.3 Knowledge engineering

In a similar manner, knowledge engineering is software engineering applied to the design of KBS.

The coining of the phrase 'knowledge engineering' has been attributed to various sources: Donald A. Michie is sometimes accredited with the first use of the term in 1972, although others assign the same honour to Edward A. Feigenbaum in 1977. Whoever originated the phrase, it is safe to say that since it appeared in the 1970s, there have been those working in the field who have been content, and even proud, to name themselves 'knowledge engineers', that is, practitioners of knowledge engineering.

Knowledge engineering is a term (like many in computing) that can be, and often is, used in a number of different ways. In its widest (and today perhaps the most widely accepted) sense, knowledge engineering can be thought of as the process of developing knowledge-based systems.

Knowledge engineering includes:

- acquiring from experts the knowledge that is to be used in the system (a process known as knowledge acquisition);
- choosing an appropriate method of representing the knowledge in a symbolic form, known as knowledge representation;
- software design;
- implementation in an appropriate computer language.

Like software engineering, knowledge engineering is the application of rigorous software engineering approaches to the development of knowledge-based systems. But do knowledge engineers deserve the title 'engineer'? Are they really applying professional, rigorous approaches to the development of an engineering product? Are they using recognized techniques to ensure quality? Are they working to standards? Indeed, do such standards exist? Are the products they produce really of high quality? In particular, is the software which they produce reliable?

In the early days, there were very few tools and methods applicable to the work of a knowledge engineer, since the technology itself was still in its infancy. But the same argument could be applied to software engineering;

particularly in the early days. The process of establishing methods that are widely adopted in the real world is a long one. The field is now becoming mature, and methods and techniques are now appearing and being used in industry and commerce.

The growing interest in knowledge engineering throughout the 1980s and up to the present day means that there is now an increasing number of professional knowledge engineers in universities, government departments, commerce and industry. They are working towards a professional, engineering approach to the development of standardized, quality-assured knowledge-based systems.

The aim of this book is to provide a course in practical knowledge engineering. The books covers all of the stages that a knowledge engineer must follow when designing and building a KBS.

1.4 The role of the knowledge engineer

1.4.1 Background

Those involved in KBS production come from a wide range of backgrounds, reflecting the various different technologies that feed into knowledge engineering. As mentioned in section 1.3.3, knowledge engineering is a multi-stage process during which knowledge is elicited from human experts (knowledge acquisition) and this knowledge is built into a working system. The latter stage involves translating the expertise into a form in which it can be understood by the computer (knowledge representation) and designing, programming and testing the system.

Those involved in the production of KBS can therefore be:

- computer scientists
- knowledge specialists
- software engineers
- systems analysts
- psychologists
- project managers
- experts in the particular application domain (domain experts)

1.4.2 The skills of the knowledge engineer

A recent survey which was undertaken in the UK by Smith and Ross (Smith *et al.*, 1994; Ross, 1993) set out to closely scrutinize the skills and personality attributes of the knowledge engineer. The survey was based upon a similar one undertaken by Awad and Lindgren in the USA (Awad and Lindgren, 1992).

The survey was designed to identify any similarities and differences between knowledge engineers and traditional software engineers, to examine the

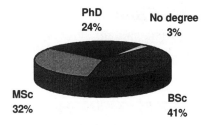

Figure 1.4 *Qualifications of respondents.*

skills and personality attributes required in each discipline, and to look at the
methods and technology in use in KBS development.

Figures 1.4 and 1.5 show the qualifications and salary range of the
respondents to the UK survey. As you can see in Figure 1.4, most knowledge
engineers are well qualified; usually to degree level. The salary which a
professional knowledge engineer can command is also quite attractive (Figure
1.5).

Certain human skills and personality attributes are important for knowledge engineers. Knowledge engineers are expected to have a number of
human and interpersonal skills in order to deal with experts, as well as with
users and other members of the project team. Project management is an
integral part of the knowledge engineer's role.

Knowledge engineers have to be able to elicit knowledge from experts
through interviews and the application of other techniques, so that they can
understand a problem as well as the real experts do. They must also be able
to translate this knowledge into a form in which it can be represented in a
computerized system. This means that a thorough appreciation of knowledge
representation techniques is vital, together with an awareness of current
trends in KBS technology.

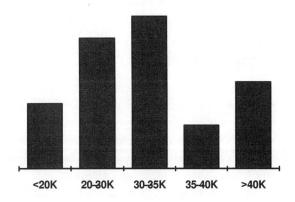

Figure 1.5 *Breakdown of respondents by salary range (in US$).*

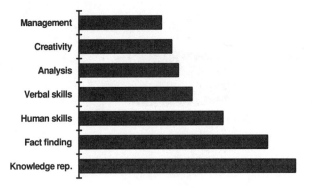

Figure 1.6 *The seven most important skills for a knowledge engineer.*

Furthermore, it can also fall to the knowledge engineer to market the KBS product: knowledge engineers often play a role similar to the IT (information technology) champion. This is the person who really believes in and pushes a new IT system within an organization. He or she must really care about the success of the system and see it as his or her job to make sure that everyone accepts the new technology.

The knowledge engineer has to be a KBS champion, to both users and to management. Knowledge engineers are also expected to be creative, have the ability to think logically and possess enough experience to enable them to solve real problems.

The knowledge engineer must possess skills in many different areas. Figure 1.6 gives a breakdown of the seven most important skills and attributes associated with the knowledge engineering role. The size of the bar in each case represents the importance of that particular attribute.

To summarize, the knowledge engineer is a versatile creature, with numerous skills in project management, software development and systems analysis. The knowledge engineer also requires considerable human and interpersonal skills, and skills particular to the development of KBS, such as knowledge representation techniques.

1.5 Knowledge engineering around the world

Knowledge engineering is now a recognized discipline in countries throughout the world. A recent survey of the current state of professional knowledge engineering undertaken by Lansbury and Smith revealed some interesting findings (Gillies, Smith and Lansbury, 1994; Lansbury, 1993). The survey covered several countries including the UK, Spain, Holland, Mexico, Brazil, the USA, Japan, France and Belgium.

The aim of the survey was to ascertain the current state of knowledge engineering and the role of the professional knowledge engineer from an international perspective. The results are summarized below:

1.5.1 The people

- The positions the knowledge engineers held were of a managerial or equivalent level, ranging from Dean of Computer Science to a knowledge engineering group co-ordinator.
- Salaries were relatively high and surprisingly very similar around the world, with an average of US$35K.
- They had all worked in their appropriate positions for under 10 years, 60% for 2–5 years.

Most knowledge engineers had a high level of previous professional experience. Salaries were comparable with those of other professionals, showing the high value that the market places on such skills. The time spent in the present position highlights the fact that knowledge engineering is quite new in comparison with other software disciplines.

1.5.2 Education

- All respondents had a degree level qualification or equivalent. Many had a higher degree.
- 85% gained their grounding in knowledge engineering during their degree courses.
- However, there were no respondents who had gained a particular specialised knowledge engineering qualification as part of that training.

The educational background of knowledge engineers worldwide seems to be very strong. This is important if knowledge engineering is to emerge as a highly regarded scientific discipline worthy of the title engineering.

1.5.3 Terminology

- 72% replied 'YES' that the term knowledge engineer is widely used in their own country.
- Of the 28% who replied 'NO', terms used in its place included systems analyst and software engineer.
- 57% of respondents had held previous positions in software engineering, whilst other positions included project manager, senior engineer and lecturer.
- All of the respondents felt that they followed engineering standards in the course of their work.

The replies suggest that the term knowledge engineer is becoming widely accepted throughout the world. Importantly, for the progression of knowledge engineering into a true 'engineering' discipline, there was a universal response from respondents that they consider themselves to be operating in an engineering field.

1.5.4 Specialization

- 72% replied that they worked as part of a team.

- Only 28% said that they specialized and this was in the area of knowledge acquisition.

An emphasis on teamwork was noted, highlighting the need for firm project management and standardized approaches to system development. An increasing specialization of knowledge engineers in one part of the development process was shown (knowledge acquisition).

1.6 Summary

The knowledge engineer is a multi-skilled, multi-talented individual with experience and expertise in a number of areas including KBS technology, computer science, systems analysis, human and interpersonal skills, software engineering and information gathering.

The view of KBS development as an engineering activity is still a relatively new one, with some of the principles of formal development only just beginning to be understood and applied by many practitioners.

One has to be aware of the fact that engineering as a discipline has a long history and that any specialized engineering discipline must draw upon a large store of information developed over time. Knowledge engineering does not, at present, have such a level of maturity, but it does have many characteristics in common with other engineering disciplines, particularly software engineering.

The debate is likely to go on for some time as to the worthiness of the term 'knowledge engineering'. There is, however, little doubt as time goes on that the arguments for the title will outweigh those against more and more.

1.7 Exercises

1. Ensure you understand and can differentiate among the following terms:

   - data
   - information
   - knowledge

   Look up the above terms in a dictionary and see if the dictionary makes a clear distinction between them (it may not!).

2. Try to find a professional engineer to interview (any discipline will do). Make a list of the most important factors in his or her job.

Chapter 2

An introduction to knowledge-based systems

OBJECTIVES

In this chapter you will learn:

- ❏ about the different forms of knowledge based systems (KBS);
- ❏ the history of KBS;
- ❏ about some of the applications of KBS;
- ❏ how to choose an application area for KBS treatment;
- ❏ the structure of a KBS;
- ❏ something about the case studies which we are going to use in the remainder of this book.

2.1 Introduction

2.1.1 Background

The earliest computers were extremely large awe-inspiring machines which were used by scientists to perform rapid calculations. In order to obtain an answer from these strange looking beasts the user would first have to decide on a method of solving a problem. He or she would then have to translate the method of solution into a set of instructions called a computer program. The program would invariably have to be written in a language that was unintelligible to the average human being and would consist of a series of strange commands which related to the way in which the computer's electronic components operated.

Since those early days computer designers have striven to make computers easier to use, to bridge the gap between the human and the machine (Figure 2.1).

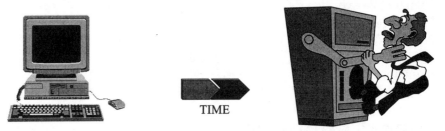

Figure 2.1 *Over the years COMPUTERS have moved more closely to HUMANS.*

The languages in which the user has to write a computer program have been designed so that they resemble, as closely as possible, the English words and phrases and mathematical symbols which we use in everyday life. The computer hardware itself has seen dramatic reductions both in price and size, accompanied by similarly dramatic increases in its capacity to store and process data.

But still the computer is only a machine. We cannot (yet) talk to it in English as we would a human being. (There is, however, much progress in this area of research and systems are now appearing that can understand natural language). We cannot give it an everyday problem to solve unless it has already been programmed with an appropriate method of solution. We cannot expect it to learn from its mistakes and apply previous experience and common sense to the solution of problems. Or can we?

Is it even sensible to begin to try to emulate the human brain? The brain is an extremely complex machine. It contains about 10^{32} neurons. This is more cells than there are stars in the Milky Way. The brain deals with sight, hearing, taste and touch all at the same time. In addition it has the ability to store and retrieve vast quantities of information and to control our emotions, feelings and desires. Can a computer ever truly emulate such a complex structure?

Artificial intelligence (AI) is the name given to a field of research which is attempting, with varying degrees of success, to produce computer systems which can accomplish the above. In other words, the aim of AI research is to provide computers with similar intellectual abilities to those of a human being. This is obviously an awesome task, particularly as many of our own intellectual abilities and mental processes are not yet fully understood, even by experts in psychology.

One area of AI research which is quite advanced, however, is that of producing knowledge-based systems (KBS). Indeed, KBS development, or **knowledge engineering**, is one of the few areas of AI which has moved out of the research laboratory and into the real world. Knowledge engineering is beginning to fulfil a real potential in industrial and commercial applications.

As discussed in Chapter 1, a KBS is a computer system which embodies knowledge about a specific problem domain and can thus be used to apply this knowledge to solve problems from that problem domain. Many KBS are often termed **expert systems**, as they behave in a similar manner to a human expert when solving a problem. In fact, the terms KBS and expert system are often used interchangeably. This isn't quite right, as there are many KBS which do contain knowledge, but are not really expert systems. For instance an intelligent database system may be knowledge based, but it is not an expert system, because it has not been designed to apply expertise to solve problems. We will stick to using the term KBS throughout this book, to mean any system which has knowledge embedded within it.

2.1.2 Categories of KBS

Knowledge-based systems include:

- **Expert systems** – this is probably the most common category of KBS. As we mentioned above the terms KBS and expert system are often used interchangeably. An expert system is any system which emulates the thought processes, decision-making processes and/or actions of a human expert (or group of experts). Most of the examples which we will meet in this book could be categorized as expert systems.
- **Intelligent database systems** – these are database systems which have added intelligence. This often takes the form of an intelligent front end which makes it easier to access the information in the database.
- **Intelligent tutoring systems** – these are educational systems which attempt to model a human tutor.
- **Intelligent CASE tools** – CASE (computer-aided software engineering) involves the use of computers to automate parts of the software development process. In recent years, some CASE tools have had intelligence (knowledge) added to them. Such tools try to replicate the knowledge of a software engineer and are the integration of CASE and KBS.
- **Integrated or hybrid systems** – these are systems which integrate KBS approaches and traditional information systems approaches. One of the case studies which you meet later in this chapter concerns an integrated system.

Waterman (1986) suggests the following categories of expert systems:

- **Interpretation** – systems which can be used for interpreting data in an expert manner.
- **Prediction** – systems which can be used to predict the outcome of a particular scenario.
- **Diagnosis** – systems which can diagnose the cause of a particular problem.
- **Design** – systems which can be used to design and configure objects.
- **Planning** – systems for planning and scheduling sequences of actions and events.
- **Monitoring** – systems which can monitor the state of a physical system by comparing observed data to expected values.
- **Debugging** – systems which can be used to prescribe cures for faults.
- **Repair** – systems which can implement repairs.

- **Instruction** – systems which can instruct users how to perform a particular action or groups of actions.
- **Control** – systems which can control and govern overall system behaviour.

The above categories covers most possible KBS. Some of the above categories of knowledge overlap and many systems can fit into more than one category.

A KBS will take the knowledge and experience of a human (or group of humans) and make it available 24 hours a day, every day of the year. The decisions made will be consistent and reliable, and it is possible for the system to be used from a number of different locations and by relatively inexperienced staff.

Many KBS can also learn from their mistakes and gain experience from their successes and failures, just as a human would. The system may also be able to explain the reasoning behind the way in which it has arrived at a particular conclusion.

You may ask 'Why do we need a computer to do such tasks for us? We have plenty of human experts to solve our problems for us.' But is that true? Consider the following properties of human experts:

- They are scarce.
- Their services are expensive.
- They are usually very much in demand and are therefore very busy.
- They are mortal.

Computer systems do not suffer from the above drawbacks.

Consider the following scenario:

Many human experts spend a lot of their time solving trivial problems, some of which are very similar (Figure 2.2). These are the day-to-day problems which they may meet all of the time, but cannot be ignored and still have to be dealt with. Because of their specialist training and expertise such experts are also in heavy demand not only to help solve day-to-day problems, but also to help with more difficult and interesting problems.

In many cases these very experts are the only people we can approach to help solve problems of a certain type. This may be because only they possess the specialist knowledge needed to solve the problems, or simply because they

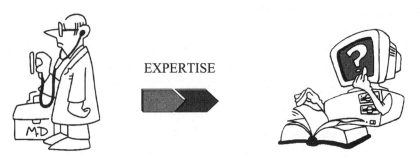

EXPERTISE

Figure 2.2 *Many tasks undertaken by professionals could be done by a KBS.*

are the only people who are, by law, allowed to undertake such work. Without doubt these experts would be much happier if they could devote more of their time to solving more of the really interesting problems and have some help with the trivial day-to-day problems.

Professional experts who might fall into the above category include:

- lawyers
- solicitors
- doctors
- architects

All of the above professionals are expensive to hire and extremely busy. Wouldn't it be useful, and indeed sensible, if at least some of their expertise could somehow be implanted within a computer system? A copy of this system could then be held at public places such as libraries and supermarkets and it could then be used as a cost-effective consultant on day-to-day problems. Of course for more difficult problems the system would need to advise the user to consult a real professional.

Consider the scenario below:

John is a solicitor who deals largely with divorce cases. This is quite a lucrative business, particularly in current times where divorce is becoming more and more common. Many of the cases which he deals with are, of course, relatively straightforward and hence he finds them quite boring to deal with. He often boasts to his friends that he could deal with them 'in his sleep'. Yet he clearly can't turn cases away just because they are straightforward and uninteresting. These people need help and he may be the only one who can give them the help that they need. He would also be turning away lucrative business, and anyway he needs the money to help pay for his large mortgage and two cars.

What John really needs is a KBS which could screen for the trivial cases and help answer a lot of the straightforward questions for him. This KBS would have implanted within it some of the more basic knowledge relating to divorce law. It would also have a bank of case studies which it could draw on, thus bringing the benefit of past experience to bear on a case. Perhaps John could even get his assistant to help operate the system.

This would free up John's time for other things. He could then concentrate on more interesting cases, or take on even more cases and increase his salary. Either way, the benefits of such a system are quite obvious.

There are many other fields of enterprise where such a system would be of immense value. There are just as many other fields of human expertise where a computer system will never be able to match the capabilities of a human being (Figure 2.3). These include those activities which involve originality, intuition, creativity and artistic ability. For example, one could never imagine a computer being able to paint a great master, write a (good) play or compose music. That is how it should be. There need to be some things which only

Figure 2.3 *Fields where a computer will never be able to match a human.*

humans can do, or we enter into the dangerous scenario of the computers being able to really think for themselves and trying to replace us.

There are also legal implications of using a computer to give advice and solve human problems. These legal implications have yet to be really examined. For example, if a doctor uses a KBS to advise as to the treatment of a patient suffering from an infectious disease, and that patient dies, who is responsible? Is it the knowledge engineer who programmed the KBS? Is it the human expert(s) from whom the knowledge was extracted in the first place? Is it the company who sold the KBS? Is it the doctor who used the KBS as a basis for a diagnosis? Such questions as these remain unanswered for the time being. This means that great care must be taken when deciding upon an application area for a KBS.

The next sections of this chapter discuss some of the applications of KBS technology in more detail.

2.2 A history of KBS

2.2.1 Early systems

Early work on AI began in the 1950s and 1960s. This work was trying to make computers which could think as humans. However, much of the work did not produce any really practical results, and AI began to get itself something of a bad name.

Some of the earliest KBS were developed during the 1970s and earlier. These included one of the most well known and well documented systems, namely MYCIN.

MYCIN is a KBS which was designed at Stanford University in the USA to deal with problems in the treatment and diagnosis of infectious diseases. The system, therefore, comprises a large knowledge base which contains facts and rules about the forms and causes of infectious diseases and can thus be used to aid the clinician in diagnosis.

Another system which was developed around the same period as MYCIN is PROSPECTOR, which was designed by SRI International in association with the United States Geological Survey, to assist geologists during mineral exploration work. Both of these early expert systems contain large amounts of knowledge which have been drawn from well understood and researched problem domains.

Another famous early expert system was DENDRAL, which acted as a chemist's assistant in interpreting the data from mass spectrography. DENDRAL was developed by Ed Feigenbaum of Stanford University in the United States. Feigenbaum is seen by many as the father of expert systems.

In developing DENDRAL, Feigenbaum and his colleagues discovered that human chemists carried around enormous amounts of specialized knowledge in their heads, and it was impossible to do the job without having that specialized knowledge. The difficult task was to sit down with these chemists, watch them work and ask them questions about how they made decisions. Of course, they weren't always able to answer these questions as, although they knew how to do these things they found great difficulty expressing them in words. It was then necessary to figure out some way of representing the knowledge, these 'rules of thumb', in the form of a large KBS.

'In DENDRAL', Feigenbaum says (Feigenbaum and McCorduck, 1984), 'we looked not only for the relatively hard chemical knowledge about stability and mass spectral processes, but also for the relatively soft knowledge: how a particular scientist makes a particular kind of decision when he's not really sure, when there's a variety of evidence, a lot of ambiguities. How does he select?'

Each of the above systems, although successful as a research project, did not have any real success in business or industry. Probably the first real commercial application was XCON, which was developed by DEC (Digital Equipment Corporation) to configure their computers. Table 2.1 lists some early KBS.

Table 2.1 *Some early knowledge-based systems*

Year	System	Author(s)	Task	Fate
1956		Newell, Simon and Shaw	Proved logic theorems	Laboratory prototype
1961		Minsky and Slagle	Solved mathematical calculus problems	Laboratory prototype
1973	DENDRAL	Feigenbaum	Derived chemical structures from mass spectrograph	Algorithmic version sold well
1976	MYCIN	Shortliffe	Medical diagnosis of blood disorders	Given to hospitals, but not in everyday use
1978	PROSPECTOR	Duda	Prospecting for mineral ores	Used a few times in a commercial situation

Generation one (mid-1940s)
Large valve-based mainframe computers

Generation two (mid-1950s)
Much more compact transistor based machines

Generation three (mid-1960s)
ICs appear and we have much smaller, yet more powerful computers

Generation four (early 1970s)
LSI produces birth of the microcomputer

Generation five (1990s onwards)
Knowledge processing computers

Figure 2.4 *The five generations of computers.*

2.2.2 The AI wilderness

In 1972 the *Lighthill Report on Artificial Intelligence* appeared (Lighthill, 1972). Sir James Lighthill, a distinguished physicist, was commissioned by the Science Research Council of Great Britain to evaluate the state of AI and recommend whether further funding should be given.

The Lighthill Report said that AI was too theoretical and that it had little potential for real use in the business world. This report virtually stopped the support of AI research in the UK in the 1970s. Similar situations arose in other parts of the world, making the road for people working in KBS a long and hard one.

However, AI did recover from this setback and much useful work has been undertaken in recent times. The remainder of this section gives you an idea of some of the most important developments in KBS over the years.

2.2.3 The Japanese fifth-generation project

It is often said that the history of computers can be divided into four generations, stretching from their inception in the mid-1940s to the present day (Figure 2.4). These four generations are each described below.

2.2.3.1 Generation one

The first generation of computers emerged in the mid-1940s. These were extremely large, valve-based machines which were so vast that they filled an entire room and needed several people to operate and look after them.

2.2.3.2 Generation two

In the mid-1950s advances in electronics resulted in the valve being largely superseded by the much smaller transistor. This enabled computer manufacturers to construct what was to become known as the second generation computer which was a much more compact, transistor-based machine.

2.2.3.3 Generation three

Further advances in electronics during the mid-1960s enabled component manufacturers to combine entire circuits on a single device. These devices were known as integrated circuits (ICs). The use of ICs in the production of computers heralded the advent of the third generation computer, which was, once again, much more compact than its direct predecessor.

2.2.3.4 Generation four

In the early 1970s another new age dawned with the mass production of much more powerful ICs. Each of these ICs contained a much larger amount of circuitry and a corresponding larger number of individual components. This new technology was known as large scale integration (LSI) and the resultant devices were termed 'chips'. The fourth generation of computers thus consisted of machines which were constructed entirely of such chips and were, once again, much more compact than previous models. It was also around this period that the first microcomputers began to appear. This was the birth of the personal computer (PC).

2.2.3.5 So what is a fifth generation computer?

In 1981 the Japanese announced the Fifth Generation Computer Project, whose aim was to produce machines which would form the next generation of computer systems. However, unlike the previous four generations of computers, the fifth generation machine was not seen as being purely a result of advances in computer hardware. Rather, the vision of the fifth generation computer was that of a computer system which not only used all of the recent advances in both hardware and software technology, but also took a very different and new approach to the way a computer system was built and worked.

All of the previous generations of computers were essentially data-processing and/or number-crunching engines. In order to use such machines, the operator had to program the computer with an appropriate method of solution to the problem in hand. The philosophy behind the fifth generation computer was that the user would be able to communicate with the machine in natural language (for example English) and that the computer would contain sufficient knowledge to be able to understand and solve real problems. The fifth generation computer was thus seen as a highly sophisticated and powerful knowledge-processing and problem-solving machine.

Basically what the Japanese were attempting to produce was a system which resembled, as closely as possible, a human being in its intelligence and knowledge. Such a computer system was obviously a bold leap from the systems which were available at that time. Now, over a decade later, such systems are still not available. However, many advances have been made in KBS and 'thinking' machines, and the Fifth Generation Programme kick-started the rest of the world to think very seriously about KBS and AI.

2.2.4 ALVEY

Although the ALVEY programme has now reached completion, its impact on KBS (and information technology) research in the UK has been so great in recent years that no review of the area would be complete without mentioning it. The ALVEY programme for advanced information technology was launched in 1982 as a direct response to the Japanese Fifth Generation Programme. The programme encompassed many different aspects of information technology (IT), one of which was KBS. The budget for the programme was around £350 million over a period of five years and it was based upon the concept of promoting joint collaborative research projects between universities and industry.

The ALVEY programme succeeded in starting off research in all areas of KBS/AI including work on vision systems and image processing (to produce computers which can 'see'), natural language processing (to produce computers which we can converse with in English), robotics and industrial KBS. These developments were supported by the funding of collaborative research projects, workshops, conferences and technology transfer and development clubs.

This resulted in many exciting advances and helped to forge real links between industrial organizations and universities. Unfortunately, subsequent funding was not provided at a similarly high level and hence many research ideas and prototype systems were not able to be transformed into real products.

The KBS component of the ALVEY programme comprised four large projects known as 'demonstrator' projects as well as numerous smaller research projects. The four demonstrator projects were so named because their aim was to demonstrate how useful KBS technology can be to business and industry. The projects involved:

- the development of a KBS to aid in the formulation of chemical mixtures;
- the use of KBS techniques in the production of mechanical systems (in particular diesel engines and helicopter gearboxes);
- the development of a decision support system for air crews and a flight-deck simulator;
- the use of KBS techniques for stock control.

2.2.5 KBS research within Europe

The European Union (EU) has also set up a number of large research programmes in the information technology area. One of the most important of these programmes is the ESPRIT (European Strategic Programme of Research in Information Technology) programme.

In 1988, the British Minister for Industry and Consumer Affairs commented on the role of ESPRIT:

> Britain is part of Europe and is working with other member states to secure the single market. This surely means it is right to put emphasis on European collaborations. European-scale effort is often needed when large investments will be required for the research itself or for the subsequent production and marketing of the product. ESPRIT provides the opportunity for both our companies and our universities to participate in research on a European scale and to develop the commercial relationship that will be needed.
>
> (Smith and Rada, 1994)

The ESPRIT programme has provided funding for a large number of multinational collaborative KBS projects involving universities and commercial companies since the programme began in the early 1980s. ESPRIT has thus been of enormous significance in creating a truly collaborative community of European researchers, developers and users (Smith and Rada, 1994). Through programmes such as ESPRIT, Europe has gained a lead in KBS development methodologies such as KADS (as discussed in Chapter 3).

Current ESPRIT projects are focusing more and more on producing practical computer software which can be used to benefit European industry. The EU is particularly keen to fund projects which will not only undertake useful research, but will also result in products that can be used in business and industry. This means that the KBS projects which are currently being funded by the ESPRIT programme are likely to result in more real, working KBS.

One example of such a project is CIM.REFLEX. The CIM.REFLEX project (ESPRIT 2 Project 6304) used KBS in the production planning process in order to enable manufacturing companies to respond in a more flexible and dynamic manner. The project aim was to specify, develop, implement and evaluate a KBS for production planning which also addresses the tasks of product configuration and costing.

CIM.REFLEX had six partners. Two of these were universities, two were manufacturing companies and two were software houses. The project team covered three EU countries: Denmark, France and the UK.

CIM.REFLEX addressed the need for manufacturing companies to react quickly and with sufficient flexibility to customer demands. A core issue for the project was to meet practical industrial requirements as well as applying the latest research from KBS technology.

The complete CIM.REFLEX system gives knowledge-based decision support at the time a sale is made, using data which reflect the current situation in the factory. A combination of an expert-system programming language (Prolog) and the DECIBAC expert system shell has been used to develop the CIM.REFLEX system.

In order to do this the project team spent many months working with a large number of staff in manufacturing companies. Many knowledge-acquisition sessions were held to capture the knowledge of these staff. This included staff from the shop floor, from the planning department and from the accounts department. The system was designed to enable sales staff to use this knowledge when they make a sale.

Other programmes such as AIM (Applied Informatics in Medicine) have also provided funding for KBS work. For instance, the project GALEN has built a large KBS for medicine.

2.3 KBS applications

2.3.1 KBS in the UK

In order to identify current practices in KBS in the UK, the Department of Trade and Industry commissioned a survey of companies using KBS (DTI, 1992). The survey, which involved telephone interviews with 199 companies, uncovered many interesting findings about KBS users. The main findings were:

- KBS and expert systems are not just used by a few, very large, companies. Rather, KBS applications were found in both large and small companies in many different market sectors. In fact, 10% of the companies who were found to be using KBS were small companies with less than 100 employees. This indicates that KBS technology has the potential to help businesses of every shape and size, and that we are going to see more smaller companies using them in the future.
- The diversity of KBS applications is very large. This is because KBS technology is so versatile, and can be used in almost any field where human knowledge exists. The most popular application areas in the UK were found to be manufacturing and financial services, which together made up 62% of the sample.
- Applications currently in operation span a wide range of business areas. Manufacturing, production, marketing and customer service, and accounting/financial management are the most common application areas, but there are many other applications in areas such as training and regulation compliance.
- Systems performing diagnostic, advisory and assessment task types are most popular. Diagnostic systems are used to provide a diagnosis as to the cause or source of a particular problem, for instance why a particular part

for a car is not being manufactured correctly. Advisory systems give advice as to how to perform a particular task, for instance how to set up a piece of complex machinery to make a new product. Assessment systems might be used for assessing the status of a particular manufacturing process or, in financial application areas, for assessing the risk involved in insuring someone or something.

- KBS can make knowledge widely accessible and can be used at many levels within an organization. Around one third of the companies who were using KBS said that their systems were being used by more than 50 people.
- KBS development does not have to take too long or be too complicated. Twenty nine per cent of the systems identified by the survey had been developed in less than six months.
- Personal computers are most frequently used for the development and operation of KBS. Many surveys have identified a trend towards using PC-based packages known as expert system shells for the development of small (and even some large) scale systems. We will cover the use of shells in Chapter 6.

Many of the companies interviewed were planning future work to enhance their KBS, and almost two thirds had new systems in development or planned. Thirteen per cent were even planning to sell their KBS as a commercial product. This means that, in the coming years, more and more KBS will be made available on the market.

2.3.2 Current applications

In one survey by Fahnrich of the use of KBS in the USA, the UK and Germany, the USA was credited with about two thirds of the systems, the UK had a little over one sixth, and Germany had a little less than one sixth (Figure 2.5). Particularly interesting was the difference in what the KBS were being used for.

The USA and UK concentrated on data processing, manufacturing and electrical engineering. The majority of the German systems were for mechanical engineering and plant construction. In a classification of Japanese expert systems by industrial field the top areas were all in heavy industry

KBS are now moving into the mainstream of computing. That is, more and more KBS applications are being integrated with traditional IT systems such as personnel systems, banking systems and so on. This means that KBS technology is becoming more widely used and that the skills of knowledge engineering are becoming more and more important and valued in the world-wide market place. It is these skills which we will aim to develop in you, the reader, throughout this book.

2.3.2.1 Social applications

In recent years, there has been a large amount of research into the social applications of KBS; that is, systems which can be used to improve both the

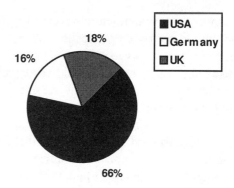

Figure 2.5 *Proportion of KBS applications in the USA, UK and Germany.*

quality and quantity of advice and expertise available to the person in the street.

Systems include:

- a system which was designed to advise expectant mothers as to their maternity rights, including knowledge about eligibility for maternity benefit, maternity pay, etc.;
- a system, currently available on a PC, which gives advice on an employee's rights with respect to dismissal, redundancy pay, etc.;
- a system which is designed to give home owners advice on planning law and answer such questions as 'Is my plan for an extension likely to be approved?'.

2.3.2.2 Financial applications

The area of financial applications is currently one of the most popular applications for the use of KBS. KBS are in current use in many large financial institutions such as insurance companies, banks and finance houses. The type of systems which are in common use include:

- KBS which aid bank managers when they are deciding whether or not to grant a loan to a particular customer;
- systems which give advice as to whether to grant a mortgage or not;
- systems which advise insurance companies as to the risk factor involved in insuring a particular individual or item;
- systems which are used by credit card companies to help them decide whether or not to issue an individual with a credit card;
- systems which have been devised to recognize and guard against computer fraud. This is becoming an increasingly large area. As computer fraud may often be difficult to detect, the knowledge which is encapsulated within such a KBS can be quite complex.

A survey by Kingston (1991) reported over 100 KBS applications in this sector in the UK and over 400 worldwide. Much of the work in this area remains secret. Companies are, without a doubt, developing (and using) some very sophisticated KBS 'behind closed doors'. They are not likely to want to tell their competitors about pieces of computer software which are earning them lots of money and giving them a market advantage.

2.3.2.3 Industry, manufacturing and the military

Many UK industrial and manufacturing companies have now introduced KBS into their daily operations. Applications in this area include:

- KBS which are capable of diagnosing various industrial faults, such as faults in aircraft, gas turbines and helicopters;
- systems which are designed to minimize plant downtime and avoid shutdowns, by identifying any potential problems as rapidly as possible – this is very important as, in large factories, a lot of money can be lost if things go wrong and the plant has to be shut down for any length of time;
- systems which are used to design and make small mechanical parts (such systems may form part of a much wider plant automation system which may also use robots) – this moves us some way towards a goal of total factory automation, where much of the day-to-day work within a factory is undertaken by computers, machines and robots;
- military applications of KBS such as the identification of targets and potential threats to security – the applications of KBS in defence are wide and varied; it is often difficult to find out any details of such systems as the defence authorities around the world are not likely to go around giving away their secrets.

During 1989, the UK Department of Trade and Industry undertook a large survey of the use of KBS in manufacturing (DTI, 1989). The survey reported that, although the UK was somewhat behind developments in technology in the USA in the field of manufacturing, there were currently more live applications (54) than found in, for example, Japan (where 32 such applications were identified).

2.4 The components of a knowledge-based system

This section describes the major components of a typical knowledge-based system (Figure 2.6):

- knowledge base
- inference engine
- user interface
- explanation facilities
- learning facilities

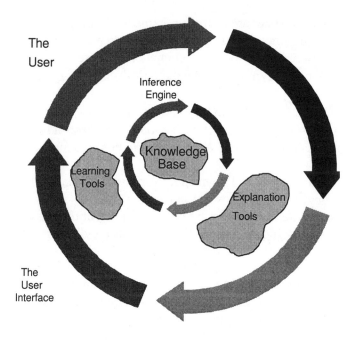

Figure 2.6 *Diagram of a typical KBS.*

2.4.1 The knowledge base

The knowledge base is obviously the heart of any KBS. It comprises human knowledge represented in some form. There are many ways which have been devised to represent knowledge within a computer and these are covered in detail in a later chapter.

One of the most common ways to represent knowledge is in the form of facts and rules. These facts and rules contain knowledge about the particular problem area from which the system draws its expertise (often termed the problem domain).

A fact is a clear, concise statement which expresses something which is true within the particular problem domain. For example, the following statements are all facts:

```
John is a man.
Susan lives in a house.
Tony drives a car.
Mary has brown hair.
```

A rule is generally of the form:

If *statement1* **then** *statement2.*

where *statement1* and *statement2* are both expressions which may or may not be true. The rule is simply stating that if *statement1* is true then this implies that *statement2* is also true.

Examples of rules are:

If a person marries twice **and** he/she has not been divorced **then** he/she is a bigamist.

If a person has $1,000,000 **then** he/she is a dollar millionaire.

A KBS which is designed to aid medical practitioners in the diagnosis of abdominal pain would have a knowledge base which contained facts and rules about the likely causes of such pain and the particular symptoms related to each of these causes. Such rules might take the form:

If the patient has pain to the lower right of the abdomen
and the patient has vomited
then the patient may have appendicitis.

These facts and rules will usually be represented within the knowledge base in a form which the computer can recognize and deal with. This might involve the use of an expert system shell or an expert system language such as Prolog. Figure 2.7 shows some rules which are written in the form required for an expert system shell. The rules are taken from one of the case studies which is used in the remainder of this book.

2.4.2 The inference engine

In order to make use of the expertise which is embodied in the knowledge base, the system must also possess an element which can scan facts and rules, and provide answers to the queries given to it by the user. This element is known as the inference engine.

This is the thinking part of the KBS. The inference engine has the ability to look through the knowledge base and apply the rules to the solution of a particular problem. It is, therefore, the driving force of the KBS. It acts in a similar manner to the human brain in that it uses the knowledge from the knowledge base to provide an answer to a particular question (or a solution to a particular problem).

2.4.3 The user interface

The user interface is the means by which the user communicates with the computer system. Ideally this interface should be as English-like as possible to make it easy to use for inexperienced users. That is, an ideal system would

```
Find-Employee-Rule:   If  first priority group
                          and skills consideration
                          and recommended moves and preferred work areas
                      Then  display search result


First-Priority-Group-Rule:     If staff type = internal
                               and   staff resource centre=vacancy resource centre
                               and  staff location=vacancy location
                               and  staff grade=vacancy grades required
                               and  staff availability = yes
                           Then staff selected as first priority group staff


  Staff-Type-Rule:  If staff_type$="CS"
                    Then staff type = internal


  Resource-Centre-Rules:  If res_cent$=vres_cent$
                          Then staff resource centre=vacancy resource centre


  Location-Rule:  If site_code$=vsite_code$
                  Then staff location=vacancy location


  Grades-Value-Convert-Rule:  If convert grade descriptions into values
                              Then grade evaluation

  Grade-Evaluation-Rule1:  If req1_value>=req2_value
                           and curr_grade_value<=req1_value
                           and curr_grade_value>=req2_value
                           Then staff grade=vacancy grades required

  Grade-Evaluation-Rule2:  If req1_value<=req2_value
                           and curr_grade_value<=req2_value
                           and curr_grade_value<=req1_value
                           Then staff grade=vacancy grades required
```

Figure 2.7 *Sample rules.*

allow the user to type (or speak) his or her questions to the system in English. The system would then recognize the meaning of the questions, and use its inference engine to apply the rules in the knowledge base to deduce an answer. This answer would then be communicated back to the user in simple English.

Such an ideal system is, however, not likely to be available in the immediate future due to the difficulties which arise in trying to program a computer to recognize, and understand the meaning of, even the most simple English sentences and phrases.

One way in which AI is used in user-interface design is in the construction of **adaptive user interfaces**. As the name suggests, an adaptive user interface is one which adapts to the different needs of different groups of users. For instance a medical KBS might present a different series of screens and questions to an experienced consultant from those which it presents to a trainee doctor. In order to construct an adaptive user interface the computer must have knowledge about the different users of the system. It can then present each group of users with an interface which has been specifically designed to match their needs. A really clever adaptive interface will also be able to learn about users from the way in which they interact with the system. The interface can then change dynamically (i.e. over time) as it becomes more familiar with (i.e. gains more knowledge about) those people who are using it to communicate with the computer system.

The user interface is, in many ways, the most important part of any software system. It can make or break the system. A good user interface will be easy to use and even encourage users to use the system. A poor user interface will mean that the users will not enjoy using the system and will find it difficult to use. This may mean that the system will be rejected by its potential user community and will, in many instances, not get used at all.

The subject of user-interface design is a very large field of study, and much research has been undertaken to try and improve the way in which humans can communicate with computers. This has involved a lot of experimental work in which human subjects have been observed using different forms of interface.

2.4.4 Explanation and learning facilities

Any really useful KBS should be able to explain the answers that it gives to its users. That is, the system should be able to explain exactly why it has given a particular answer, and what knowledge it has used to reach a particular conclusion. It should also be able to explain why it has been unable to give an answer.

This is very important if the KBS is going to be really accepted by the users. That is, users often want to know why a particular answer has been given. If the KBS cannot reassure these users by letting them know how it arrived at a particular answer or conclusion they are unlikely to really trust it. This may mean that it will not get used as much as it should and it may even not get used at all.

A good KBS should also be able to learn from its experiences, just as a human does. Human knowledge does not stand still. Our knowledge changes over time as we learn from our past experiences and from our mistakes. A really useful KBS should be able to do the same. That is, the KBS should develop with time as it learns from its own experiences and mistakes. This means that the knowledge base will grow as the system is used. This is how it should be. After all, your own knowledge is growing and changing all the time. For instance, when you have finished reading this book, you should possess more knowledge than you did before you picked it up.

2.5 Which problem areas are best suited to KBS treatment?

2.5.1 When to use a KBS

As we have learnt in this chapter, KBS are gradually finding their way into many areas of modern life. So should we expect to see a KBS appearing in every office, shop and factory in the near future?

Perhaps not. Only certain types of application are suited to KBS implementation. But how do you determine whether or not a particular problem area is suitable for the 'KBS' treatment? It is the aim of this section to answer this question.

The following rules give an indication of the sort of criteria which must be satisfied in order for a particular application area to benefit from KBS treatment:

- The field under study should be able to be reduced into a series of rules rather than mathematical formulae or equations. In particular, a KBS may not be applicable if the problem involves a large number of complex calculations.
- The field under study should be well understood so that well-defined knowledge can be formulated and represented in computer form.
- The field under study should not encompass problems which take too short (i.e. less than half an hour) or too long (longer than, say, one week) a time to solve.
- There should be general agreement among recognized experts in the field. It is no use if all the experts have different ideas or theories – in such a case whose knowledge would you computerize?
- The knowledge within the problem domain should be sufficiently large to warrant the development of a KBS of, say, more than about a dozen rules – for less it is probably more efficient to solve the problem manually.
- There should be one or more 'tame' experts who are agreeable to their involvement in the project.

Notwithstanding the above rules, however, any application that requires access to specialist knowledge is a potential area for the introduction of KBS technology.

2.5.2 Benefits

But what exactly are the benefits that can be gained by the introduction of a KBS?

There are many benefits that can accrue from the introduction of KBS technology within a particular application area. Some of the more obvious benefits include:

- A KBS can make knowledge and expertise much more accessible than would otherwise be possible.
- Using a KBS can be much cheaper than hiring the services of a real human expert.
- A KBS can be used to preserve knowledge which would otherwise be lost over time.
- Computers are not prone to human error in the application of their knowledge.
- KBS can be used to facilitate communication between humans themselves and hence improve their own knowledge.

2.6 The practical case studies

Throughout this book we will use four practical case studies to illustrate the major concepts of knowledge engineering. We will start here by introducing you to each of the case studies. The case studies have been chosen to illustrate the development of four different, but commonly found, KBS applications.

As you progress through the book, you will meet the case studies again and again. Each time, however, we will move a little further towards the development of the final KBS. By the time you have finished reading the book, we will have covered portions of the actual computer programs which were used to implement the KBS.

The case studies are:

1. a **quality control system**, which illustrates how KBS technology can be used to give workers advice on how to recognize (and rectify) faults in the products they are making and thus exercise good quality practices (Hardy, 1993);

2. a **forecasting system**, which shows how a KBS can be used to predict future trends (Leonard, 1992);

3. a **monitoring system**, which demonstrates how a KBS can be used to check on the status of an important piece of equipment (Jawad, 1991);

4. an **integrated system**, which shows how KBS technology can be integrated with conventional computer software technology (Lin, 1993).

Each of the systems are taken from genuine practical experiences. They are based on KBS which were developed for the companies concerned.

2.6.1 The quality-control system

The company concerned in this case study is part of an international group of companies associated with the manufacture and distribution of vending and food services packaging. The particular problem which we will look at in this case study is the manufacturer of plastic cups, the sort of cups which are used in vending machines and which we drink our coffee or hot chocolate out of.

Each and every stage of product manufacture is handled by the company, from the raw materials through to packaging and distribution. One of its central concerns is the quality of the final product. This is monitored manually both by the operators and the Quality Assurance Department. Since the output of the machines can exceed 80,000 cups per hour, it is very important to keep the product within its specification, and to avoid having to stop the machines to put things right. This is because once a machine starts making cups incorrectly, it will continue to do so. This will soon result in a large number of spoilt cups and a lot of wasted production time.

Currently, the operators are sufficiently well trained to be able to deal with most of the common problems which can arise. However, when problems are unfamiliar, or do not respond straight away to adjustments to the machines, expert diagnosis is obtained either from more experienced operators or from production/development personnel. As is typical of such situations, having to bring someone in takes valuable time, costs money and takes the expert away from whatever he or she was involved in.

The task in this case study was, therefore, to develop a knowledge-based diagnosis and fault-finding system that could be used by the operators to assist in their operations. In particular, the aim of the KBS was to find any faults in the production of cups.

Whilst visually the problems affecting the cups are not large, even with very small problems the product is still flawed, and this can lead to problems and customer dissatisfaction. It is also hard to determine the cause of the problem, since it can happen at any point in the production process. There are nine typical problems that can occur with a cup, and the KBS was developed to recognize each of these and then give the operator appropriate advice.

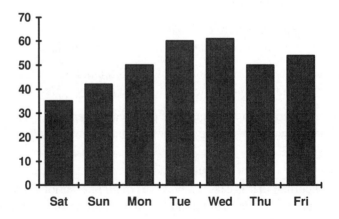

Figure 2.8 *A KBS designed to estimate gas demand.*

2.6.2 The forecasting system

Forecasting is the practise of estimating, as closely as possible, future trends. This KBS aimed to improve and enhance the forecasting techniques used in British Gas, and in particular within one region. Its aim was to improve the accuracy of estimation of gas usage. This project aimed to investigate the use of a KBS to improve the accuracy of the short-term forecasting that is carried out daily within each region of British Gas (see Figure 2.8).

British Gas buy their supplies of natural gas from over forty privately owned gas fields situated around the coast of Great Britain, and transport it through its network of steel pipes to the gas regions and then to the customers.

The amount of gas needed daily must be ordered from the suppliers twelve hours in advance, and as the gas day traditionally runs from 6 a.m. one day to 6 a.m. the next, this means the gas wells are notified by 6 p.m. The amount of gas needed is calculated by British Gas Headquarters, primarily by summing the estimates of the amount of gas that each region expects to sell the next day.

To allow Headquarters time to firm up their estimate they require each region's estimate by 4 p.m. Each region is therefore required to forecast their estimation of the volume of gas for the following day 14 hours in advance of that day starting. Not only have they to estimate this far in advance but they are required to forecast as accurately as they can, as they can lose money if they get it wrong. It was, therefore, vital to develop a KBS which could accurately forecast the gas demand required by the region for the following day.

This is not easy as gas demand can depend upon several factors:

- seasonal factors (we use more gas in the winter than in the summer);
- the weather on a particular day;
- other factors, such as, for example, on the afternoon of the Cup Final most people will be in the house with the central heating on.

2.6.3 The monitoring system

This case study concerns a KBS which was designed to give advice on the initial setting and subsequent adjustment of a mechanical ventilator used in a hospital intensive care unit.

The ventilator is used to control the breathing of seriously ill patients who have often been rushed into hospital. Previous manual systems relied heavily on the intuition of the doctor as to how to set the ventilator, so as to stabilize the patient in as short a period of time as possible.

A ventilator is a mechanical device which ventilates a patient's lungs or in other words 'does the breathing for the patient'. All modern ventilators achieve this by periodically forcing gas into the patient's lungs.

In normal clinical practice, the initial settings of the ventilator are decided by the doctor on the basis of a number of known or estimated physiological factors such as weight, height, age, lung condition, heart condition or disease.

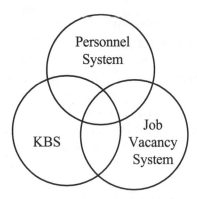

Figure 2.9 *The integrated HRM system.*

Ventilator adjustments by the doctor tend to be made according to rules that are not hard and fast, and there always exists an element of 'inspired guesswork' in the process. Measurements of blood gases, patient condition and ventilator adjustments must be made as frequently as necessary to keep the patient stable.

The goal of the KBS described in this case study is to assist the doctor in the intensive care unit by performing the following:

• predicting the initial setting of the mechanical ventilator;
• suggesting adjustments to the settings of the ventilator;
• summarizing the patient's status.

2.6.4 The integrated system

This case study concerns an application where a KBS in integrated with a conventional software system. This situation is becoming more and more common as KBS are accepted in the everyday business world. The system in this case study is a human-resource management system which was developed for a large organization. A human-resource management (HRM) system is a software system which is designed to make the best use of the people in the organization. In this case the main aim of the system was to identify which staff were best suited for particular projects and to identify the training needs of those staff.

The department employs approximately 4000 staff, and is sub-divided into a number of areas, each responsible for specific services. Each of these areas has a resource manager who is responsible for a number of projects. The duty of the resource manager is to fit a suitably qualified person to a specific job within each of the projects which they are responsible for.

Any vacancy not filled within any one area is then made available across the whole department. This involves staff being transferred between areas. If no suitable staff are available internally, the resource manager must turn to the use of external consultants. Because of the expense involved, these are usually only employed on high-priority, short-term projects.

The main task to be done by the KBS is to match staff with suitable projects. The KBS must, then, hold knowledge relating to staff skills, location, availability and other personal factors. The new system was required to use the existing personnel database and job vacancy database (Figure 2.9).

2.7 Summary

This chapter has given a feel for the field of knowledge-based systems. The history of KBS has been covered along with common application areas, both past and present. We have also introduced the case studies which are to be used as the basis for much of the following text.

2.8 Exercises

1. Using the categories defined by Waterman (section 2.1.2), place the following KBS into the most appropriate categories.

   - A KBS which checks the condition of turbines in a power plant and informs the operators when there are possible problems. The operators must then make the decision as to whether the turbine needs shutting down and repairing.
   - A KBS which asks a car buyer the attributes of the car which he/she is looking for. The system will then try and match a car to the customer's exact requirements.
   - A KBS which is used by a shop-floor manager in a factory to generate work schedules.
   - A KBS which is used by a personnel manager to produce a shortlist of applicants for a job.

2. Categorize the four case studies described in sections 2.6.1–4 according to Waterman's categories.

3. Following this question is an extract from the instructions for a new portable colour television. Study the extract and identify:

   - five facts
   - five rules

Write these facts and rules in English.

Your new colour television

Safety
1. **Moisture.** Avoid positioning the set where extreme dust or moisture is likely. The unit should not be exposed to dripping or moisture such as rain, dew, condensation, etc.

2. **Vibration.** Place the unit on a stable, level surface, avoiding places subject to strong vibration.

3. **Magnetism.** Do not position the set near strong magnetic fields such as loudspeaker enclosures as they can adversely affect the picture quality.

4. **Accidents.** Keep such things as flower vases, coffee cups, etc., which may get spilt, away from your television. If liquids should be spilled into the unit serious damage may result. If you spill any liquid into the machine, disconnect the mains plug from the wall socket or remove the car battery lead and consult qualified service personnel before attempting to use the equipment again.

5. **Cleaning.** Do not spray cleaner or wax directly onto the unit.

Power Indicator

Plug the mains lead into the wall socket before switching on the power. When the power is switched on a power indicator will glow constantly during operation and standby modes. If the power indicator doesn't glow check the fuse in the plug and confirm power is available at the wall socket.

The Aerial

Your television is fitted with a built-in telescopic aerial. The aerial should be extended and rotated for best reception.

When using the unit in a caravan or car, or in areas of poor reception, an alternative aerial may be required. The type of aerial needed depends on the position of your television, its distance from the transmitter, local interference, etc. If you don't already have a suitable television aerial and your are uncertain of what to buy, you should seek the advice of a local professional aerial contractor.

If an alternative aerial is used, make sure that it is correctly installed. Take the aerial plug and insert in into the 75 ohm aerial socket which can be found on the back of the television.

Remote Control

The remote control handset has an operating range of approximately 7 metres. For best effect it should be pointed directly at the remote sensor on the front of the television. However, operation is possible up to an angle of 30°.

The remote control may not work if:

- The batteries are low.
- The batteries are inserted incorrectly.
- The path from the Handset to the television is obstructed (by furniture, etc.)

Chapter 3

The knowledge-engineering life cycle

OBJECTIVES

In this chapter you will learn:

- ❏ about the traditional software-development life cycle;
- ❏ the stages that a knowledge engineer will go through when developing a KBS;
- ❏ the importance of prototyping in KBS development;
- ❏ the importance of methods for KBS development;
- ❏ about the key structured methodologies which can be used for knowledge engineering.

3.1 Introduction

> It must be remembered that there is nothing more difficult to plan, more doubtful of success, nor more dangerous to manage than the creation of a new system. For the initiator has the enmity of all who would profit by the preservation of the old institution and merely lukewarm defenders in those who could gain by the new ones.
>
> Machiavelli (1513) *The Prince*

This chapter focuses upon the role, and importance, of taking a staged and methodical approach in the process of KBS development. In particular, lessons regarding the importance of taking a structured prototyping approach to KBS development are illustrated by reference to one of our case studies.

The chapter begins with an overview of the traditional software-development life cycle. This is followed by a discussion of one of the most common approaches to knowledge-based system development: prototyping. Following this is included a brief history of methods, followed by an overview of some of the most important methods which can be used by knowledge engineers. The chapter closes with a series of problems for you to work through.

3.2 The traditional software-development life cycle

In common with any other product, software goes through a number of stages from initial conception through to the final finished article. These stages are commonly termed the software-development life cycle. For the purposes of this book a typical life cycle is depicted in Figure 3.1.

3.2.1 Analysis

This stage consists of analysing the user's problems and is one of the most difficult, creative and intuitive stages in the software-development process. This is because analysis consists of trying to get to the real heart of the problem; which may not be at all straightforward. The user may not really grasp what the problem is. In knowledge-engineering terms, this is equivalent

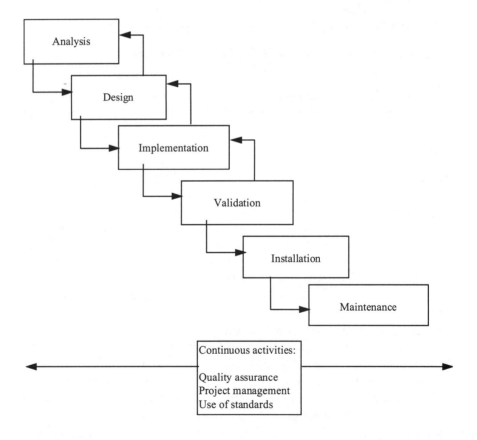

Figure 3.1 *The traditional software development life cycle.*

to the knowledge-acquisition and representation phases. These are discussed fully in Chapters 4 and 5.

The questions to be answered at this stage may include:

- 'What is the real problem to be solved?'
- 'What do the potential users of the software really need?'
- 'What computer and programs are needed?'
- 'What data are to be used and what results are to be presented (and in what format)?'

This stage will involve extensive discussions and consultations with the people who are going to use the software in the future. The output of this stage will be a detailed specification which will spell out exactly:

- the inputs and outputs of the system;
- the hardware and software to be used;
- the functions to be performed by the system;
- the form and structure of the user interface (i.e. how the system is to interact with its users).

3.2.2 Design

This stage entails the design of the software. Here the software engineers will decide how many programs need to be written and describe their overall structure. During this stage the software engineer may be using a semi-formal methodology to help ensure a well-structured software system. This might result in a diagrammatic representation of the software system to be produced, known as a structure chart.

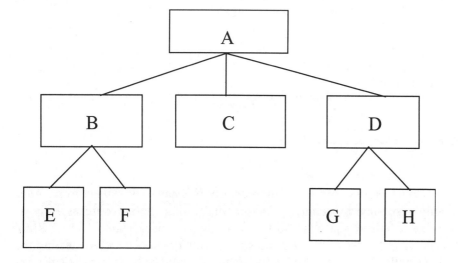

Figure 3.2 *Example of a structure chart.*

The structure chart in Figure 3.2 shows a program A which consists of three parts B, C and D. Part B in turn consists of two parts, E and F, while part D consists of parts G and H. Structure charts can be very useful during design and give a pictorial view of the structure of the software.

KBS design is usually undertaken in an iterative rather than a staged manner, using a prototyping approach. The prototyping approach is discussed in detail in section 3.3 of this chapter.

3.2.3 Implementation

The implementation (or coding) stage involves taking the software design and converting it into the instructions of a programming language, such as C, COBOL, Ada or FORTRAN. For a knowledge engineer this will mean translating the design into an appropriate language such as Prolog or Lisp, or using an expert system shell. This is discussed fully in Chapter 6. Examples of code follow:

```
CRYSTAL     (an expert system shell):


            [   2]  adjust dailydiff for precipitation
          + IF    [ 27]    test for mild weather today morning
          + AND   [ 26]    test for mild weather today afternoon
          + AND   [ 29]    test for mild weather tomorrow morning
          + AND   [ 28]    test for mild weather tomorrow afternoon
            AND DO: Assign Variable
                  base3:=base3
```

```
Prolog:

run(y):- nl,
write("EXPERT SYSTEM FOR THE DIAGNOSIS AND MANAGEMENT OF
RESPIRATORY FAILURE"),
write("Ensure all your responses are typed in lowercase!"),
write("What is the patient's unit number ? > "),
readln(Number),
inputcond(Condition),
inputsex(Sex),
inputwt(Weight),
inputage(Age),
write("Enter the patient's height in feet and inches"),nl,
inputft(Feet),
inputins(Inches),
diagnosed(Condition,Sex,Age,Weight,Feet,Ins).
```

3.2.4 Validation

Any quality product is only of high quality if it has been subject to rigorous quality assurance procedures. This entails testing the software as fully as possible to ensure that it performs according to specification and does not 'crash' or fail when it meets some strange input data. As well as testing the product at this late stage, checks and reviews should be built into the software life cycle at every stage.

The prime objective of KBS validation is to produce a system that is more reliable, of a higher quality and generally more usable than it otherwise would be. So does this happen? Are knowledge engineers really validating their systems well?

Unfortunately the answers to the above questions are currently not clear. This is because:

- few methods exist for KBS development or validation;
- KBS validation is difficult;
- no one really knows how to validate a KBS!

The subject of validation is discussed more in Chapter 8.

3.2.5 Installation

Once the software has been fully tested it should be installed on the user's computer. This can be a relatively simple process for small pieces of software, but may be much more complicated for larger, more complex systems. It may also involve training the users of the software exactly how to operate it. The software should also be accompanied by a user manual to tell the users how to operate it, and a technical manual which will enable other knowledge (or software) engineers to maintain the system in the future.

3.2.6 Maintenance

Now that the software has been installed, it must be maintained. This entails correcting any bugs that the users may subsequently find in the software and ensuring that it continues to work correctly in the future. This may also involve updating the software to meet new user requirements and changes in the environment in which the software operates.

3.2.7 Continuous activities

Throughout the software life cycle it is necessary to ensure that:

- The software-development process is tightly managed and controlled. Like any other large project, it is necessary to apply good project-management techniques to ensure success.
- Each stage of the process is carefully documented. This is particularly important for very large projects which may go on for a long time. Over the life of the project, the staff working on the development of the software system are quite likely to change. Good documentation will make it so much easier for new members of a project team to pick things up and gain a rapid understanding of the project and its current status.

- Everything produced is subject to some form of quality assurance (QA), including preliminary designs, documents and manuals. This QA should ensure that each document or piece of software which is produced adheres to the standards which have been set by the company and that they are consistent with the overall aims of the system. QA might consist of regular review meetings where members of the project team go through the latest documents which have been produced by their colleagues and look for errors and omissions. It is particularly useful if such meetings include members from outside the project team, as they are often better able to spot any problems or mistakes.

This means the production of **deliverables** at a number of natural checkpoints (the end of each stage). Deliverables are outputs which must be produced by the project team at various points during the life cycle. These will be marked on the project plan and subject to a review process. Examples of deliverables are:

- pieces of prototype software
- screen designs
- design documents
- draft user manuals
- progress reports

These can then be used for the regular monitoring, evaluation and review of the project (and hence for project management and quality assurance).

3.2.8 Benefits of the staged approach

The benefits of adopting such a life-cycle approach to software development are now widely recognized.

These benefits include:

- The ability to carefully plan the project and estimate the resources which are required to complete it. These may include the cost of personnel, hardware and software.
- The ability to estimate the size and complexity of the software project. It is important to be able to work out a realistic estimate so that this can be used to estimate how long it will take to complete the work and how much the whole project will cost.
- Availability of documents for monitoring and control. Using a life-cycle approach with plenty of deliverables will make sure that there are always documents available. These can then be used to check the progress of the project.
- The ability to update estimates on the basis of this monitoring. This might mean changing the project plan because the project is running behind schedule. This is quite common in the case of large projects.

• It is easier to fit the project into a quality-management system.

Some software developers have taken other approaches to software system development in various attempts to improve the engineering of information systems. In reality information system development is not the straightforward process that the traditional software-development life-cycle model suggests. It usually consists of a number of iterations through each of the stages. There are, therefore, several alternative approaches which involve some sort of reorganization of the various stages of analysis, design, implementation, validation, installation and maintenance.

Each of these methodologies (for example, SSADM: see Eva, 1992) has been used successfully in conventional software development. Each approach has its own advantages and disadvantages and not one has been proven to be universally better than the others.

Information system design is by no means easy or simple, but KBS development brings with it another set of problems.

In general, knowledge-based systems:

• have incomplete system/user requirements at the start of the project – it may be that the users do not fully understand what the system can do for them; the expertise which the system is aiming to capture may be difficult to categorize and represent;
• are complex and are often poorly structured;
• need to cope with uncertainty and/or incomplete knowledge.

The task of the knowledge engineer is to adapt existing software-development life cycles to the problems of KBS development and to produce new methodologies that deal with the particular difficulties associated with knowledge engineering.

Up until now, most knowledge-based systems have been developed on an *ad hoc* basis, with rapid prototyping providing a popular means of (often unstructured) system development. Rapid prototyping is discussed in the next section.

3.3 Rapid prototyping

3.3.1 Background

Rapid prototyping (or, more simply, 'prototyping') is a relatively recent technique that was first developed for traditional information-system development. It is often (quite unfairly) described as a 'quick and dirty' method that allows for the creation of a prototype version of part (or all) of the system.

Prototypes are an important concept in all branches of engineering, including software development. They have been said to be '…indispensable vehicles for obtaining irreplaceable hands-on experience with a system, be it a chair or a ship or a software product' (Jorgensen, 1984).

Prototyping has been described as 'a revolutionary change in the development process' (Naumann and Jenkins, 1982) because it departs from the traditional software engineering approach.

There is no standard definition of prototyping. This reflects the many diverse ways in which it is applied during software development. It does, however, have some generally accepted characteristics (Edwards *et al.*, 1991):

- There is involvement with the user throughout system development, from specification of requirements to the actual implementation of the system.
- The aim of the prototype is to present the user with a working model of the system.
- The model of the system developed as the prototype may not be the system which is ultimately developed. However, since it is a working model developed early in the software life cycle it provides the users with the opportunity to alter and further specify their requirements.
- The working system is evaluated by users as it is being created, so that any alterations can be made in either the requirements specification or design.
- It is an experiment that tests hypotheses.
- By creating a vehicle for communication between users and developers, this stimulates learning about the system for both parties.

3.3.2 The iterative approach

The prototyping approach consists of an iteration of a set of basic steps (Figure 3.3):

- Identify the users' basic information requirements and establish prototyping objectives. This ensures that both developers and users know what the prototype will achieve. The requirements need to be established but at this stage do not have to be complete. The user must specify exactly which parts of the system are to be prototyped.
- Design and develop a working prototype. This must be achieved quickly to give rapid feedback to the users and to allow them to make changes before progressing further. The system will not be complete at this stage.
- Implement and use the prototype system. The users have to operate the prototype and evaluate it. This allows them to gain an understanding of the working system while still allowing future changes.
- Evaluate, revise and enhance the system. Here evaluation sessions allow both users and developers to learn more about the system. Errors should be reduced and missing features (for example) should be identified.

The iterative steps shown in Figure 3.3 offer wide scope for changing requirements. They also bring the users and developers into closer working contact, which in itself ensures the design of a system which fulfils the users'

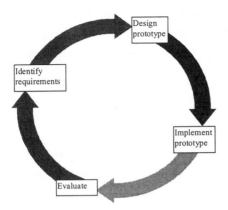

Figure 3.3 *Prototyping is an iterative technique.*

needs. The approach also allows the users to see the development of the system, unlike conventional methods in which users are subjected to more abstract specifications.

3.3.3 Types of prototyping

Ince and Hekmatpour (1987) list three types of prototyping:

- **Throw-it-away** – this involves the rapid development of an early working design and is used to develop the users' requirements to expand the original specification. This helps identify the required system and eliminates errors in understanding. The prototype is subsequently discarded.
- **Incremental** – here the technique is used after the normal design stage of the system. It is developed in stages and each stage is evaluated before continuing on to the next. The user can suggest changes at any stage; however, once the design of any stage is completed it is frozen and no further changes are allowed.
- **Evolutionary** – the technique is applied in stages as the design of the system is carried out with suggestions from both users and developers contributing to the development. This is a flexible approach which reflects the rapidly changing requirements that are often needed in software development (contrasting with the more rigid traditional approaches).

3.3.4 Why use prototyping?

When developing software it makes sense to let the user of the software see and 'get a feel' for the software as soon as is humanly possible. That is, it makes sense to develop a prototype version of the system and to let the user 'play' with that version at the earliest possible opportunity. The prototype will not be fully functional. It will not do all of the things that the final version of the system will have to. But it will have the initial screens so that the user can see what the final software will look like. In this way he/she will be able to try out the system and see if the development is going the right way.

Prototyping thus serves to (Edwards *et al.*, 1991):

* clarify user requirements
* validate the specification
* evaluate the design
* evaluate part of the development

3.3.5 Benefits

The main benefits of prototyping can be broken down into two main categories:

* achieving the required system
* developing a cost-effective system

3.3.5.1 The required system

One major problem of the traditional software-development life-cycle approach is that it would often take a long time for a system to be developed and delivered to the users. This often meant that by the time the system got into the hands of the users their requirements might well have changed. They would then either reject the system or just never bother to use it.

In either of the above cases the system is clearly a failure and a large investment will have been wasted. Prototyping avoids such failures by involving the users at every stage during the development. This significantly raises the chances of the system meeting their requirements. This is achieved through the close interaction of users and developers.

Thus, benefits are:

* The opportunity exists for amendment of the system during design. This helps both the elimination of errors and ambiguities and the addition of new ideas.
* User involvement results in a recognition of the system's true worth.
* The co-operation of users and developers improves morale and motivation of staff.
* The end result is user-friendly.
* The amendments to the final system should be minimal as these have already been made to the prototype.

3.3.5.2 The cost-effective system

Prototyped systems have been found to be more cost-effective than conventionally designed systems.

* The final system is easier to maintain because of peer group evaluation.
* The human–computer interface tends to be more user-friendly, enabling users to understand the system more quickly.

- In an experiment discussed by Boehm (cited by Ince and Hekmatpour, 1987) teams were smaller by an average of 40% and the product was developed with 45% less effort.
- The prototyping approach reduces the workload when coming up to project deadlines.
- Less time is required to develop the system.

Balancing these benefits there are also drawbacks to the use of prototyping.

3.3.6 Drawbacks

Any development approach has its drawbacks and prototyping is no exception. Some of these drawbacks are (Edwards *et al.*, 1991):

- Management may be reluctant to adopt an experimental technique. Linked with this is the fear that users will constantly change their requirements making project control difficult.
- If changes are made to the prototype the developers must ensure that these are incorporated throughout the whole system.
- Problems can arise if the users and developers do not agree (or conversely agree too quickly) on the prototype, as some requirements may then be missed.
- Costing and setting a time limit can prove difficult.
- The users must be willing to accept that prototyping involves iteration and that the software developed may be discarded. Associated with this users also need to understand that once prototyped the product may still take several months to develop.

Despite these potential obstacles, there is some indication (Tozer, 1987) that users do not become too demanding, nor do they expect the product to be delivered rapidly. Instead there appears to be increased co-operation and communication between users and developers which helps in the development of better systems.

3.3.7 Prototyping in KBS design

Prototyping is thus an iterative, evolutionary and sometimes exploratory technique. It has been criticized as being unstructured, as lacking control and documentation and as being suitable only for small projects. However, it has become the most popular medium for developing KBS systems. The case studies discussed in this book were all developed using a prototyping approach. Some of the lessons learnt from one of the case studies are presented in section 3.5.

Prototyping has been so successful in KBS development because knowledge engineering depends, perhaps more than any other form of software development, on the involvement of the users of the system. Another reason is because of the speed with which you can develop a system when using an expert system shell.

Prototyping has thus been seized upon by many knowledge engineers as the ideal vehicle for KBS development. Practical development can be begun almost immediately and the technical feasibility and commercial desirability of a knowledge-engineering project can be demonstrated to senior management early in the process. This is a very important factor considering the level of resistance to KBS technology that is often experienced.

Prototyping also seems to be perfectly suited to the types of problems often encountered in KBS development, where the initial requirements are typically ill-defined, and the problem itself often ill-structured. In knowledge engineering the prototype provides a sounding board for management, users and experts alike, and can be important in crystallizing system specifications, user requirements, human/computer interfaces, and the problem domain itself, i.e. exactly what knowledge must be obtained from the expert or experts to allow the system to function correctly.

That is, prototyping can be used to help identify the real requirements of the KBS and to get a better understanding of the knowledge which is to be captured and represented.

The prototype can be evaluated by users and management in conjunction with the knowledge engineer in terms of:

- **Project viability** – is the knowledge-based system likely to be of real use?
- **Systems/user requirements** – will it do what is required?
- **Human–computer interfaces** – will the users be able to use the system?

Users and management are thus presented with something concrete early on in the project. They can then suggest refinements and improvements and these can be incorporated into later versions of the KBS. This is important if the system is to be successful.

The major criticism of the prototyping approach to KBS development is that it has too often been used in an unstructured, undisciplined, *ad hoc* manner. Prototyping has not been used as a method but rather instead of a method. Whereas this may be acceptable in the research laboratory, in the real world of commercial applications KBS must be developed according to QA procedures and standards, giving full regard to commercial considerations.

Prototyping should not be used at the expense of quality or as an excuse for not applying a sound methodical approach. If KBS development is to succeed it is important to use prototyping alongside a set of QA procedures and good sound management practices.

3.3.8 Summary

KBS development using the prototyping technique can be effective in generating a product which gives users the features they require. By its nature it is a flexible approach and it can be incorporated with conventional systems-development methodologies. This gives the knowledge engineers and users the benefits of both approaches: the more rigorous specification from the traditional methods coupled with the user-driven requirements definition.

3.4 Structured KBS development methodologies

3.4.1 Background

All branches of engineering have a set of methods and tools with which to work. For instance, civil engineers have methods to aid in the calculation of the stresses and strains on bridges, electronic engineers have methods to help in the layout of electronic components on a circuit board, and chemical engineers have methods based on chemical equations to help when working with chemical reactions. Software and knowledge engineering are no different to any other branch of engineering in this respect. Methods are as important during the design and implementation of software as during the design and construction of any other engineering artefact.

Knowledge engineering has developed from the discipline of software engineering which has, in turn, developed from the art of programming. It must not be forgotten that it is not that many years ago that there were no methods for the programmer to work with. Indeed, in the early days of computing, programming was truly an art and not a science. The early programmer had no methods to help him/her in the task of software construction.

Table 3.1 illustrates the way in which system development has matured over the years. It should, however, be stressed that software and knowledge engineering are still relatively immature disciplines in comparison with many of the more established and traditional branches of engineering. Indeed, it is only in quite recent times that methods have become available for designing and constructing software systems. Even today, there are a lot of methods around and little real agreement as to which is the 'best' method (if there can ever be said to be such a thing).

It was the so-called 'software crisis' of the late 1960s which brought a realization that methods were needed if software development was ever to become a truly professional engineering discipline. Out of this realization a series of methods were born. An overview of the history of information-system development methods is presented in Table 3.1 and Figure 3.4.

So it is now the case that the software developer has a set of methods with which to work. In general, these methods provide the software designer with a set of rules, procedures and diagrams which help in the design of a software system. But which methods should one choose for a particular project?

This is often a difficult question to answer as there may be many factors involved in making such a decision. For instance, it is likely that one must first also answer the following questions:

Table 3.1 *A tabular history of methods*

Period	Methods	Application
1950s	None	
1960s	MASCOT	Real-time systems where time is a critical factor such as defence systems or aircraft control systems
1970s	JSP (Jackson structured programming)	Commercial systems which deal with large quantities of data such as payroll systems
1980s	SSADM (Structured systems analysis and development method). SSADM is the standard method used by the UK civil service	Commercial
1980s	JSD (Jackson system development)	Real-time
1990s	Object-oriented design methods	Any
1990s	Formal, mathematical methods such as VDM (Vienna development method) and Z which use mathematics to ensure software quality	Any
1990s	KADS (see later)	KBS

- What methods do I (and any other people involved) already know?
- What are the characteristics of the problem environment? Is it real-time? Data processing? Safety critical?
- What tools do I have available to support the methods?
- Are any methods required either by the client or because of legislation?

Methods are now widely accepted and used throughout the software-development community. A study of 230 organizations undertaken in the UK by market analyst Spikes Cavell in 1992 revealed that 73% of companies use one form of method or another. The survey also showed that almost 19% of those

Programming No methods Black art	1950s
Software engineering	1960s
Advent of structured programming	1970s
Knowledge engineering	1980s
Structured methods Object oriented design KBS methods Prototyping	1990s

Figure 3.4 *A history of methods.*

companies which were not currently using a method were planning to do so in the future. The results are shown in Figure 3.5.

This represents, then, a major commitment to the use of methods within the UK software-development community. However, one common statement which is still made is 'It doesn't matter what method you use, as long as you use a method.'

There is certainly some truth in this statement but certain methods are better suited to certain application areas. For instance, methods such as SSADM are ideal for the development of large commercial systems such as payroll systems and formal methods such as VDM are well-suited to systems which particularly require mathematical rigour during their development in

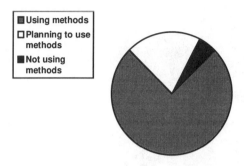

Figure 3.5 *Use of methods in the USA in 1992 (Cavell, 1992).*

order to ensure high quality and reliability (such as aircraft control or defence systems).

Most knowledge engineers would agree that the particular requirements of KBS render traditional software-development life cycles inappropriate. However, this by no means implies that they would agree on the best way to tackle the problem: the chances are that they will have widely differing opinions.

In fact, a debate continues with regard to the relationship between knowledge engineering and software engineering. Some argue that there is a need for the two fields to move closer together. This could be important in the future because KBS will increasingly be integrated with existing information systems to form integrated or hybrid systems. The time has thus come to forge stronger links between the two disciplines.

One major barrier to KBS uptake in commerce and industry is lack of confidence in the technology. Through the adoption of structured methods, tools and techniques, knowledge engineers can show that knowledge-based systems are useful, efficient, reliable, maintainable, worthy of investment and of great value to business and industry.

Advocates of knowledge engineering suggest that the discipline holds the key to creating intelligent information systems. Detractors claim that knowledge-based systems divert a large amount of time, energy and money into a 'scientific cul-de-sac'. The truth of the matter is perhaps somewhere between these two extremes.

Whilst this debate rages at a conceptual level, others have been busy developing methods to tackle the practical problem of producing knowledge-based systems of a consistently high quality. But there are many approaches in evidence.

The approaches can be separated into two major groupings. The first grouping, rapid prototyping, has already been discussed in section 3.3. Prototyping is characteristic of much of the actual KBS development in UK industry. According to a recent report by Touche Ross (1992), 45% of companies said that this was their preferred means of KBS development. Only 25% claimed to use a structured methodology. Figure 3.6 shows the results of this survey.

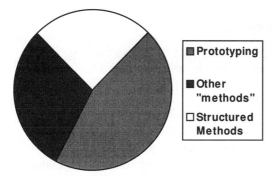

Figure 3.6 *Almost half (45%) of UK companies use prototyping for KBS development.*

The second set of approaches can be grouped under the umbrella term 'structured methodologies'. This includes methods such as:

- GEMINI
- POLITE
- KADS

which are briefly described in sections 3.4.2–4.

3.4.2 GEMINI

GEMINI (General Expert systems Methodology INItiative) (Montgomery, 1988; Thompson, 1990) is a project that has been sponsored by UK government and industry. The aim of GEMINI was to combine KBS techniques, traditional software-engineering methods, and incremental prototyping techniques with the SSADM method. GEMINI was designed to be particularly useful in the development of hybrid systems (systems which integrate traditional information systems with knowledge-based elements). GEMINI incorporates into its life cycle six stages which come directly from the SSADM method:

1. **Current system investigation** – which (as the name suggests) examines the current system.

2. **Requirements specification** – which sets out the requirements of the KBS.

3. **Technical options** – this stage examines the different technical options and asks questions such as 'which hardware and software should we use for the KBS project?'

4. **Data design** – this is the equivalent of knowledge representation and involves defining the knowledge on which the KBS will operate.

5. **Process design** – this is the equivalent of defining the rules which will exist within the KBS.

6. **Physical design** – this stage defines the structure of the system and how it will run on the user's hardware.

Progress through the life cycle is not sequential, but iterative: before passing on to the next stage, deliverables from the current stage must be validated using one of a number of tools and techniques. These include prototyping and methods borrowed from conventional SSADM.

The GEMINI method has been used for the development of some large knowledge-based systems in the UK, particularly in the public sector.

3.4.3 POLITE

Another methodology that has been developed centres around the POLITE system-development life cycle, which has evolved from the Run–Understand–Debug–Edit (RUDE) technique (Bader *et al.*, 1988). The RUDE cycle is shown in Figure 3.7.

The originators of the POLITE method have criticized the prototyping approach to KBS development that is used by most knowledge engineers in the UK. However, they argue (from experience) that rapid prototyping is a valuable technique for KBS development, in that it allows 'validation of the analysis and design by the expert and the prospective user… Only through this iterative process can the performance objectives for the system be obtained' (Bader *et al.*, 1988).

The POLITE life cycle joins the traditional software-development life cycle with the RUDE cycle, by adding a RUDE stage between each of the major phases.

3.4.4 KADS

KADS (knowledge acquisition and design process) is another methodology that has been developed for KBS construction (Hickman, 1989; Porter, 1992; Schreiber, Wielinga and Brenker, 1993). It is probably the most successful

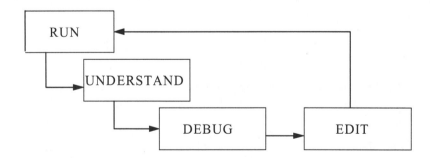

Figure 3.7 *The RUDE prototyping cycle.*

and widely known knowledge-engineering method; certainly this is the case within Europe.

The KADS project was initiated in 1983, funded by the European Commission under the ESPRIT programme (European Strategic Programme for Research in Information Technology). KADS is a model-based method that has gained widespread acceptance throughout Europe and inspired worldwide interest. Certainly there has been a large amount of investment in the method, but it has been criticized for being large and difficult to understand and apply.

It was formulated with the intention of taking the best practices from traditional system development and combining them with additional tools and techniques to enable KBS builders to tackle the particular problems associated with knowledge engineering.

In KADS, there is a thorough and rigorous problem analysis before design and implementation is undertaken. Rapid prototyping is used as an experimental or exploratory tool to investigate specific areas of interest in the project, rather than as a development methodology itself.

It is a modelling methodology. The finished KBS product is an operational model that incorporates models of expertise, user–system interaction and the organization in which the system will operate. The modelling approach allows complex knowledge-based systems to be built to exacting requirements, in a framework that helps with project management and the application of quality assurance techniques.

KADS is based on five principles:

1. a four-layer framework for modelling expertise (the domain, inference, task and strategic layers);

2. refinement of simple models of the system into more complex ones;

3. use of intermediate models as a means of coping with the complexity of the knowledge-engineering process;

4. structure-preserving transformation of expertise into design model and system code;

5. reusability of partial models as templates for top-down knowledge acquisition.

3.5 The development of hybrid information systems

A new and important development is in the area of hybrid information systems (HIS). These may well be the next generation of information system and will consist of traditional information or database systems linked and integrated with knowledge-based systems. Current methodologies for software engineering and knowledge engineering cannot meet the requirements of HIS development and techniques for their design and implementation are currently a very active research area. The integrated system case study describes a simple kind of HIS.

Chen and Kendal (Chen *et al.*, 1995) propose a hierarchical architecture for HIS development which is based on a four-level model (Figure 3.8). The four levels are:

1. **Code and repository level** – the lowest level. This deals mainly with technologies for the design and implementation of databases, knowledge base and procedures.

2. **Modelling level** – this consists of all models that integrate data, knowledge and procedures based on modelling objects and entities.

3. **HIS level** – this implements combinations and linkages of objects to build a HIS. Conventional information systems or knowledge-based systems are subsets of a HIS.

4. **ICIS (intelligent and co-operative information systems) level** – the top level. This integrates existing software systems.

From a technical viewpoint these four levels are independent of each other. From a system viewpoint they are interrelated. Chen and Kendal suggest a process for developing HIS which starts with preliminary requirements analysis from the view of the whole system at the HIS level. It then performs detailed requirement specification and model design based at the modelling level. Finally design and implementation of the HIS takes place at the lowest level.

They propose a life-cycle model which incorporates many of the concepts of the evolutionary prototyping approach (Figure 3.9). The methodology has been used in the development of a medical HIS (Figure 3.10).

3.6 Lessons from one of the case studies

In this chapter we have discussed the role and importance of taking a methodical approach to KBS development, given an overview of the traditional software-development life cycle and shown the importance of prototyping. Following this was as overview of some of the most important methods which can be used by knowledge engineers.

It has been seen that the most popular approach to knowledge engineering is prototyping. This certainly matches the author's own experiences. All of the four case studies discussed in this book were developed using a prototyping approach.

The following comments (Hardy, 1993), which were made by the knowledge engineer who developed the quality control expert system for finding faults in plastic cups, illustrates some interesting points about prototyping.

Given that it was one of the aims of this project to involve the user at every stage, the knowledge acquisition phase, and the associated documentation were intrinsic to the software development. The pro-

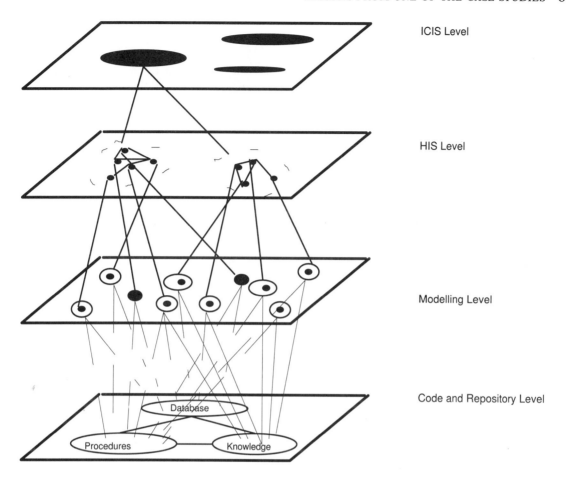

Figure 3.8 *The hierarchical architecture of complex software systems (Chen, 1995).*

totyping approach to client-centred development has recently been taken up widely by knowledge engineers, which may suggest that developments are moving away from research, into the market place.

The project was intended to provide a diagnostic expert system for three of the most common problems encountered at the rim curler. It was envisaged that by the Christmas break, two of these problems would have been covered. However, there were a number of unavoidable postponements of knowledge acquisition sessions. In addition, Mr A. Black (the client, but not the key expert) managed to free sufficient time to look at the software that I had developed. Unfortunately, what the expert (Mrs D. Whyte) had found acceptable as a user interface, was not what the client required.

Consequently, I cancelled the following three knowledge acquisition sessions, in order that I could make the necessary changes to the prototype. This was the first occasion where the client had stated exactly what he wanted, and I felt that it was important to make an effort to give him a program that

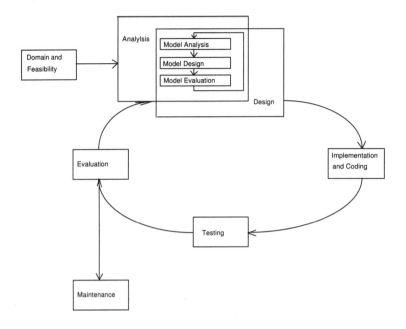

Figure 3.9 *Process model for the development of HIS (Chen, 1995).*

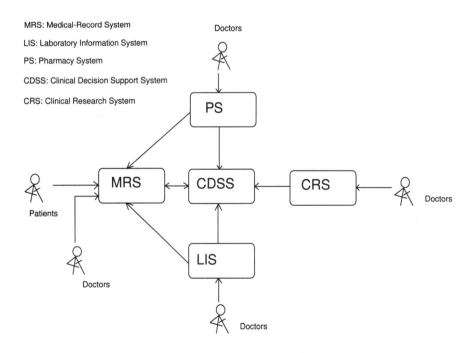

Figure 3.10 *The medical HIS (Chen, 1995).*

he would feel confident with. The result of this, is that one problem area was thoroughly covered before Christmas. Since I had deliberately timetabled myself to allow for such eventualities, this did not adversely influence my schedule.

The program prior to the changes was primarily a system based on menu choices. This placed the onus on the operator to follow the instructions provided, make judgements about the outcome of the changes that he/she had made, and then make another menu choice, which would then repeat the sequence of 'choice, adjustment, judgement'. The client argued that this required the operator to make too many decisions, and that the program should be telling the operator to make particular changes on the basis of the input.

Knowledge base development is something that is never really complete. There is always the opportunity to add something, in order to give it that little bit more, such as another series of options. Consequently, in the current development, I had to clearly and completely stop development at a particular point. That does not mean that the current KBS is incomplete, nor that it is not possible to go back to it at a later date. I believe that the 'clean break' is the best approach in such situations, otherwise further prototype development can become a process of diminishing returns.

In the current development I was requested to carry out a presentation to a group of technical and senior managers. I was therefore able to use this as the finishing point for the software, since it was intended that the presentation should include a software demonstration. I based the presentation on what I believe to be the key factors that businesses should consider in any KBS development, and how I then applied those considerations to the current project.

The presentation was followed by a demonstration, and then a discussion about KBS development, software and the approaches that they might take in future developments. The development has proved to be a success, and has exceeded the anticipations of both client and sponsor.

These comments highlight a number of important factors:

- The user and the expert can often have very different views of the same system. It is the knowledge engineer's job to try to produce a system which will represent the true knowledge and be of real use to the users.
- You have to agree (or decide on) a cut-off point at which you stop software development. Otherwise, prototyping may go on indefinitely, forever trying to match the ever-changing requirements of users.
- Knowledge acquisition and software development may be combined in prototyping. As further knowledge is captured this will be incorporated within the latest version of the prototype. The distinction between knowledge acquisition and software development is often blurred. This is also an argument for the use of prototyping rather than a staged life-cycle approach which forces the knowledge engineer to adhere to a series of rather false and often stifling stages.

3.7 Summary

This chapter has focused upon the knowledge-engineering life cycle. The stages that a knowledge engineer will go through when designing a KBS have been discussed, along with the importance of using methods for software development. The importance of the prototyping approach and why it is so appropriate for KBS development, has been covered. Finally some practical lessons from one of the case studies have been presented.

3.8 Exercises

1. Prototyping and structured methodologies both have positive and negative aspects, and each one's success depends upon the situation in which they are used and whether the knowledge engineer has correctly thought out which approach will suit the particular development. It is certainly more feasible to apply a prototyping method to small rather than large scale projects. For example Kingston (Kingston, 1991) notes that 'KADS has been criticized for the overhead which it places on small and medium-sized KBS projects where the risk of KBS development becoming unmanageable are relatively low'.

Complete the table below listing the pros and cons of prototyping and structured methodologies.

Prototyping		Structured methodologies	
For	Against	For	Against

2. The knowledge engineer needs to be aware that there cannot be one rigid strategy for development that can be applicable in all circumstances. One may have to compare methodologies in order to establish the suitability of the particular project. This can be very difficult. Try to produce a list of important criteria for a methodology which is to be applied to the development of a KBS for air traffic control.

Chapter 4

Knowledge acquisition*

OBJECTIVES

In this chapter you will learn:

❑ the importance of the knowledge acquisition process;

❑ the major techniques of knowledge acquisition;

❑ the do's and don'ts of interviewing;

❑ some lessons from the case studies.

4.1 Introduction

Knowledge acquisition is the process of acquiring knowledge from a human expert (or group of experts) and using this knowledge to build a KBS. It is also seen as a 'critical bottleneck' and recognized by many to be the most difficult stage of the knowledge-engineering process. Indeed it is often compared to 'hard' engineering and terms like mining, quarrying and extracting have been used to describe it.

If this is true human experts must look forward to the visit of the knowledge engineer as much as they would look forward to a visit to the dentist! This certainly shouldn't be the case: the knowledge engineer should aim to be as 'user-friendly' as possible.

Human experts are often seen as being inarticulate, argumentative and quickly bored. This is, in most cases, a myth. Most experts are so involved with and interested in their own subject area that they will be delighted to talk about it to anyone and will exhaust any knowledge engineer.

Knowledge acquisition involves elicitation of data from the expert, interpretation of these data to deduce the underlying knowledge and then creation of a model of the expert's domain knowledge in terms of the most appropriate knowledge representation mechanism. In other words, the knowledge engineer must familiarize him/herself with the domain of the expert, clearly identify the

* The author would like to thank Colin Hardy and David Leonard for their contributions to this chapter.

area of the domain that needs modelling and then represent this knowledge in a form that can be computerized.

Although there have been several moves to use computer software tools for knowledge elicitation the majority of expert systems developed have used some form of structured or unstructured interview to obtain information. A recent survey in the UK revealed that 77% of knowledge-based systems had been developed after the use of interview sessions (Smith *et al.*, 1994). Most of these started out with informal discussions to explain the project and to gather preliminary information, followed by more formal structured interviews.

Opinions about the use of interviews vary widely. Kawaguchi, Motoda and Mizoguchi (1991) said that they are 'essential in eliciting new knowledge from domain experts' while Cooke and McDonald (1986) called them: 'a less than optimal knowledge acquisition technique'.

Rightly or wrongly, and regardless of personal preferences, the interview process remains the most frequently used method for obtaining domain knowledge from human experts. Hence much of this chapter is devoted to a discussion on the subject of interviews and how best to go about the interview process. There is also coverage of some more structured and formal approaches to the knowledge acquisition process.

4.2 Printed sources

The simplest form of knowledge acquisition is gaining the knowledge from printed sources. This includes searching through documents, books and other items of printed material to find the knowledge necessary to build a system. The types of printed sources that may be of use include:

- **Procedures manuals** which describe how certain procedures are carried out in an organization.
- **Records** of past case studies which can be analysed in order to work out general principles and rules.
- **Standards documentation** which describe the particular standards an organization must adhere to.

In general, printed sources should be used as back-up or supplementary material, to support the knowledge gained from talking to and observing real human experts. They can also be used if an expert is not readily available. They are, however, extremely important in the initial stages of knowledge capture, for gaining initial concepts and learning the language of the problem domain.

Indeed, it is probably very wise for knowledge engineers to read as much as they can about the problem area which is going to be explored before approaching any human experts. In this way they can make sure that they have an understanding of the problem, terminology and major concepts before taking up the time of any of the experts. This will result in less time wasted and more effective interview sessions.

4.3 Interviews

One useful definition of an interview is given below:

> An interview is a verbal and non-verbal interaction between two parties, with the mutually agreed purpose of one party obtaining information from, or about the other, in order that it may be used for a particular purpose.
>
> (Hardy, 1993)

This draws a distinction between an interview and a discussion (Figure 4.1), in that the flow of information in an interview is primarily, and explicitly, in one direction. Similarly, an interview is not an interrogation since the situation and the outcome should be mutually agreed.

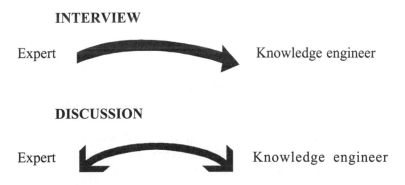

Figure 4.1 *The distinction between an interview and a discussion.*

However, an interview should not be assumed to be a 'natural' form of interaction and the management of an interview is not as straightforward as you might imagine. It is important to approach the interview in an organized, structured and professional manner if it is to succeed as a tool for knowledge acquisition.

To the expert, a knowledge-acquisition interview may be perceived to be just another activity. However, in terms of the knowledge-engineering process it is crucial and it is the responsibility of the knowledge engineer to ensure that the time is used as effectively as possible.

An interview can so easily degenerate into a discussion, since the latter is a more 'comfortable' form of social interaction. However, this defeats the aim of the session and wastes both the expert's and the knowledge engineer's time, because for a relatively large proportion of that time information passes in the wrong direction.

Conversely, interviewers who demand too much of an expert may believe that they are interviewing when they are actually carrying out an interrogation. Such interviewers run the risk of losing the expert's willing involvement.

Interviews have the advantage over the use of observation (section 4.6) and printed sources in that knowledge engineers can satisfy both themselves and the expert that they have grasped the points that the expert has been making. There are however a number of disadvantages, one of which is the length of time that it will take the knowledge engineer to transcribe and analyse the taped interviews.

Another disadvantage is that there may well be discrepancies between the method of problem solving outlined by experts and the actual method that they use in practise. They may well decide to introduce extraneous points to impress. They may find it difficult to describe the process that they undertake during problem solving.

There can also be problems with the knowledge engineer introducing bias through the phrasing of the questions, which can lead to misunderstandings and a misconstruction of the domain. The interviewer must also avoid making assumptions which may apply to the world in general but are incorrect in the narrower world of the expert's domain.

It has been argued (Hoffman, 1986) that the inefficient use of interviews may be one of the reasons why the knowledge-acquisition phase has been regarded as the major 'bottleneck' in KBS development. This may well be because of the knowledge engineer's inability to establish and maintain the formality of the interview.

Nevertheless, with a little effort, and perhaps a little assistance, the interview can be a very efficient knowledge-acquisition tool. Between the extremes of discussion and interrogation, there are a number of very useful interviewing techniques. These are described in the following sections.

4.3.1 Unstructured interviews

This is probably the most widely used knowledge-acquisition method and consists of free-flowing dialogue. Here, the knowledge engineer asks spontaneous questions and there has been little planning prior to the interview. The popularity of this method with knowledge engineers is a result of the lack of formality and the lack of preparation required. It certainly results in more relaxed interactions than using other, more structured, methods.

However, if the knowledge engineer does not take primary responsibility for the development of the interview, this will fall to the expert, who is unlikely to have a clear idea of what he or she is supposed to be doing. This means that the interview will tend to take on a life and direction of its own. Things may become unfocused and time may well be wasted discussing issues and concepts which are actually tangential to the real problems. Consequently, the output from such unstructured interviews will rarely provide complete or well-organized descriptions of the knowledge and processes involved.

There are, thus, a number of distinct disadvantages to the use of unstructured interviews and they should be used with caution, apart from in the early stages of the knowledge-acquisition process. In particular, they can be useful in setting the agenda for future, more structured, interviews and for establishing a rapport between the knowledge engineer and the expert. They can be used for exploring areas that focused interviews may miss and their unstructured nature may often cause the expert to stray into areas which would not otherwise have been discovered.

4.3.2 Structured interviews

The concept of the structured interview is not easily defined and there are many different forms. Some of the most useful forms are discussed below.

4.3.2.1 Focused interviews: lessons from the quality-control system

Carefully focused interviews were used during the knowledge-acquisition phase of the design of the quality-control system. Focused interviews should be like normal, interesting and informal conversations. They should be relaxed and unhurried in nature. However, they should not be 'off the cuff' and the knowledge engineer should prepare for them well. They normally consist of three parts.

The first is an introduction where the knowledge engineer does most of the talking. This involves setting out the goals for the project, introducing the expert to the purpose of the interview and agreeing a sequence of topics. The knowledge engineer should also try and motivate the expert and put him or her at ease.

In the second part the topics which have already been agreed are discussed. The expert should do most of the talking and the knowledge engineer should (hopefully) listen attentively.

The interview should always end with a review by the knowledge engineer to ensure that he or she has understood everything correctly and fully. The interview should provide the knowledge engineer with factual knowledge about the types of problems solved by the expert and the expertise involved.

The use of knowledge-acquisition forms can be extremely beneficial during focused interviews. The forms can be used to broadly itemize the aims of the session and if they are given to the expert in advance of the session they can be used as an agenda. The form shown in Figure 4.2 was designed by the knowledge engineer and used during knowledge-acquisition sessions for the quality-control system.

KNOWLEDGE ACQUISITION FORM

Fault Diagnosis Expert System
Knowledge Acquisition Form

KA Session #: 5	**KA Session Date:** 23/11/92

Session Topic: Hot wrinkle problem

Knowledge Engineer: C. Hardy	**Knowledge Source:** B. Hepple
Session Location: CupCo	**Elapsed Time:**

Session Type:	
	Interview
	Observation
	Tutorial
	Teachback
	Twenty Questions
	Other

Major Session Goals:

To discuss KA sessions to-date.
To confirm the accuracy of prior transcripts.
To discuss how the expert would approach this problem.
To summarise the outcome of the current KA session.

Session Summary:

Figure 4.2 *Knowledge acquisition form.*

KNOWLEDGE ACQUISITION FORM

<table>
<tr><td colspan="4" align="center">**Fault Diagnosis Expert System**
Knowledge Acquisition Form</td></tr>
<tr><td colspan="2">**KA Session #:** 14</td><td colspan="2">**KA Session Date:** 6/1/93</td></tr>
<tr><td colspan="4">**Session Topic:** Cold wrinkle problem</td></tr>
<tr><td colspan="2">**Knowledge Engineer:** C. Hardy</td><td colspan="2">**Knowledge Source:** D. Good</td></tr>
<tr><td colspan="2">**Session Location:** CupCo</td><td colspan="2">**Elapsed Time:** 1 hour</td></tr>
<tr><td rowspan="6">**Session Type:**</td><td colspan="3">**Interview**</td></tr>
<tr><td colspan="3">**Observation**</td></tr>
<tr><td colspan="3">**Tutorial**</td></tr>
<tr><td colspan="3">**Teachback**</td></tr>
<tr><td colspan="3">**Twenty Questions**</td></tr>
<tr><td colspan="3">**Other**</td></tr>
</table>

Major Session Goals:

To obtain a description of one case in which the expert had solved a cold wrinkle problem.

Session Summary:

From experience, the expert has solved all instances of cold wrinkle by carrying out the following:

Go to rim curler.
Raise the temperature of the oven nearest the scroll (Choice of oven is one of personal preference through experience).

Whilst this invariably solved the cold wrinkle problem (for this expert); by doing so, it may produce a hot wrinkle problem on what would have been good cups. He would then:

Go to the former.
Reduce the thickness of the rims.
Go to rim curler.
Reduce the oven temperature incrementally.

Figure 4.3 *A completed knowledge acquisition form*

Having an agenda for each interview keeps the expert's responses within the appropriate problem area. The knowledge-acquisition form can be completed during the interview and agreed by both parties. A completed form from the development of the quality-control system is shown in Figure 4.3.

In addition to a knowledge-acquisition form, the expert should receive (where appropriate) a transcript of the previous session, a knowledge-acquisition form itemizing the procedure for the coming session and, as the development progresses, an updated version of any software which is being prototyped. A sample transcript session can be seen in section 4.10.

Introducing software into interviews from the earliest stages will save the knowledge engineer from major restructuring of that software at a later date. This idea is similar to that proposed by software engineers who often stress that it is a mistake to wait until the analysis stage is complete before implementing a trial system and emphasize the importance of representing knowledge as soon as possible in order to avoid the risk of having to start again.

4.3.2.2 Tutorial interviews

These are used as a means of familiarizing the knowledge engineer with the problem domain, as well as focusing the mind of the expert on how he/she actually identifies and solves problems. They differ from many other types of interview in that the knowledge engineer takes a much smaller part in the process.

The expert is asked to prepare or record a short presentation or talk on the subject under investigation. This should last for about 15–30 minutes. This presentation is then given to the knowledge engineer. From this, the major concepts of the problem under discussion are identified. The presentation should bring out the main terminology and concepts that the expert uses. This will give the knowledge engineer a better understanding of the problem area and improve communication with the expert.

4.3.2.3 Twenty questions

A specialized form of structured interviews is to ask questions to which the expert can only answer yes or no. This is sometimes called the 'twenty questions' technique. The aim is to gather quickly the major characteristics of the concepts of the domain.

A variation on this theme is when the knowledge engineer supplies a set of previously solved problems in the domain and the expert poses the questions. From this the knowledge engineer should be able to ascertain what information the expert needs to solve the problems and, to some extent, the structure used to solve the problems.

4.3.2.4 Teachback interviews

This technique is where the expert takes the lead and the knowledge engineer must respond. The expert will describe a procedure to the knowledge engineer who must then 'teach' it back to the expert. Teachback continues until the expert is satisfied with the knowledge engineer's version of things. When they agree they are said to 'share the same concept'. Strengths of this technique include:

- There is a relative absence of confusion caused by any preconceptions about the domain which the knowledge engineer might have had.
- It is non-judgmental in nature.
- It is very often successful in gaining and retaining the expert's interest.
- There is no doubt about the expert authenticity of the data.

On the other hand, it is extremely tiring for the knowledge engineer and it is not a very structured technique.

4.3.2.5 Trigger-type interviews

In this type of interview the knowledge engineer uses materials within the interview which are intended as triggers to stimulate the expert's responses. These triggers can include structure diagrams derived from earlier knowledge-acquisition sessions and archive data from past instances ('test-cases') of the problem or activity.

4.3.2.6 Introspective (or 'think aloud') interviews

These essentially involve asking experts how they would solve a problem that they are familiar with. They are then encouraged to verbalize their thoughts with the knowledge engineer only intervening to ask probing 'how' questions.

4.3.2.7 Retrospective case description

The expert is asked how he or she solved specific problems in the recent past. This can lead to problems with the expert feeling they have to justify the approach taken instead of just outlining the approach. Also the knowledge engineer has to make a subjective decision concerning which problems are the most representative. The problem must be in the recent past as long-term memory cannot always be relied upon.

4.3.2.8 Critical incident

The expert is asked to describe his or her experience with remarkable or difficult cases. Because these are the most memorable cases in the expert's mind they are likely to produce more detailed and accurate recall than retrospective case descriptions. However, problems can occur because re-markable cases, although increasing domain awareness and understanding, may not be of help in developing the expert system. That is, remarkable cases are, by definition, few and far between. They may not, as a result, be very representative and may not be much use in compiling any general rules. On the other hand, they will be very useful for setting up exceptional rules and the limits of the problem domain.

4.3.3 Tips for good interviewing

There are a number of general principles which can be applied to all branches of interviewing. But perhaps it would be better to start by highlighting some of the problems.

4.3.3.1 Ambiguities

In order to explain how a problem is solved the expert has to resort to the use of the English language. This language becomes a tool for representing the experience of the expert. The degree to which the expert's language accurately reveals his or her internal thought processes will vary depending upon the expert's ability to explain things clearly and the knowledge engineer's skills in clarifying what the expert has reported.

Juan Pazos, a well-respected Spanish knowledge engineer, has identified seven common ambiguities which can occur during knowledge acquisition. These are outlined below. They can quite easily occur, and should be guarded against.

Ambiguity 1 – the words that the expert uses may miss out key parts of the reasoning process
In everyday speech, the use of words like:

- 'it'
- 'that'
- 'they'
- 'item'
- 'substance'
- 'process'

is very common. These words do not really help in describing the real content of the knowledge. For instance, if an expert states: 'This is the root of the problem' it is not really clear what the root is! When faced with such a situation the knowledge engineer should ask:

- 'What, exactly, is the root?'
- 'The root of what?'
- 'How do you know that?'

Ambiguity 2 – words frequently have unspecified references
For example, the expert may say: 'ABC provides a dampening function'. In this case the word 'dampening' is not clear. Appropriate queries are:

- 'What, exactly, do you mean by dampening?'
- 'Exactly what is dampened?'
- 'What does ABC dampen?'
- 'How do you know ABC does this?'

- 'What parts of the system, if any, are not dampened?'

Ambiguity 3 – comparative words like 'better', 'bigger', 'lighter' are not helpful and precise
So, if an expert states: 'This is a better system', clarification is required. Appropriate questions are:

- 'How is it better?'
- 'What criteria are you using?'
- 'How do you know that?'
- 'Better compared to what?'
- 'Better for what purposes?'

Ambiguity 4 – from time to time, words are used to summarize complex processes; these may sound complete but are not
For example, if an expert says: 'The inadequacy of the results requires that we look back through the system' the word 'inadequacy' has reduced several steps. Appropriate queries for this response are:

- 'Why are they inadequate?'
- 'What is inadequate about them?'
- 'What steps did you take to determine that they are inadequate?'

Ambiguity 5 – this includes language which implies a connection between events that is either insufficiently detailed or does not exist
For instance, an expert might say: 'If we continue to run this voltage through the system, we may end up with some expensive repair bills.' The relationship between voltage and repair bills involves the assumption that a certain voltage will damage the system and repairing the damage is going to be expensive. This may be so, but the specific relationships are not detailed. That is, it is not clear how the high voltage will result in an expensive repair bill. Appropriate questions are:

- 'How do you know this is so?'
- 'How, specifically, does a certain voltage cause repair bills?'
- 'What would make the repairs expensive?'

Ambiguity 6 – several commonly used words imply relationships without providing an explanation
These include:

- 'can/can't'
- 'possible/impossible'
- 'will/won't'
- 'should/shouldn't'

- 'must/mustn't'
- 'necessary/unnecessary'

These words are often inadequately specified when used to describe relationships. For example, an expert might say 'The ABC part shouldn't be used here.' Appropriate queries would be:

- 'What would happen if it was?'
- 'What makes ABC a poor choice?'
- 'How do you know that?'

Ambiguity 7 – certain commonly used words may erroneously imply universality in principles
These include words like:

- 'always'
- 'never'
- 'every'
- 'none'

For example, an expert might say: 'This system will never work.' The knowledge engineer will want to know:

- 'What prevents this system from working?'
- 'How do you know it won't work in all cases?'
- 'Would it work in any other situation?'
- 'Do you really mean never?'

4.3.3.2 Good questions

Asking good questions well is an art. The interviewer must actively question the expert. The worst pitfall is to fail to ask for information. Since the questions one asks clearly influence the answers one gets, knowledge engineers need to pay special attention to question formulation. A lack of awareness of different types of questions makes it difficult to conduct a good interview.

Knowledge engineers must have at their command a repertoire of good questions. These can be divided into:

- good questions to begin with
- good questions to continue with
- good questions to end with

Good questions to begin with are:

- 'How do you do your job?'

- 'Can you remember the last case you dealt with…?'
- 'What kind of things do you like to know about when you begin to think about a problem?'
- 'What facts or hypotheses do you try to establish when thinking about a problem?'
- 'What are the factors that influence how you reason about a problem?'
- 'What type of values can this object have?'
- 'What range of values is permissible?'
- 'Does this factor depend on other factors? If so, which ones?'
- 'Is this factor needed for solving all problems in the domain or for just some?'

Good questions to continue with are:

- 'Tell me more about…'
- 'Can you describe what you mean by that?'
- 'I do not understand, could you explain?'
- 'How does that relate to our topic?'
- 'How/Why/When do you do that?'
- 'What do you do next?'
- 'How is this achieved?'

Good questions to end with are:

- 'Is there anything else?'
- 'Let me summarize…'
- 'What do you think we should cover in the next session?'
- 'Thank you for your help.'
- 'Have we covered everything we should have?'

4.3.3.3 Further comments on interview methodology

Successful interviewing requires negotiating and maintaining a balance between obtaining data, information and knowledge and acknowledging the expert as a person and a professional. Interviewing also requires maintaining a balance between being directive and being responsive.

Some knowledge engineers seem to perceive interviews as trivial or, worse yet, a matter of common sense. There is a connection between the knowledge-acquisition bottleneck and the apparent reluctance to take seriously the question of interview methodology. This has major implications for KBS development because interview technique may affect the quality of the data gathered as well as the time it takes to collect them.

Because interviewing takes place through the medium of conversation and because the latter is an everyday activity, people sometimes assume that knowledge acquisition is just a matter of chatting with the expert. To the uninitiated, interviewing is 'Just talking to people!' In fact, it is very easy to interview badly, with the result that one may learn little and/or alienate the expert.

Interviewing does not just happen. The knowledge engineer must make it happen successfully. Interviewing is a difficult task that requires:

- planning
- stage management
- technique
- social skills
- a lot of self control!

Experts are people with personalities and an agenda of their own and they often have the authority to refuse further interviews. There are examples of interviewers who were highly personable but did not learn much about their topic and others who were topic orientated but made the expert felt irritated and even abused.

Referring to a knowledge engineer in the former category, the expert commented: 'He wasted my time.' Referring to one in the latter, the expert said: 'He treated me like an idiot.'

The knowledge engineer must find a middle ground between deciding upon an approach and a list of questions beforehand and being completely open to changing his or her approach on the basis of what the interviewee says and does.

Similarly, they must consciously weigh the cost in time and efficiency of letting an expert carry on at will, versus the possible cost in goodwill (and possible data) of interrupting repeatedly to keep the expert on course.

Some interviewers do not allow the expert sufficient time to speak. Novice knowledge engineers may confuse an interview with an examination and waste time unnecessarily trying to demonstrate their own competence to the expert. It is imperative to learn to listen. Silence is better than firing questions at the expert without really listening to the responses.

The backgrounds of both the interviewer and the expert are likely to affect the interview situation. An interview is a social encounter as well as a professional one. It is impossible to prescribe a particular strategy or style. Experience shows that the tactics appropriate in any particular situation depend on both of the individuals involved.

Clearly, face to face knowledge acquisition demands considerable sensitivity and flexibility on the part of both partners. This is particularly true on the part of the knowledge engineer who must be able to assess and adjust to the social constraints posed by the interview. Juan Pazos recalls one experienced knowledge engineer who said that: 'Experts are a cantankerous lot.'

The knowledge engineer should beware of the following:

- Do not ask long, complicated, repetitive questions. Ask one short, clear question at a time and then stop talking. Resist the temptation to repeat and elaborate on questions.

- Do not use a vocabulary which is unfamiliar to the expert. Try to speak the expert's language.

Interviewing is difficult because it requires the knowledge engineer to pay attention on many levels at once. In addition to asking questions and monitoring progress, knowledge engineers must constantly be aware of:

- time
- personality attributes
- human factors
- political factors

Given these demands the interviewer may miss, or fail to grasp, the significance of some of what the expert says. Therefore, it is necessary that some sort of objective record of each interview be maintained.

The easiest and least obtrusive recording device is a small tape recorder, but before using such a device you must ask the permission of the expert. Too often knowledge engineers seem to trust their memories and their handwritten notes.

4.4 Questionnaires

Questionnaires can be used in two ways. First, they can be mailed to experts to complete. Second, they can be used as the basis for an interview and to act as an agenda to provide structure for the interview. Questionnaires were used in both ways during the development of the forecasting system.

Four regional sites were visited by the knowledge engineer. A questionnaire was used as the basis for the interview. The questions were asked in order but the interviewees were encouraged to reply at length and the knowledge engineer allowed them to digress from the questions. All interviews were tape recorded. This technique did not cause any problems and all interviewees were happy with the arrangement. Typing up the tape transcripts was, however, very time consuming.

A questionnaire was also sent to the gas regions (see Figure 4.4 for an extract). From the replies the following knowledge was obtained:

- All regions used some formula as a means of forecasting gas delivery.
- The formula for the effective temperature was individual to each region.
- Most regions used some form of computer program for helping with the forecasting.
- All thought that the modelling process that they used could be improved.
- All agreed that, after temperature, the most important factors were type of day and wind.

- All regions used, and could provide, percentage figures for the effect of weekends on gas consumption. These were all individual to each region.
- Most regions also used percentage figures for the effect of wind.
- No region used percentage figures for the effect of other misery factors such as rain, snow, cloud, etc. These were dealt with on an *ad hoc* basis with the individual Shift Control Officer using his/her own experience to amend the forecast to take these into account.
- All regions ended up with several, rather than one, estimates for the following day value. The Shift Control Officer then used his/her own experience to decide on a figure.

4.5 Formal techniques

4.5.1 Introduction

Most of the more formalized techniques currently used for knowledge acquisition have their origins in Kelly's theory of the psychology of personal constructs (Kelly, 1955). The basic ideas behind this theory are that people perceive the world in terms of their own **constructs**. A construct is a specialized form of conceptualization.

An individual's constructs are personal. No two people will have the same set of constructs. Kelly proposed that individuals act like scientists in that their thoughts and actions are the methods by which they tests their constructs of the world. *The Psychology of Personal Constructs* is a thoroughly developed and well respected theory of human behaviour, personality and perception (Kelly, 1955).

A number of knowledge-acquisition techniques have been developed from Personal Construct Theory. Sections 4.5.2–3 cover two of these techniques which have been widely used in knowledge engineering:

- repertory grids
- card sort

4.5.2 Repertory grids

Repertory grids use a two-dimensional matrix to display a picture of the relationships between various objects and concepts from the problem domain. Along one axis are placed a list of people, objects or situations familiar to the individual (these are termed **elements**). The other axis consists of a set of elicited **constructs**.

Constructs are generally elicited by means of a repertory test. This consists of presenting three randomly chosen elements to the expert and asking in what way two of them are similar. The response forms one pole of a construct. The expert is then asked for the opposite of that pole, which would characterize the third element. This would then form the other pole of the construct. This

---

FORECASTING SYSTEM

Questionnaire

1. How do begin your estimating of the next days delivery? (please tick which applies):

Do you: a. Consider the type of day that tomorrow will be ❑

(i.e. weekday, weekend, holiday)

b. Start with the weather forecast ❑

c. Start with the estimate for today ❑

d. Start at some other point – please outline below ❑

2. Do you use? (please tick which applies):

a. Model day estimates ❑

b. Weather estimates ❑

c. Computer program estimates ❑

d. Others – please outline ❑

Model Day Forecasting

3. What percentages do you allow for the effect of tomorrow over today? (please enter %):

a. Tuesday over a Monday ❑%

b. Wednesday over a Tuesday ❑%

c. Thursday over a Wednesday ❑%

d. Friday over a Thursday ❑%

e. Saturday over a Friday ❑%

f. Saturday over a Weekday ❑%

g. Sunday over a Saturday ❑%

Figure 4.4 *Extract from questionnaire.*

4. How do you deal with Bank Holiday Mondays? (please tick which applies):

     a. Treat the Monday as another type of day   ❏

     b. Use a special percentage   ❏

     c. Use some other method – please outline   ❏

5. How do you deal with Tuesdays following Bank Holiday Monday?s (please tick which applies):

     a. As a normal Tuesday   ❏

     b. Use a special percentage over   ❏

     c. Use some other method – please outline   ❏

6. How do you deal with Statutory Holidays – Easter, Christmas, New Year?:

     a. Do you use comparisons with previous years?   ❏

     b. If so how many years do you go back   ❏ years
     c. Use some other method – please outline   ❏

Figure 4.4 *Extract from questionnaire. (continued)*

process is repeated for different groups of three elements until the options are exhausted. The expert is then asked to rate each element on each of the constructs. This is generally on a scale with an odd number of points. Examples of constructs are shown in Figure 4.5. These constructs can then be rated on a scale of 1 to 5 or 1 to 3.

heavy ──────────▶ light

small ──────────▶ large

tall ──────────▶ short

Figure 4.5 *Examples of constructs.*

Figure 4.6 *Rating scale for blood gases in the monitoring system.*

For instance, in the monitoring system, one element of interest, blood gases, read in order to set the ventilator, could have a rating scale like the one in Figure 4.6.

In the quality-control system, the knowledge engineer was concerned with the acquisition of the expert's procedural knowledge about how he or she solved particular problems. The choice of what sort of elements to use, and consequently what the grid was going to be about, was determined in discussion with the expert. It was decided to use 'adjustments necessary to solve the problem' as elements. The expert was given the opportunity to elicit his or her own constructs. The grid consisted of nine elements and five constructs. The elements were:

- scroll timing
- material
- scroll head position
- locators changed
- punch and dies changed
- separator opened
- scroll and cooling rails cleaned
- cutter feed
- adjustment to straighten sheet offset trim

The constructs were:

- affect timing and feed before scroll
- all of product
- bad rim before curler
- affects good or bad rim in curler
- ragged trim at curler

The constructs and elements can be seen in the repertory grid in Figure 4.7. This grid formed the basis for several useful discussions with the expert. This concerned the apparent associations between the possible actions that could be taken to solve the problem.

The use of grids as a medium for the expert to examine his or her reasoning processes can reveal beliefs about the problem domain that were not previously apparent. However, the grids can be difficult to construct and, having done so, they may not really help in the construction of rules.

	Comparison of causes of hairs and dust	E1	E2	E3	E4	E5	E6	E7	E8	E9	
C1	Affect timing and feed before scroll	3	1	3	1	1	1	3	1	1	Affect in scroll
C2	All of product	3	1	3	3	3	3	3	3	1	Rim of product
C3	Bad rim before curler	3	1	3	1	1	3	3	1	1	Damage to a particular area
C4	Affects good or bad rim in curler	1	2	1	3	3	1	1	3	3	Affects the cutting of the cup
C5	Ragged trim at curler	3	1	3	1	1	3	3	1	1	Scuffing and pin-point damage to rim at curler

Scroll timing

Material

Scroll head position

Locators changed

Punch and dies changed

Separator opened

Scroll and cooling rails cleaned

Cutter feed

Adjustment to straighten sheet offset trim

Figure 4.7 *A repertory grid for the quality-control KBS.*

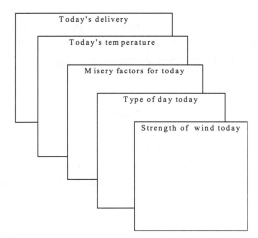

Figure 4.8 *Card sort*

4.5.3 Card sort

Card sorting is a means of eliciting concepts from elements. The name of an element is written on each card and the cards are then sorted into groups representing similar characteristics (Figure 4.8).

If the knowledge engineer is interested in understanding the associations between elements, then the expert could be asked to group the cards into piles, according to a criterion of his or her choice. It is proposed that this reveals one dimension of classification. The process can then be repeated until the expert is unable to provide any more dimensions.

The technique can also be used to obtain a binary tree (Figure 4.9). The expert is asked to sort the cards into two piles and then subdivide each pile in turn until no other divisions are possible. It is also possible to carry out this process in reverse, whereby the expert has to form as many piles as possible and then determine reasons as to why piles should be consolidated.

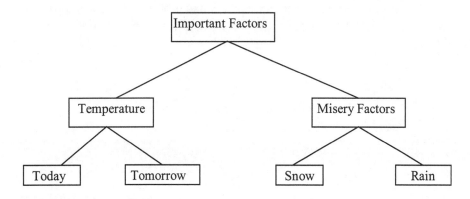

Figure 4.9 *A binary tree*

This technique is sometimes called concept sorting. When the major concepts have been isolated from the interview transcript, they are each written on a separate card, and given to the expert in a totally random order. They are then sorted through and laid out in clusters, showing relationships into which they naturally fall.

In the forecasting system, the knowledge engineer chose this technique in order to be able to rank the importance that the experts held individual concepts, rather than gathering actual knowledge. It was hoped there would arise from the ranking of the concepts a consensus of agreement of the importance of the pieces of knowledge used in arriving at the forecast.

The experts were asked to rank the following basic entities, in order of importance of their effect on the following day's delivery of gas:

- today's delivery
- yesterday's delivery
- yesterday's temperature
- today's temperature
- type of day it was today (i.e weekday, saturday, etc.)
- type of day it will be tomorrow
- strength of wind today
- strength of wind tomorrow
- misery factors for today
- misery factors for tomorrow
- living day
- overnight delivery

Each of the above factors were written on a card and presented to the expert who then sorted them into order. ('Misery factors' is a term used within the industry to describe the effect of rain, snow, frost, drizzle, sunshine, cloud, fog, etc.) The gas day traditionally runs from 06:01 a.m. one day to 06:00 a.m. the next day. The 'living day' is used to describe the hours between 6:01 a.m. and 10:00 p.m., and 'overnight' is between 10:00 p.m. and 6:00 a.m. The top ranking entities were taken individually and broken down where possible, and again ranked. For instance, 'misery factors' can be broken down into the following:

- rain
- heavy rain
- light rain
- drizzle
- showers
- snow
- sleet
- frost
- fog

- cloud
- broken cloud
- overcast
- sunshine
- sunny spells
- sea fret

These were again written on cards and the expert was asked to sort them into order. This process was thus used to gain a clearer picture of the factors which are taken into account in estimating gas demand.

4.6 Observation techniques

4.6.1 Introduction

So far the knowledge-acquisition methods described have relied on the abilities of experts to recall how they applied their knowledge in the past or to guess how they would do so in future. Observation is concerned with those methods which are carried out at the same time as the real problem solving. What is common amongst each of these methods is that the knowledge engineer is present at the exact time that the expert applies his or her knowledge. Consequently, this allows for the observation of the expert's behaviour.

4.6.2 Protocol analysis

In the method of protocol analysis, behaviour (verbal or otherwise) is recorded as the expert works through a problem. The 'protocol' is then transcribed and analysed to extract a set of rules.

The technique is useful for eliciting procedures that experts use in problem solving and which they may not be able to articulate. The limitations of protocol analysis have been well documented. An obvious point is that online protocol analysis may interfere with the process of problem solving.

Protocol analysis was used quite extensively in the development of the monitoring KBS. In this case, the knowledge engineer recorded the protocols which the clinicians followed when setting and adjusting the mechanical ventilator. This was used as the basis for subsequent interview sessions and enabled the knowledge engineer to get a firmer grasp of the way in which the procedure was undertaken.

4.6.2.1 Verbal protocol analysis

In this technique the expert is asked to work through a case, describing what he or she is doing. Welbank discusses some of the main disadvantages of protocol analysis:

> Protocols collected on the job do not cover every situation that could arise. The subject cannot verbalise as fast as he/she reasons, which makes for important deficiencies in the type of material collected. He/she may not report what is obvious to him/her. He/she may leave out steps in his/her reasoning. Most importantly he/she does not naturally give 'if *x*, then *y*' type rules, or explain his/her reasons for deciding to do one thing rather than another. He/she may not have time to explain even if he/she is asked to.
>
> (Welbank, 1987)

It is generally agreed that the process of transcribing protocols is insufferably time consuming and that analysis is a skilled and difficult task demanding a good understanding of the domain on the part of the knowledge engineer.

On the positive side, one of the major advantages of collecting protocols is that the situation can be completely natural. As a technique it also takes up a minimum of the expert's time. Verbal protocols are probably best used in combination with other sources of information such as interviewing.

4.6.2.2 Behavioural protocol analysis

This technique can be distinguished from verbal protocol analysis in that it attempts to capture additional non-verbal protocols by such methods as video recording. The expert can be called upon to do a later evaluation of tapes and videos as, when asked to evaluate their performance, experts may find it easy to give reasons for their actions and articulations. However, experts may provide justifications for their decisions and give reasons which they believe to be appropriate, but which do in fact play no part in their reasoning.

Behavioural protocols suffer from the same underlying disadvantages as those listed for verbal protocols. Particularly prominent is the large amount of time required for analysing tapes. In addition video recording an expert at work may not always be feasible.

4.6.3 Summary

Observational techniques are frequently used by knowledge engineers and can be applied at a number of stages throughout KBS development. Protocol analysis is generally regarded as the most common of these techniques, but it has been argued that it suffers from a lack of definition. Protocol analysis techniques are regarded as useful tools for knowledge engineers, due to their ability to access expert heuristics at the actual time of their use.

4.7 Other factors

4.7.1 Introduction

We have discussed the merits and problems associated with a number of manual knowledge-acquisition techniques. There are additional factors which need to be considered; these are introduced in this section.

4.7.2 Expert talkers?

There are two factors which can impair a knowledge engineer's ability to access expert knowledge:

1. the expert may be unwilling to part with the knowledge

2. the expert may have difficulty accessing the knowledge and/or describing his or her knowledge.

4.7.2.1 Expert willingness

This problem is primarily one of diplomacy and the experience of the knowledge engineer in choosing suitable expert/s (if there are more than one available) and gaining their support. However, assuming that resistance is still present, it may be useful to use some more formal techniques because they are unfamiliar and may excite the expert's curiosity!

4.7.2.2 Knowledge access

As has been noted, expert knowledge is often deeply hidden in the expert's mind and, as such, can be difficult to access. Knowledge-acquisition techniques have been specifically designed to access information that was not readily available. However, as discussed, there are limitations in their use. Another alternative may be the use of observational techniques such as protocol analysis.

4.7.3 Multiple experts

As La Salle and Medsker state:

> knowledge acquisition involving multiple experts is fraught with the problems of dealing with single experts compounded with the obstacles and risks of trying to co-ordinate human interactions and integrate multiple knowledge bases
>
> (La Salle and Medsker, 1991)

In a survey carried out in the UK by O'Neil and Morris in 1989, 59% of companies building expert systems recommended using only one major expert for the kernel of knowledge (O'Neil and Morris, 1989). Other experts were brought into the project later to validate the system. The principal reason given for this approach was that it was easier both to elicit the knowledge and to avoid contentious issues and conflicting opinions. In fact, it was reported that one company that was using an expert committee came to the conclusion that it was absolutely incapable of agreeing on anything and ended up redesigning the project using one expert.

With reference to the forecasting system, there were a number of experts geographically spread throughout the country in several regions. Using computerized conferencing to gather all the experts together would have been nice but was not feasible. The 72 experts work differing shift patterns and so could never be together (even remotely) at one time. The knowledge engineer decided that the only sensible approach would be to concentrate on building a system for one region but would approach as many regions as possible personally to interview the experts on duty and also to send other regions a questionnaire.

Even narrowing down the knowledge acquisition to one region the knowledge engineer was left with six experts. The problems which the knowledge engineer needed to overcome were:

- How can experts reach an agreement about vocabulary and definitions? The knowledge engineer may use voting to reach a consensus. Although this solution is simple, it can be risky if only a few experts are involved.
- Should the expert system try to find a consensus among a given set of experts when recommending solutions? The knowledge engineer may have to rely on his or her own judgement about when a consensus seems to have been reached.
- Experts in the same area who try to solve the same problem may use different techniques. These differences in technique and solutions make it difficult to use several experts to build an expert system.

4.8 Knowledge-acquisition tools

Manual acquisition methods are expensive and time consuming. One further disadvantage is that the knowledge engineer must almost become an expert in the domain in order to understand and model the domain expert. Domain experts themselves may lack the ability to clearly explain the problem to the knowledge engineer.

There is an increasing trend for domain experts themselves to work directly with a shell or to be 'interviewed' by a computerised acquisition tool which will write the rules directly. The principle of rule induction is that the expert supplies a set of domain examples of different types of decisions. A computer program using an inductive algorithm then uses these examples to induce a set of rules.

Knowledge acquisition tools are also being developed to overcome the problem of multiple experts. Experts in the same area who try to solve the same problem may use different techniques and arrive at the same or different acceptable solutions. The expertise transfer system (ETS) interviews experts, analyses the elicited knowledge, builds knowledge bases to test the knowledge, uses feedback to help refine the knowledge bases and helps the expert combine his or her knowledge with that of other experts. A number of other tools are now being developed, and these include the following:

- **AQUINAS** – elicits and models information using a knowledge-acquisition workbench including repertory grid-based interviewing.
- **MOLE** – exploits information about how problems are solved to elicit diagnostic knowledge and use feedback to fine tune knowledge.
- **OPAL** – performs knowledge acquisition for the cancer treatment domain.

4.9 Summary

This chapter has covered a number of techniques for knowledge acquisition. It has focused largely on interviews as these are the most widely used, and most useful, technique. However, it is advisable to use a combination of techniques for the best results. In particular, it is useful to apply interview techniques alongside observation techniques.

The advent of software support for the process will aid efficiency in the future.

4.10 Exercises

There follows a full knowledge-acquisition session transcript for the quality-control system. The exercises which follow are based on this transcript.

1. Draw a flowchart which represents the identification of the hot wrinkle problem.

2. Derive a set of rules (in English) for the identification of the hot wrinkle problem.

3. In your opinion has the expert explained the problem well, and fully?

KNOWLEDGE ACQUISITION SESSION TRANSCRIPT

Interview carried out with B. Barrow relating to the hot wrinkle problem, and how he would respond to it.

> On any wrinkle problem, the first thing I look at is the product itself. This would usually be taking a full set of the product, from the trim press and feeding them through the rimmer. They would then be laid out to see where the wrinkles are, how many there are and how they are associated.
>
> It is sometimes best if you feed two sets through, because then you can get an indication if the problem is following through on certain numbers, or whether it is becoming random.

At the same time, I would do a quick check around the rimming machine itself to see that the water is flowing correctly, that the temperatures look stable and that the line itself is feeding cups in a constant stable manner.

In a hot wrinkle situation, the problem is not usually in the rimmer, but you have got to take those steps to ensure that you are not moving backwards, when you are at the machine already.

There are three parts to a rimming machine; there is the water unit which feeds the scrolls, and controls the temperature of the scrolls and guide rods. There is the drive unit, which feeds the cups through and drives the scroll. There is the oven, controlling the temperature stability. There is an indication of the temperature of the water.

There is also 'show flows', which is a unit with a little ball in it, and when the water passes through, the ball bounces about. You also have temperatures on the oven. The ovens are dual ovens, so you have a first and second zone, so you can have the zones at different temperatures. Normally, the temperatures are higher in the second zone, so you give pre-heat, and then a blast before the rimmer. Apart from that, there is only the speed of the rimmer. In a lot of cases it gives you an indication of the speed of the unit, but in a lot of cases we use two start threads, so for one revolution it would pick up two cups.

The double start threads are only used on the small vending cups. For larger pots you go back to the single thread, because you don't put as many through.

The in-feed belt is also driven off the same motor, so you don't get an over-drive into the unit.

Assuming there is nothing out of the ordinary about the rimming machine, then I would look at the cups themselves. Normally, it is either all over the place and random or it is in designated areas in the tool.

If it is in random areas, then the next thing to do is to check the product weight, because that probably means that you are not leaving sufficient material in the cup to give you a decent curl. In the rim of the cup, you need to have the correct thickness of material right round.

If you find that you have random wrinkles across the set, then the next thing is to check the product weight. The ideal way to set these machines is to have the pots slightly heavier on the outside, and slightly lighter than the specification in the middle.

This is because the outside of the set of the cups normally cools quicker than the inside, because of the direction of the extrusion. The extrusion driving through the middle keeps the inside of the sheet hot. Therefore, use the volume of the sheet. The greater the volume of the sheet, the greater the heat retention.

If you are over-heating (which is probably one of the possible reasons for hot wrinkle) you could decrease the temperature over-all. You could do that by altering the position of the cooling rollers. We have one cooling roller which can be adjusted to give greater or lesser contact with the sheet. If you are over temperature, then you would increase contact. This would reduce the temperature across the sheet.

This may give you an improvement to the curl situation, but not do the whole job. What you can then do is a secondary control, which is the water flow itself. You can restrict the water flow, which then gives you control of temperature across the sheet. This is important, because it is normally still hotter in the middle than the outside.

If you slow the water down, it is chilled water entering the centre of these rollers, and it cascades both ways. You can restrict the water entering the rollers, that is still chilled water at the centre, but it is in the roller longer and consequently takes less heat out of the outside of the sheet. This is sometimes the case where you are either chilling or over-heating the end rows. It is usually the end rows where you get this kind of problem.

This is the same approach if it is in individual rows. This is because you have so much control gained there, you can adjust the temperature for particular rows by increasing or decreasing the flow of the water. You feed out of the die, and you control linear temperature by either increasing or decreasing the contact with the sheet. Whereas, you get traverse control by control of the water flow itself.

There can be instances where adjusting both of these is not enough. You would use both of these in conjunction with control of the plug speed. To increase the material in the top of the cup (this is always the problem) you will then either decrease the speed of the plug, so it doesn't drive through as quickly, and therefore pulls material up the top of the pot. Or, you will bring the timing of that action to be later into the process, so that the mould is actually on the sheet coming through as the tool closes. The mould is actually on the sheet when you set the helper away, and the mould itself will pick up more material as it reaches the top.

If the problem is in a located area, the solution is in the setting of the die. It is possible that during weight adjustment one area of the die has been closed off too much. You can usually check that by taking those pots, cut them in half and weight the two halves. You can also measure the thickness down the wall.

There can be occasions where opening the die at a certain point will not allow material to flow out. It may need the die closing down in another area, to push material into that point. It is also useful at that point to check that all the cartridge heaters are working. It could be that one of the heaters is dubious, and the die is not hot enough in that spot; therefore you are getting preferential flow.

There can be times when you get problems with just one pot in an area, but not necessarily the same pot. That can come from the cooling roller damage. It is also possible to get problems from water or oil condensing on the cooling rollers themselves. Occasionally you will get a build up of the monomer as it weeps from the sheet. The consequence of that is that some of the sheet does not touch the roller.

This will result in random wrinkle, and in this case, it is merely a matter of shutting the machine down and cleaning the rollers.

However, if the monomer builds up again you have to go back and look at the materials.

Another area which can cause hot wrinkle is in the trim press. If you get a poor cut, you will get feathering of the edge. This will cause a piece of 'rag' to be attached to the rim, and as it goes through the rim roller it will burn away. This in itself will cause a hot spot, and can cause a bad curl. This would be a consistent problem. It can be caused by a number of things.

You may find that one cup is cutting out badly, although a cutter cuts out six pots. This would come back to the forming machine, and you may have a damaged mould. If you have a damaged mould on the top of the cup, it may not be able to get hold of the cup properly, and distort it and twist the rim. You can also get the same problem because the trim press hasn't been set up true to the sheet. In this instance the locators can't move the sheet far enough and the extreme cups (usually the opposite corners) are trimmed badly, and that one doesn't curl. This would probably be picked up at the rimmer.

Even if you believe that the problem is in the former, it is policy to check the profile of the pots as they come out of the trim press. It is possible to have it formed poorly which results in a poor trim. Or you can get it where there is a damaged locator. The locator twists the cup, and trims it out poorly each time. They may have had problems in the trim press when it has been cleaned out, but in the cleaning out something has got damaged. So you end up with a punch that has a true edge, but the locator has a dent in the side. This may cause shearing of the side of the cup.

If a problem occurs which is across the sheet rather than down a row, then I would go straight to the cooling rollers, or the 'dancing rollers'. Particular note would be paid to the two rollers on which the sheet remains stationary prior to going into the press. It could be the result of a damaged roller.

There is also the possibility that a leakage has occurred from the air inlets to the former. This would normally cause cooling to the front of the set. If it was further back, you would tend to look at the rollers. What may happen is that the tool piles up, and you get plastic all over the tool. So the sheet would be cut along the roller in order to clean it, but in so doing, the roller is damaged.

If the problem occurs on the outside of the sheet, it is usually the result of an incorrect setting. For example, one of the outside rows is a lot lighter. This is merely the result of die adjustment.

If the problem occurs on one pot consistently, then this may be the result of a bent or damaged plug. Changing the plug would be the first option, since it is a relatively simple and quick operation, compared to problems with the mould.

In terms of air leakage onto the sheet, this can come from any source including roof fans.

There is also the possibility of contamination on the sheet. This may be from the extractor fans which draw the fumes from the extruder. It would also draw off the monomers etc., and these would build up inside. In that event, you might get a drop dripping out of the hood. This would result in contamination on one row, but at unpredictable times. If it was coming from the extruder die, it would probably be visible as a yellowish mark.

On a hot day, the chilled water pipes may have condensation form on the outside, and this may drip on the sheet. This may cause a hot wrinkle.

Chapter 5

Knowledge representation*

When we seek knowledge we are bounded by only our imagination.
J. Durkin

OBJECTIVES

In this chapter you will learn:

❏ about the different knowledge-representation schemes which are available to you;

❏ how to choose between these schemes;

❏ the advantages and disadvantages of these schemes;

❏ how to represent knowledge in a form suitable for a knowledge-based system.

5.1 Introduction

Knowledge is humanity's first frontier. Since the dawn of time our curiosity has tempted us to find out about things. We have sought to obtain knowledge, to apply that knowledge to solve everyday problems and to expand on it to improve the world around us and our environment. It has been the pursuit of knowledge that has taken us from kneeling over a fire in a cave to walking on the moon.

The key to the efficient implementation of a KBS is finding a suitable representation for the real problem-solving knowledge which is to be incorporated in the system. Whereas conventional computing uses data and usually concentrates on efficient techniques for representing numbers and file records, knowledge representation is concerned with the efficient representation of everyday concepts, situations and common-sense knowledge from a particular application domain.

*The author would like to thank Dimitrios Markakis for his contributions to this chapter.

A good definition of knowledge representation is: 'Knowledge representation is formalizing and storing knowledge in some suitable structure to allow for subsequent computer processing.' A KBS is only as good as the knowledge which the knowledge engineer has captured and then represented in the knowledge base. It is therefore very important that the knowledge engineer represents the knowledge in the best way possible. This involves writing down, in some language, descriptions or pictures that correspond as closely as possible with the real knowledge from the problem domain in which he or she is working.

It must be noted that none of the knowledge-representation techniques discussed in this chapter can be considered to be the best form of knowledge representation. Rather, there are quite a few competing candidate representations and it is up to the knowledge engineer to select the most appropriate.

Some knowledge representations will be more appropriate for one problem than other. The language in which you are going to implement your system may also place restrictions upon the kinds of knowledge representation which are available to you.

Before describing some of these different representation schemes, it is important to define the two most common types of knowledge which are employed by an expert during the problem-solving process. These are:

- heuristic knowledge
- descriptive knowledge

These are each discussed below.

5.1.1 Heuristic knowledge

Many of the problems which are tackled by experts are difficult and poorly understood. It is often not possible to solve them by following a methodical or well-formulated procedure. One of the things which differentiates an expert from others in his or her field, is their ability, when faced with a specific problem, to apply a problem-solving strategy which leads them quickly to an acceptable solution for the problem.

Problem-solving techniques applied by an expert often have no formal basis but are based on observations and empirical associations gathered by the expert over time. On the basis of his or her experience, the expert develops rules of thumb which allow him or her to focus attention on the key aspects of the problem. These rules of thumb are called **heuristics** and this type of knowledge is often called **heuristic knowledge**.

Heuristic knowledge is generally considered to be 'shallow' (section 5.1.2). That is, heuristics often ignore the formal laws and theories of a problem domain. They simply express surface relationships which an expert has observed to be of use when tackling problems in the domain. They can often be stated in terms of rules. For example, the forecasting case study might have the following rule:

```
IF    the temperature tomorrow is higher than the temperature
      today,
THEN the demand for gas will be less
```

This heuristic states a relationship between the temperature tomorrow, the temperature today and the demand for gas. It does not refer to the exact relationship between these factors. Through experience, the engineer has noticed the surface relationship between these factors. He or she knows this to be the case from past experience and uses this rule of thumb as the basis for future calculations of gas demand.

5.1.2 Deep and shallow knowledge

The level of knowledge which an expert has about a particular problem domain can be categorized as 'shallow' or 'deep'. Similarly, the level of understanding that is encapsulated within a KBS can also be considered to be shallow or deep.

Shallow knowledge is when the expert has a superficial, surface knowledge of a problem area, but does not have a deep understanding of the way in which the problem domain operates. That is, he or she does not have a powerful mental model of the problem environment.

On the other hand, deep knowledge is when the expert has a thorough understanding of the very basics of the problem in terms of the fundamental laws on which it is based (such as the laws of physics, chemistry, nature, mathematics, etc.)

For example, we know that if we drop a dinner plate it will crash to the ground. Simply accepting that state without understanding why it happens can be said to be shallow knowledge. Deep knowledge would involve a fundamental understanding of the laws of gravity and how they cause the plate to be attracted towards the earth.

Deep knowledge allows the knowledge to be applied to a wider range of situations and allows for more powerful reasoning. However, to build this level of reasoning into a KBS will be costly and time consuming and may be prone to errors. On the other hand, shallow knowledge can be quite limited in application but is probably easier to obtain and makes the KBS easier to maintain.

5.1.3 Descriptive knowledge

The formulation of the heuristics used by an expert highlights concepts in the problem domain which are central to the problem-solving process. In effect, these concepts represent a distilled version of the expert's background knowledge. This knowledge is termed descriptive knowledge. It provides a description of the problem domain, which suppresses irrelevant detail but which makes explicit those features and characteristics which are important in the problem-solving process.

The problem-solving knowledge captured within an expert system is, therefore, a combination of heuristic and descriptive knowledge. The heuristic knowledge captures the active problem-solving strategies employed by the expert. However, it cannot be considered in isolation from the descriptive knowledge, since it would not be possible to express the heuristics without this supportive background knowledge.

5.2 Rules

Rules are the natural way of representing certain forms of knowledge, especially heuristic knowledge. Rules are generally represented as IF–THEN statements. The general form of a rule is:

```
IF <situation> THEN <action>
```

A simple rule could be:

```
IF    Christmas Day falls on a Monday
OR    Christmas Day falls on a Tuesday
THEN  Many factories will close for one week and gas con
      sumption will be reduced significantly
```

In the example rule above the right-hand side indicates a conclusion about the probable outcome of Christmas Day falling at the start of a working week, given the information contained in the left-hand side. The left-hand side of a rule may contain a number of clauses, combined using logical connectives such as AND and OR.

For instance, the left-hand side of the above rule contains two clauses:

```
Christmas Day falls on a Monday
```
and
```
Christmas Day falls on a Tuesday
```

linked together by an OR connective.

Additionally, a NOT operator may be used to indicate that the rule should fire if the clause is not true.

There is no direct interaction between rules; rules cannot activate (or 'fire') each other directly. The only mechanism for communication between rules is through the conclusions which can be inferred by a rule. When a rule has been successfully activated, it adds its conclusions to the set of facts in the knowledge base. These facts then fire other rules and their conclusions can be used in turn to activate yet more rules.

Knowledge-based systems that use production rules for knowledge representation are termed **rule-based systems**. Their main characteristics are that:

- They represent practical human reasoning in the form of conditional if–then rules.
- Their knowledge grows as more rules are added.
- They solve complex problems by combining groups of relevant rules.
- They dynamically select the best rules to execute.

An important aspect of any KBS employing rules is the use of **inference techniques** to manipulate the expertise when solving a problem. The inference engine is the software system that locates knowledge and from it **infers** new knowledge. The most common and proven inferencing strategies are **forward and backward chaining**.

5.2.1 Chaining

Forward chaining operates from the facts in the knowledge base and uses these to work towards conclusions. Thus, it will 'fire' rules when conditions are satisfied by the facts in the knowledge base.

The reasoning method used in forward chaining is:

```
REPEAT
```

- Select all rules whose left-hand side is true.
- Choose one of these rules.
- Execute the right-hand side of the rule, updating the current knowledge base and reaching conclusions.

```
UNTIL no more rules match
```

Backward chaining operates by selecting a possible conclusion and working backwards to prove that the conclusion is true. The reasoning method used in backward chaining is:

```
REPEAT
```

- Select all rules whose right-hand side are to be proved. That is, select those rules whose conclusions are possible targets to be inferred.
- Choose one of these rules.
- Examine the left-hand side of the rule. If it is true, then the conclusion is proven.

```
UNTIL no more rules match
```

For example, consider the following rules:

```
Rule 1: IF  B  AND  I  THEN  X
Rule 2: IF  I  AND  J  THEN  Y
Rule 3: IF  C  AND  K  THEN  Z
Rule 4: IF  J  THEN  K
```

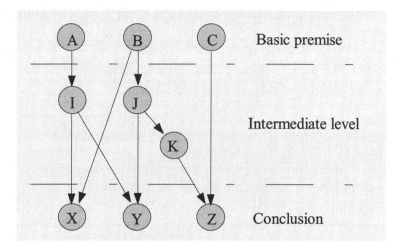

Figure 5.1 *Forward chaining.*

```
Rule 5: IF B THEN J
Rule 6: IF A THEN I
```

Figure 5.1 shows the operation of forward chaining. The reasoning process works from basic premises to intermediate conclusions and forward to the final conclusions.

XCON, the system for configuring and designing VAX computers mentioned in section 2.2.1, is a typical forward-chaining system. The configuration work which takes place in order to locate the various computer parts in their correct position is very complex, because a computer system will consist of more than one hundred parts. The searching strategy of XCON is to find all of the possible situations in a first layer of basic premises and then go on to the next layer for further searching.

Figure 5.2 is an example of backward chaining. It works backwards from a conclusion until an answer is discovered.

MYCIN is a typical backward-chaining system. The order of a given question from MYCIN is determined by the present assumption and the answer to previous questions. For each patient the order of questions can be different. Strictly speaking, MYCIN uses a combination of forward and backward chaining. MYCIN uses backward chaining to discover what organisms are present; then it uses forward chaining to conclude what treatment is required.

5.2.2 Certainty factors

In many problem domains the expert may use some form of judgmental or inexact reasoning. For example, he or she may use heuristics such as:

```
When conditions X and Y occur, Z is likely to be the
case.
```

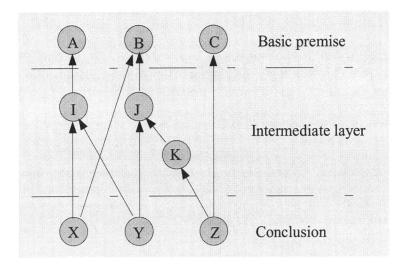

Figure 5.2 *Backward chaining.*

In some cases the information used by experts may be uncertain, that is, they may believe that a fact is true but may not be entirely certain. This type of reasoning, where some facts suggest others and facts are known to be probably true, is very common.

To cope with this kind of uncertainty, the way of expressing rules is usually extended to include a representation of the degree of certainty with which a fact or conclusion can be considered to be true. This is usually represented as attaching a number to the rule. This number is called a **certainty factor** (CF).

Certainty factors generally range from a minimum value of 0, indicating that something is definitely false, to a maximum value of 1, indicating that it is definitely true. Intermediate values indicate the strength with which it can be believed. For example, the following rules are taken from the monitoring-system case study and illustrate the use of certainty factors:

```
RULE 1:
IF    the patient has hypothermia
THEN  he or she may have respiratory problems (CF 0.5)
AND   he or she may suffer cardiac arrest (CF 0.4)


RULE 2:
IF    there is a reduction in alveolar minute volume
THEN  the respiratory centre may be depressed (CF 0.6)


RULE 3:
IF    the arterial pCO2 rises above 12 kPa in response to
      oxygen therapy
AND   it remains at that level for more than 5 minutes
THEN  there is a substantial risk of carbon dioxnarcosis
      (CF 0.9)
```

5.3 Frames

Frames represent a way of breaking a knowledge base into modular chunks. They are closely connected with a type of design called object-oriented design (section 5.6). In 1975, M.L. Minsky described a frame as:

> the ingredients of most theories both in Artificial Intelligence and in Psychology have been on the whole too minute, local, and unstructured to account...for the effectiveness of common-sense thought. The 'chunks' of reasoning, language, memory, and perception ought to be larger and more structured; their factual and procedural contents must be more intimately connected in order to explain the apparent power and speed of mental activities.
>
> (Minsky, 1975)

Frames provide a method of combining declarations and procedures within a single knowledge-representation environment. The fundamental organizing principle underlying frame systems are the packaging of both data and procedures into a single knowledge structure. Frames are a way of organizing, as well as packaging, knowledge. They are organized into hierarchies or networks that can be used to inherit information (Parsaye, 1988).

A frame is a description of an object which contains slots for all of the information associated with that object. For instance, the frame for a cup, in the quality-control system, could have the following slots:

- what type of cup it is
- what colour it usually is
- what size it usually is
- what purpose it usually fulfils
- what it costs
- what material it is made of

This is shown in Figure 5.3.

Frames have the following advantages:

- They can be graphically represented (on paper or computer) and so allow the knowledge engineer to develop them quickly.
- They allow representation of different types of knowledge.
- They can be used to contain default values.
- They allow for easy classification of knowledge and reduce the complexity of the knowledge base.
- They can clearly document information about a domain model, for example, a plant's machines and their associated attributes.
- They can inherit procedural or declarative knowledge from other frames.
- They can constrain the allowable values that an attribute can take.

CUP FRAME		
TYPE		Small drinking
COLOUR		Brown
SIZE		Height: 8mm; diameter: 3mm
PURPOSE		Drinking
COST		0.5p
MATERIAL		Plastic

Figure 5.3 *A cup frame.*

The following is an example of a frame describing a man called Frank
Bradley who might be stored in the integrated system:

```
MANXY
IS-A        VALUE:     MAN
Name        VALUE:     Frank  Bradley
Height      VALUE:     1.90
Weight      VALUE:     95
Skills      VALUE:     Programming
Hobbies     VALUE:     Jogging,  Tennis
```

The MANXY frame represents a man whose name is Frank Bradley and
whose height, weight, skills and hobbies are described. In frame terminology
a frame is made up of four levels of description:

- frame
- slot
- facet
- data

The name of the frame is the only information represented at the frame level.
The attributes of the frame are normally represented at the slot level. The
facet level indicates different aspects of an attribute for which information
may be stored in the frame. The data level is the lowest level in the frame;
information about the attributes is stored at this level.

As indicated in the above example, slots can be used to represent attributes
or properties of a frame. However, slots can also be used to represent
relationships between frames. When the value of the slot indicates the name
of another frame, the name of the slot can be considered to be the name of the
relationship between the frames. This is precisely the meaning of the IS-A slot
in the frame MANXY; it establishes the IS-A link between MANXY and the
more general MAN frame.

Frames are normally used to represent knowledge built on well-known
characteristics and experiences. Every individual has a great deal of common-

sense knowledge and experience. They call upon this to solve problems. Frames can be used to represent this kind of knowledge. The main bottleneck when using frames is trying to establish default values for the objects on which everyone, especially all the experts, agree.

5.3.1 Facets

Facets may take many forms:

- **Values** – these describe attributes such as blue, red and yellow for a colour slot.
- **Default** – this facet is used if the slot is empty, that is, without any description. That is, the default colour value for a cup might be brown.
- **Range** – range indicates what kind of information can appear in a slot, for example: integer numbers only, two decimal points, 0–100.
- **If added** – this facet contains procedural information or attachments. It specifies an action to be taken when a value in the slot is added (or modified). Such procedural attachments are called **demons**.
- **If needed** – this facet is used in a case when no slot value is given. It triggers, much like the if-added situation, a procedure that goes out and gets or computes a value.

Facets are extremely useful in debugging, since they can turn control over to the knowledge engineer (or debugging routine) when activated. An example of a facet in the general MAN frame from the integrated system is shown below:

```
MAN
IS-A      VALUE:    MAMMAL
Height    TYPE:     Real
          DEFAULT:  1.80
Weight    TYPE:     Real
          DEFAULT:  75
```

The average height and weight of a man are now specified as default values for those slots. Now, if an effort is made to retrieve a value for a frame specifying the height and weight of a specific man and no value is found in the appropriate slots of the lower frame, the default values specified in the MAN frame can be returned in their place. In this way, one interpretation of the default values is to assert that, unless told specifically otherwise, any man can be considered to be of average height and weight.

Figure 5.4 shows a practical pump design in which the knowledge representation is packaged within a frame.

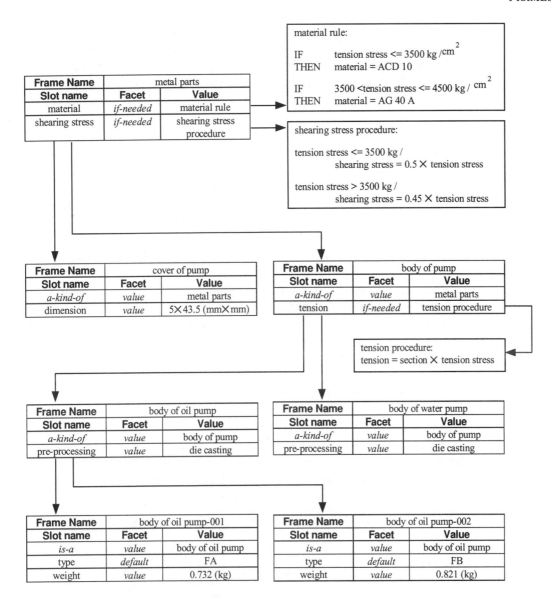

Figure 5.4 *Pump design with frame representation (Kuo, 1995).*

5.4 Semantic nets

One of the oldest and easiest-to-understand knowledge-representation schemes is the semantic network or semantic net. Semantic networks are graphic descriptions of knowledge that show hierarchical relationships between objects.

A simple semantic net, depicting relationships from the integrated system, is shown in Figure 5.5. It is made up of a number of circles, or nodes, which represent objects and descriptive information about those objects. An object can be any physical item such as a book, car, animal or person. Nodes can also be concepts, events or actions. Attributes of an object can also be used as nodes and could represent size, colour, age, origin or other characteristics. In this way, detailed information about objects can be presented.

The nodes in a semantic network are interconnected by links or arcs. These arcs show the relationships between the objects. Some of the most common arcs are of the **is-a** or **has-a** type.

An is-a link is used to show class relationship, that is, to denote that an object belongs to a larger class or category of objects. Has-a links are used to identify characteristics or attributes of the object nodes.

Semantic nets are a very flexible form of representation since new nodes and links can be added as they are needed. In addition, the structure of the net diagram provides a graphical picture of the knowledge base. However, they do have the disadvantage that large networks can be difficult to represent on a single piece of a paper or on a computer screen. Large semantic nets are also difficult and unwieldy to manipulate and you often get arcs crossing each other which can cause many problems.

Inheritance refers to the ability of one node to inherit characteristics from other nodes in the network. A special property of the is-a link is that properties can be transmitted from one node to another along it.

Although a semantic network is graphic in nature, it does not appear this way in a computer. Instead, the various objects and their relationships are stated in English-like terms and these are programmed into the computer using a software tool or a language. Searching semantic networks (especially large ones) can be quite difficult and the technique is often used for initial analysis purposes, followed by a transformation to rules or frames. Semantic nets can thus be used as a visual representation of relationships and can be combined with other representation methods.

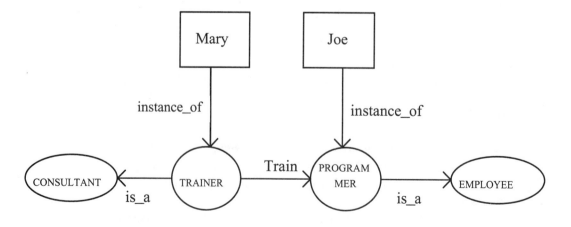

Figure 5.5 *Example of a semantic network.*

5.5 Blackboard representations

Blackboard systems are so named because they organize and process knowledge in a fashion similar to a group of people working around a blackboard. The blackboard is used as a repository for the knowledge that is being assembled by the group. Each person represents a **knowledge source**, a specialized source of knowledge about some aspect of the problem. The group leader provides a control function, guiding and focusing the activities of the knowledge sources and controlling their access to the blackboard.

Knowledge can be represented on the blackboard and in the knowledge sources in various ways (rules, frames, etc.). A blackboard system is not so much a technique of knowledge representation but more a way of organizing and processing knowledge, which may be represented in several different forms. Thus, a blackboard approach can be thought of as a problem-solution process.

The blackboard concept was the basis for the HEARSAY II speech-recognition system developed at Carnegie–Mellon University, which in turn has served as a model for a number of later blackboard-based applications. The first system for building blackboard systems (AGE) was constructed at Stanford University by Nii and Aiello in 1978.

A blackboard system can be thought of as a framework in which knowledge can be arranged so that it can be shared among a number of co-operating processes. The knowledge about a problem can be distributed to a set of specialists called knowledge sources, each of whom has a particular area of expertise. Part of the knowledge is placed on the blackboard and this is the shared portion of the knowledge base through which the specialists communicate. The remainder of the knowledge resides with the individual specialists who operate independently of each other (except for the communication that takes place through the knowledge placed on the blackboard).

The specialists can be viewed as domain experts. Each expert works to further the state of collective knowledge as represented on the blackboard. This contributes to the problem's solution. However, in addition to the domain specialists, at least one specialist must have expertise relating to the solution process. It is this specialist that provides the control function, guiding the activities of the other specialists and controlling their access to the blackboard.

The blackboard representation is a structure upon which knowledge can be placed using several different forms of representation. A variety of knowledge representations are compatible with, and can be used with, a blackboard structure.

The blackboard serves a dual role in KBS design. Like other forms of knowledge representation this structure governs access to and modification of the knowledge represented. However, a blackboard can also serve as a solution methodology, providing an approach for developing a solution to the problem at hand. The blackboard concept can be considered more as a philosophy or a set of guidelines than as another form of knowledge representation.

As stated above, a blackboard knowledge representation is constructed from three major components (Figure 5.6):

- knowledge sources (expertise)
- blackboard (knowledge storage and communication)
- control (problem-solving strategy)

These are discussed in the following sections.

5.5.1 Knowledge sources
The knowledge sources represent expertise that is captured in the KBS. Each knowledge source represents some particular specialized knowledge pertaining to the problem being solved. This knowledge may be represented in different ways, perhaps as a collection of rules and/or frames.

5.5.2 The blackboard
The operation of the blackboard system can be likened to a collection of specialists that have gathered together to tackle a problem. If they are allowed to talk freely to each other, a number of side conversations are quite likely to

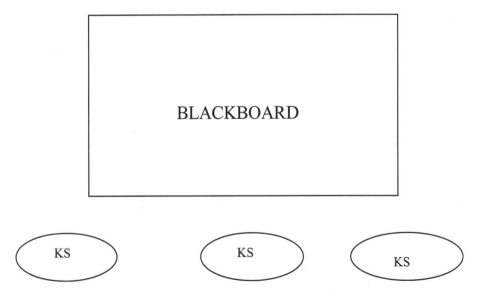

KS: Knowledge Source

Figure 5.6 *Schematic of a blackboard system.*

develop. As a result, some of the specialists will not know some of the information being developed or contributed by the other specialists.

To prevent this from happening, every specialist should be included in the 'conversations'. Every expert should work alone and then share his or her conclusions with others by 'writing them on the blackboard' for all to see. The concept of independence and yet sharing are fundamental to the blackboard approach to problem solving. The blackboard, thus, represents the communication medium through which the knowledge sources (e.g. the experts) communicate their findings to each other.

5.5.3 Control

A group of experts left in a room without direction will probably wander around, somewhat aimlessly, in their search for a solution to a problem. The solution process needs to be guided or controlled. Special knowledge sources must be present in order to provide this control. They focus on the control of the problem-solving process rather than on the domain knowledge. They provide control in two ways:

- by placing information on the blackboard that will influence the knowledge sources;
- by selecting the knowledge sources to be used.

Blackboard representations have a variety of uses. Early applications involved real-time data processing domains, including speech processing and signal processing. Additionally, the blackboard representational form is also appropriate for certain types of scheduling or planning applications. Generally, a blackboard representation might be routinely considered for problems that can be naturally broken down into a number of smaller independent problem structures.

5.6 Object-based representations

Until 1990, object-oriented technology was of minimal interest in the computing industry. Yet in recent years this situation has been changing rapidly. Today, there is a great surge of interest in what is widely perceived as one of the most interesting and potentially powerful new technologies currently available. Many software packages are now being developed to implement object-oriented technology. Object-oriented programming is well suited to KBS development. The major concepts of object-oriented technology are outlined below.

5.6.1 The object

An object has been defined by Professor Ian Sommerville (Sommerville, 1992) as 'an entity which has a state and a defined set of operations to access and modify that state.' This means that an object consists of both data and code. The code relates to the functions or rules for processing the data. Objects are independent and may readily be changed because all of the relevant information is held within the object itself. This is referred to as **encapsulation**.

Object-oriented systems embrace object-oriented analysis, design and programming. That is, using the object-oriented approach is an entirely new approach to the whole process of system design. Instead of building systems as combinations of isolated routines, object-oriented systems allow the reuse of objects. Hence, systems can be built by using the existing objects.

5.6.2 The class

The basic modular unit is the class which represents a group of objects based on similarities. An object class can also be referred to as an abstract data type, such as Account, Employee, Customer, Supplier, Stock. Classes are useful to a programmer as they are a means of reusing code. A class as such is not a tangible item in itself but a template for constructing objects.

5.6.3 Messages and methods

A procedure or method is a specification of action on data contained in the object. Messages invoke attached procedures (methods) to act upon object data. Objects respond to messages they receive by determining the appropriate procedure to execute.

For example, when a message is sent to an object (Figure 5.7), the object responds by locating an attached procedure associated with this message and executing it. Since different procedures are defined as methods for the objects, different objects might respond to the same message in different ways.

5.6.4 Inheritance

A class may inherit its structure and methods from other classes. Examples of this are the classes of PERSON and EMPLOYEE in the integrated system.

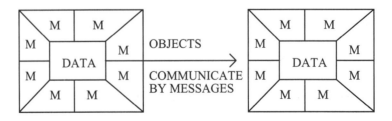

M -- SOFTWARE MODULE

Figure 5.7 *The object-oriented approach.*

The class EMPLOYEE inherits the attributes (data components) and methods of the class PERSON. Therefore, the class EMPLOYEE has similarities to the class PERSON (e.g., name, birthday, age) with the addition of other attributes specific to that type of class (e.g. employee id, dept no.).

5.6.5 Object-oriented technology and KBS

Currently, object orientation is used in a number of different disciplines within computing. These include programming languages, databases and knowledge engineering. Many experimental knowledge-representation languages have been developed to package both data and procedures into structures related by some form of inheritance mechanism.

There are several attempts to use object-oriented technology in KBS design. One such attempt is FOODM (Frame-based Object-Oriented Data Model). FOODM is the kernel of a prototype system which is known as SEDSDT (Sunderland Expert Database System Development Tool, developed by Shi-Ming Huang in 1994). The FOODM was the basis for the design of the integrated-system case study (Huang *et al.*, 1994).

FOODM is a higher-order synthesis which includes frame concepts, semantic data modelling concepts and object-oriented concepts. It can also support external modules and thus allow existing systems to communicate with each other via it.

SEDSDT is an open architecture and can be used to couple many different modules into the FOODM. These modules can be grouped into three generic classes (Figure 5.8):

- the knowledge-representation module
- the expert-system coupling module
- the database coupling module

The knowledge-representation module contains knowledge expressed in the language of SEDSDT, which is known as the K-Language. The K-Language is a menu driven language. The expert-system coupling module represents any knowledge which is encapsulated in an existing external expert system. The database coupling module represents any 'knowledge' which is encapsulated in an existing external database system.

5.7 Case-based reasoning

Case-based reasoning (CBR) is a recent technique which has been developed to overcome some of the limitations of rule-based KBS. In particular, CBR can help where the experience domain is rich but the knowledge domain is poor or inadequate. A case-based system maintains old cases in a case library so that the best solutions for new problems can be constructed through the retrieval of similar cases.

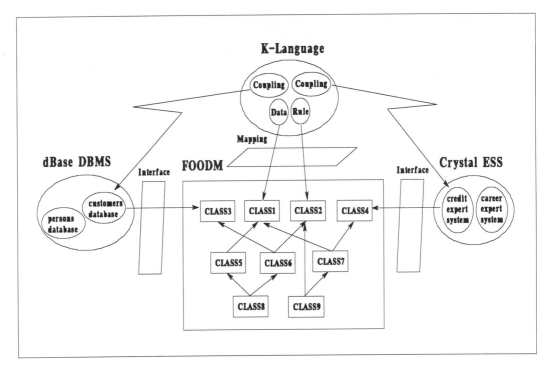

Figure 5.8 *The architecture of FOODM (Huang, 1994).*

CBR utilizes previous experiences of problems in order to solve new problems. During knowledge elicitation cases are stored in order to build up a 'case base'. In the case of successfully solved problems, the experience is stored in the case base for use when new problems arise. On the other hand, when a problem solution fails, that experience is also stored in order to avoid making the same mistakes again in the future.

In previous chapters we have discussed the knowledge-acquisition bottleneck and the problems of acquiring and formulating knowledge, especially when the size of the problem is large. With CBR we are not trying to express the knowledge in terms of specific rules. Rather, we are building up a set of cases, or experiences, which can then be referred to and used in future problem-solving activities.

When CBR cannot find an exact answer, it gives the closest answer to the problem, because CBR systems are able to report prior cases that are sufficiently similar to the new problem's requirements. It has been argued that the current surge of interest in CBR is due to the intuitive nature of CBR and its close resemblance to human reasoning (Watson and Marir, 1994).

Several definitions of a case have been given:

- A case is a contextualized piece of knowledge representation, an experience that teaches a lesson fundamental to achieving the goal of the reasoner (Kolodner, 1993).

- A case is a triple (P, S, J) where P is a problem description, S the solution for the described problem and J the justification of the solution. A case corresponds to a real event or process which can be limited within space and time (Althoff and Wess, 1992).
- A case is a relevant example rather than a general rule. Cases are applied to new problems by using an analogical reasoning process. Proponents of CBR claim that it is closer to the way in which humans reason (Luger and Stubblefield, 1989).

Similarly, there are several definitions of case-based reasoning:

- Case-based reasoning may be defined as the adaptation of old solutions to meet a new demand, using old cases to explain new situations, using old cases to critique new solutions, or reasoning from a precedent to interpret a new situation or create an equitable solution to a new problem (Kolodner, 1993).
- Case-based reasoning is a method of solving a new problem by remembering a previous similar situation (case) and by reusing information and knowledge of that situation (Aamodt and Plaza, 1994).
- A case-based reasoner solves new problems by adapting solutions that were used to solve old problems (Schank, 1982).

The essential concept of CBR is that it attempts to simulate human experts when solving problems. By using past experiences, the accumulated expertise held within the system can be applied to the solution of the new problem under consideration.

CBR is best applied in areas where problems may not be easily decomposed, or the general principles involved are not completely understood, but where a library of past experiences can be generated and employed. CBR can also be used where complex problems exist for which there is not a precise answer. In this situation only suggested solutions can be made rather than a concrete solution.

Case-based reasoning was first proposed by Schank and Abelson in 1977. Their program relied on knowledge and reasoning described as a pattern and allowed the reasoner to work out problem solutions and perform inferences. In the early 1980s, the first CBR application system, called CYRUS (Computerized Yale Retrieval and Update System), was developed by Janet Kolodner at Yale University in Roger Schank's group. CYRUS was a question–answer system with knowledge, as cases, of various travels and meetings of former US Secretary of State Cyrus Vance (Kolodner, 1993). The case memory model developed for this system has later served as the basis for several other case-based reasoning systems, including MEDIATOR, CHEF, PERSUADER, CASEY and JULIA (Watson and Marir, 1994; Aamodt and Plaza, 1994).

Table 5.1 illustrates some of the differences between rule-based reasoning (RBR) and case-based reasoning (CBR) methods.

Table 5.1 *Differences between RBR and CBR*

	Rule-based reasoning	Case-based reasoning
Knowledge content	Rules are small, independent but consistent	Cases are large chunks of domain knowledge and stored by describing the way things work
Domain	Well enough understood	well and not well understood
Matching	Exactly	Partially
Heuristic	Explicit	Implicit
Interpretation	Single	Multiple

5.8 Selecting a knowledge representation

Each of the knowledge-representation techniques described earlier has relevance to particular types of knowledge. None is applicable to all forms of knowledge. In fact, choosing the appropriate representations for a KBS is still considered to be something of an art.

It is often difficult to explain why some knowledge-representation schemes work well in some domains but not in others. Consequently, no methods exist for choosing the most appropriate representation(s) for a KBS. However, a set of five guidelines that a number of knowledge engineers have found to be very useful are (Markakis, 1994):

- Select the most natural representation.
- Break down the problem.
- Plan for the representation.
- Work to the strengths.
- Understand your tools!

The relevance and importance of each guideline to a particular KBS development will depend on the characteristics of the system being built. Not every guideline will apply in every situation. Each of them should, however, be carefully considered. They can be used to make the resultant KBS more efficient, more powerful, more understandable and less costly to maintain.

5.8.1 Select the most natural representation
The form(s) of representation chosen for the knowledge must match the structure of the problem in hand. This appears to be obvious, yet knowledge engineers often ignore it.

This may seem quite simple. The knowledge engineer has only to look at the natural forms of the knowledge and the inferencing procedures being used and then find representations to match those forms. Unfortunately, the structures of real-world problems often differ from the knowledge representation structures in use. Because of this discrepancy a number of knowledge-based systems have become unnecessarily complex. This is because an inappropriate form of knowledge representation was used.

Knowledge engineers are not always to blame for a poorly constructed knowledge base. One of the most common failings stems from an effort to force a body of knowledge into a particular representation form that a previously acquired system-development tool can handle. That is, the knowledge engineer is forced to choose a particular knowledge representation because of the tools or language available to him or her.

The fact that a development tool was suitable for an earlier application does not necessarily make it appropriate for subsequent development projects. But, because software is relatively expensive, organizations frequently pressurize their staff to use 'what's available' rather than acquire a new, more appropriate, piece of software. Unfortunately, the resulting damage in terms of complexity, development difficulty and maintainability can far exceed the acquisition costs involved.

An additional difficulty can be created by the fact that many problems do not fit neatly into any single representation. Rather than picking the best representation as the one to be applied to all aspects of the problem, the developer should divide the knowledge associated with the problem into pieces or sections. One section might best be captured in a frame representation, while another might best be captured in a rule representation.

A combination of different techniques can provide all the advantages of these representation schemes without the disadvantages associated with some of them. Figure 5.9 depicts two basic techniques in KBS development and the programming techniques that have emerged from the combination of these technologies.

If one or more techniques are to be combined, the knowledge engineer has to subdivide the problem knowledge and assign different representation methods to each component. In some cases the appropriate subdivisions and their representations are natural and obvious. In other cases, however, it may be far from obvious and the knowledge engineer will have to go through a considerable amount of trial and error.

Generally speaking, if it is difficult to place the knowledge into a particular representation, this may well be a signal to reorganize the knowledge or use one or more different representations. Furthermore, the knowledge engineer should also consider ways in which the KBS might change in the future.

5.8.2 Break down the problem

Complexity tends to increase with problem size. Coupled with this, there is a parallel increase in the effort required to develop the KBS, as well as in the testing effort involved (Figure 5.10).

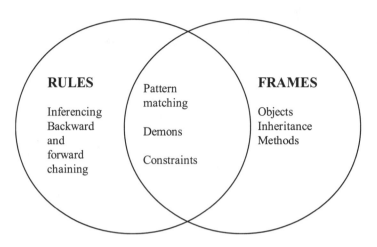

Figure 5.9 *Techniques emerging from the combination of the two basic representations.*

Because of this, the ability of the knowledge engineer to understand the entire problem decreases as the problem becomes more complex. Problems should thus be broken down into a number of smaller problems whenever possible. In general, the fact that the smaller problems are much simpler significantly outweighs the increase in the number of problems that have to be dealt with. As a result, not only is each part of the KBS easier to build, understand, and maintain, but the whole KBS becomes much more manageable.

Just as knowledge can be represented in many ways, so too can a problem be broken down in many different ways. The way in which a problem is broken down is not as important as the fact that it is broken down. Whatever the decomposition process, the result is likely to be a much more manageable system.

Not only does decomposition encourage simplification of the problem, it also helps with efficiency. A large 2000-rule KBS can be divided into 20 sets of 100 rules. Because the inferencing mechanism must consider all the rules in the set, a set of 100 rules is clearly much more efficient to handle than a set of 2000 rules.

Indeed, a 2000-rule knowledge base will be far too much for many computers to cope with. However, a KBS of 20 rule sets having 100 rules each can be processed quite rapidly. Thus, decomposition techniques can assist in producing more efficient knowledge-based systems.

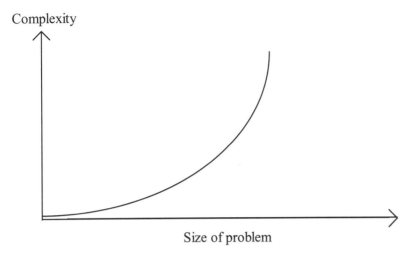

Figure 5.10 *Complexity tends to increase with problem size.*

5.8.3 Plan for the representation

It is often the case that the representation(s) that a knowledge engineer might like to use for a particular KBS development project cannot be supported by the tools he or she has available to do the job. In such a case, the availability of tools that support certain representation schemes will influence the design of the system very significantly. To avoid such problems, professional knowledge engineers first define the most appropriate set of knowledge representations and then identify the best tools for dealing with those representations.

In some cases, none of the available tools will provide exactly what is required. The knowledge engineer must then review the 'next-best choice', and so on. By not limiting selection to tools which are already available, the knowledge engineer can make sure that the resultant KBS is as powerful as possible.

5.8.4 Work to the strengths

Having selected a knowledge representation, the knowledge engineer should structure the KBS to take maximum advantage of the strengths of that representation. A typical failing of novice knowledge engineers is attempting to use a technique in a way that was not intended.

Developing a rule-based KBS is very different to programming in a procedural language such as C, COBOL or Pascal. Yet many knowledge engineers working today learnt the craft of programming with such procedural languages. As a result they may well conceptualize a problem in procedural terms. The effects of representing procedural information in the form of a rules base are not surprising. Many more rules are required to represent the knowledge in comparison with using of a declarative representation. The resulting KBS will not be very efficient or robust.

5.8.5 Understand your tools!

Even though this sounds obvious, there are a significant number of people who are using software systems that they do not really understand. This can, in part, be due to the very friendly user interfaces provided by many of the expert system shells which are now available on the market. These systems can be 'learnt' and used very quickly and easily. However, this may mean that the user does not really have a firm grasp of the full capabilities of the tool.

If knowledge engineers themselves become 'users' of the technology rather than 'experts' in it, the development and the maintenance of the resultant KBS can prove to be a very time-consuming process.

5.9 Summary

No single knowledge representation method is ideally suited for all tasks.

As a knowledge engineer you would be well advised to sacrifice the goal of uniformity and to try to exploit the benefits of multiple knowledge representations, each tailored to a different subtask. The knowledge engineer must be able to identify the strengths and weaknesses of each method and employ it to perform the specific subtask of the KBS development process that most fits it. However, this must be traded off against the constraints which are placed upon you by the tool or language which is to be used to implement the system.

There is no universal solution to the knowledge-representation problem. Knowledge engineers should not be trying to find one. Combining and choosing between the different methods is what a knowledge engineer should do to find the form of representation which is best suited to his or her needs.

5.10 Exercises

In the knowledge-acquisition phase of the development of the forecasting case study, questionnaires were used by the knowledge engineer to extract knowledge from the human expert. A sample completed questionnaire is shown below. The expert's replies are shown in bold.

Study this questionnaire and try to represent the knowledge it contains:

1. as a set of rules

2. as frames

Please note that there is no fully correct (or wrong!) solution to this problem. As is the case in most knowledge-representation problems, there are many different ways to representation the knowledge.

Knowledge Acquisition Questionnaire

Q1. What percentages do you allow for the effect of tomorrow is gas usage over that of today?

a. Tuesday over a Monday	**+10%**
b. Wednesday over a Tuesday	**+5%**
c. Thursday over a Wednesday	**+0%**
d. Friday over a Thursday	**−10%**
e. Saturday over a Friday	**−10%**
f. Saturday over a Weekday	**−15%**
g. Sunday over a Saturday	**−5%**
h. Sunday over a Weekday	**−20%**
i. Monday over a Sunday	**+10%**

Q2. How do you deal with Holidays?

  i. Bank Holiday Mondays

   a. Do you treat the Monday as another type of day?
     Treat as preceding Saturday
   b. Do you use a special percentage over
     a Weekday   % or
     a Sunday   %.
   c. Use some other method - please outline

  ii. Tuesdays following Bank Holiday Mondays

   a. Do you treat as a normal Tuesday?   **Yes**
   b. Do you use a special percentage over
     a Weekday   % or
     a Monday   %.
   c. Use some other method – please outline
  iii. Statutory Holidays – Easter, Christmas, New Year

   a. Do you use comparisons with previous years?   **Yes**
   b. If so how many years do you go back?
     Use Previous Year (i.e. One year back)
   c. Use some other method – please outline

Please answer the next 2 questions on a rating of 1 to 5 where 1 is not a lot and 5 is a lot.
Q3. How much notice do you take of a forecast which includes

rain	**4**
strong winds	**2**

snow	3
sleet	2
frost	2
wind direction	5

Q4. How much notice do you take if rain or any other misery factor is forecast to start

first thing in the morning	4
just after lunch	3
around tea-time	2
after ten at night	1

Q5. How much (as a percentage) would you add to your estimate if

a. rain is due and it is fine today	+10%
b. rain is due and it is wet today	+10%
c. snow is due and it is fine today	+15%
d. snow is due and it is wet today	+15%
e. snow is due and it has snowed today	+10%
f. strong winds are forecast and it is calm today	+10%

Chapter 6

Implementation

OBJECTIVES

In this chapter you will learn:

❏ the difference between an expert system shell and a programming language;

❏ the basics of the CRYSTAL expert system shell;

❏ the basics of the ESTA expert system shell;

❏ the basics of the Prolog programming language;

❏ how to choose the most appropriate development tool for a KBS project.

6.1 Introduction

This chapter focuses upon the implementation stage of system development. In order to implement the KBS the knowledge engineer has a range of tools available. In general, knowledge-engineering tools are software systems that help with the task of constructing a KBS. The tools that are available range from high-level programming languages through KBS shells to highly complex development environments.

Commercially available tools vary greatly in power and generality. The less expensive, simpler KBS development shells tend to provide only one inference strategy and a single form of knowledge representation. The more powerful tools, such as ART and KEE, provide environments which support multiple-inference strategies, multiple knowledge-representation techniques (rules, frames, semantic nets and so on), graphical interfaces, object-oriented programming and facilities for interfacing with external software systems.

Whilst shells are the most popular tools for KBS development, a really professional knowledge engineer should have some knowledge of the other tools which are available, including:

• KBS environments, e.g. KEE, ART and GOLDWORKS;
• KBS languages such as Prolog and Lisp;
• conventional languages such as C, FORTRAN and Pascal.

With these skills, the knowledge engineer should be able to compete in the world market where, for example, in Japan, more use is made of KBS languages than shells.

6.2 Expert system shells

The 1980s saw the appearance of several expert system shells. Shells provide an environment for the development of KBS and have certain components in common with one another, such as:

- a user interface
- a developer interface
- interfaces to other software systems/databases
- a scheme (or schemes) for knowledge representation in the knowledge base
- an inference engine to operate on the knowledge held in the knowledge base.

In a recent Department of Trade and Industry survey of the use of knowledge-based systems in the UK, which was carried out by Touche Ross in 1992, shells were found to be the most popular means of developing systems. A total of 42% of respondents used shells (the most popular of which was CRYSTAL, used by 17%), as opposed to only 10% of respondents who utilized the more sophisticated KBS development environments. Another 12% of system developers used an AI language such as Prolog or LISP, whereas 21% favoured KBS construction using conventional database/spreadsheet packages or conventional languages such as C.

These figures are undoubtedly related to the fact that at the moment 60% of knowledge-based systems are small, PC-based, stand-alone systems. Shells are a suitable (and inexpensive) means of developing small, stand-alone systems. In the future, however, the number of hybrid systems (where a KBS is integrated with, or embedded in, a conventional information system) is likely to increase. If this is the case, then the need for more sophisticated, powerful, integrated tools will increase.

Some shells are basically 'stripped-down expert systems'. That is, they are an expert system with the domain-specific knowledge removed. For example, the designers of PROSPECTOR stripped it of the knowledge of geology and turned it into KAS, a shell for building diagnostic systems.

Shells are comparatively inexpensive, can be used on PCs, and are often implemented in 'non-AI' languages, such as Pascal and FORTRAN. They provide a structure and built-in facilities which make system development fast and easy. This is why the growth of shells goes hand in hand with the use of rapid prototyping as a means of KBS development.

On the other hand, shells often lack flexibility and can only be applied to a restricted class of problems. This may reduce the professional knowledge engineer's design options.

6.3 CRYSTAL

6.3.1 Introduction

CRYSTAL is a rule-based expert system shell, marketed by Intelligent Environments Ltd. One of its principle advantages is that it is designed for users who have had minimal experience with expert systems. It is primarily menu driven and is very easy to use.

CRYSTAL is a PC-based product. Knowledge is represented in CRYSTAL by rules. Commands can be integrated with rules to carry out a variety of functions including assigning variables and testing them, displaying forms, menus and explanatory text, and controlling the processing of rules. Knowledge bases can be merged, allowing applications to be developed in manageable sections.

Command words within the language are provided from the menu or, in some cases, merely by moving the cursor position. This frees the programmer from having to manually type in the words every time.

CRYSTAL is designed to be user-friendly, and it is relatively easy to develop a basic expert system in a short period of time. Given the current trend in the use of rapid prototyping, CRYSTAL offers much to the knowledge engineer.

Hardware and software	
Hardware	PC
RAM	360K
Software	DOS

Features	
Knowledge representation	Rules, commands
Variables	Text, numeric
Inferencing	Backward
Procedural programming	No
Uncertainty management	Bayesian probabilities
Segmentation of knowledge base	Yes
External interfaces	Lotus 1-2-3, Symphony, Dbase, ASCII

Development support	
Incremental compilation	Yes
Debugging and testing aids	Yes
Training available	Yes
Telephone support	Yes

Figure 6.1 *Features of the CRYSTAL expert system shell.*

CRYSTAL offers two types of variable: text and numeric. Dates are handled as text for display purposes and as numeric for calculations. There are 98 functions provided for testing, processing and manipulating variables, including financial and mathematical functions.

CRYSTAL's method of inferencing is backward chaining and uncertainty is managed by calculating probabilities. The shell is supplied with three interface programs that allow applications to use data in Lotus 1-2-3, Dbase, or ASCII files.

Development of an application is done using the rule editor. Within the editor, rules can be entered, edited, moved and copied. New rules can be created by modifying existing ones and, where the same rule is used several times, any changes are automatically propagated throughout the rulebase. The rule editor also provides functions to assist in building applications. These include tracing the operation of an application and checking the use of rules and variables. Figure 6.1 gives an outline of the main features of the shell.

6.3.2 Building an expert system in CRYSTAL

This section will go through the development, in CRYSTAL, of part of the integrated system from our set of case studies. This system is known as JPMEDS.

JPMEDS is an expert database system which is designed to assist human resource managers in searching for the best member of staff for a vacancy.

Figure 6.2 *Crystal.*

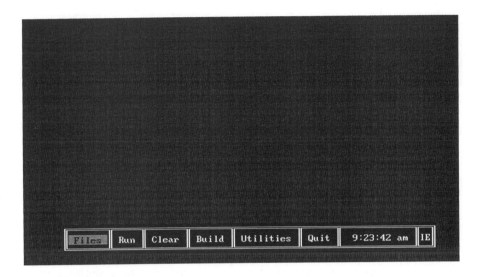

Figure 6.3 *The main menu.*

JPMEDS was built by implementing an expert system using CRYSTAL and then using its database interface to link with a personnel database system, developed in Dbase.

We are going to build a small portion of the JPMEDS expert system using CRYSTAL – one rule, in fact! This portion of the system advises members of staff who are thinking of a career change. This application is just an example and the rule used is not necessarily accurate.

When you load up CRYSTAL you will first see the screen in Figure 6.2.

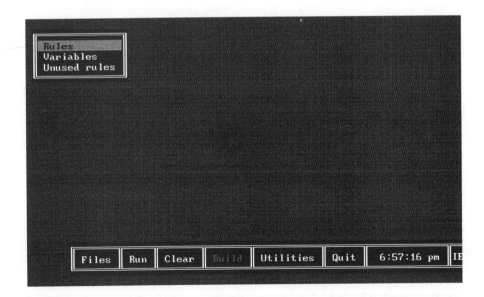

Figure 6.4 *The rules menu is in the top left-hand corner.*

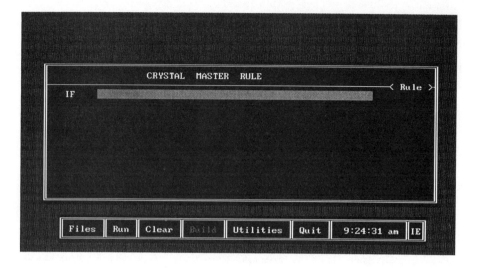

Figure 6.5 *Crystal master rule.*

When you enter CRYSTAL you will see the main menu, shown in Figure 6.3.

You must now select an option from the main menu. To make selections move along the menu using the arrow keys and then press ENTER.

We are now going to use the **Build** part of CRYSTAL to build a small part of the JPMEDS expert system. If you select the **Build** option from the main menu the screen shown in Figure 6.4 will appear.

You should now press the ENTER key to select the **Rules** option. We can now build the first rule in JPMEDS.

The display shown in Figure 6.5 will then appear on the screen.

This is the screen in which you will enter the purpose of JPMEDS.

The main purpose of this part of JPMEDS is to recommend a career for an employee. All that will be demonstrated here is how to build one simple rule. However, it quite sensible to start development in this way by building a small part of a KBS. This is the philosophy of the prototyping approach. You build small sets of rules to get going and then integrate them to form a larger KBS. In this case we are going to build a rule which will help decide whether or not an employee is suited to being a knowledge engineer.

The line preceded by the word 'IF' is highlighted, indicating that CRYS-TAL is waiting for you to begin typing in a rule. Type in the words:

```
knowledge engineer
```

The purpose of this rule is to decide, from information given by the user, whether he or she is suited to being a knowledge engineer.

Now press the F10 function key. This is the **Expand** key and allows us to expand the current condition into a full rule.

You will see that the display has changed to that shown in Figure 6.6.

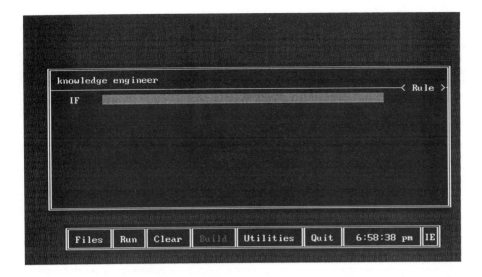

Figure 6.6 *Expanding the knowledge engineer rule.*

We now want to add some conditions to help decide whether the employee's ideal career is as a knowledge engineer. We will enter the rule that the employee is suited to being a knowledge engineer if they are sociable, logical and organized.

That is, the rule will be:

```
knowledge engineer
IF        sociable
AND       logical
AND       organized
```

CRYSTAL works by using a backward-chaining inference engine. So it would chain backwards from the conclusion:

```
knowledge engineer
```

and try to prove that the employee is **sociable, logical AND organized**. If all of these conditions are satisfied, then CRYSTAL will report that the employee is suited to the profession: **knowledge engineer**.

To enter the rule type the following:

```
sociable
```

Now press ENTER and type another condition, as follows:

```
logical
```

Press ENTER again and you will see that the word 'AND' appears on the previous line. This indicates that both of the first two conditions must be true

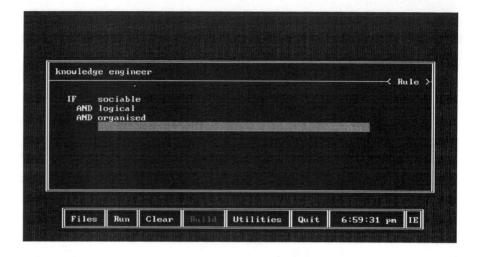

Figure 6.7 *The full knowledge-engineer rule.*

before CRYSTAL can conclude that the employee can be a knowledge engineer.

Now type:

```
organized
```

and press ENTER again.

We have now set the three conditions. All of these must be met before the master rule can be true.

The screen will now show the display in Figure 6.7.

Now press the ESC (Escape) key. This will take you back to the main menu as shown in Figure 6.8.

We have now set up a CRYSTAL rule which can be used to decide whether an employee should be a knowledge engineer. Choose **Build** and **Rules** and you will return to the master rule screen (Figure 6.9).

Now press the F10 (**Expand**) key again. The rule will appear again.

Now we need to tell CRYSTAL that if it receives the answer '**Yes**' to all three conditions, then it must display the conclusion: **knowledge engineer**. You should now be on the line which says:

```
IF sociable
```

Using the down-arrow key, move to the blank line below the one which says

```
AND organized
```

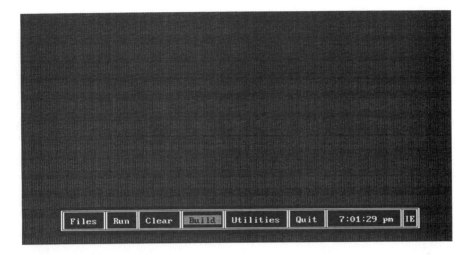

Figure 6.8 *The main menu.*

Press the F6 function key. This is the **Command** key, which brings up a list of available commands. The screen shown in Figure 6.10 will appear, with the list on the right-hand side. To make selections from this list, move up or down using the arrow keys to highlight your choice and then press ENTER.

We are going to use the **Conclusion Display** command, which allows us to tell CRYSTAL to display the conclusion: **knowledge engineer**.

Select **Conclusion Display** which is then inserted at the current cursor position, as shown in Figure 6.11.

Press the ESC (Escape) key to return to the main menu.

```
                   CRYSTAL   MASTER   RULE
                                                        〈 Rule 〉
  ◆  IF       knowledge engineer



      Files    Run    Clear    Build    Utilities    Quit    7:01:45 pm   IE
```

Figure 6.9 *Master rule.*

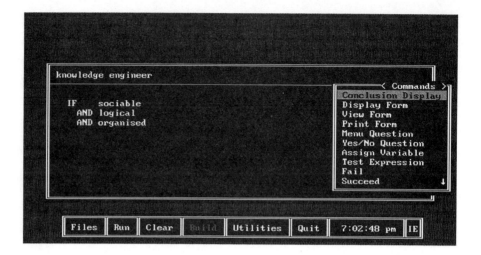

Figure 6.10 *The command menu.*

Before running JPMEDS, we need to save it. It is good practice to save to disk regularly when using any piece of software.

Select the **Files** option from the main menu. Select **Save knowledge base** and you will be prompted for a filename. Type '**JPMEDS**' as the name of the file, as shown in Figure 6.12, and press ENTER.

You have now saved the knowledge base. If you wanted to leave CRYSTAL now, you could do so without losing your work because you can load JPMEDS again when you go back into CRYSTAL.

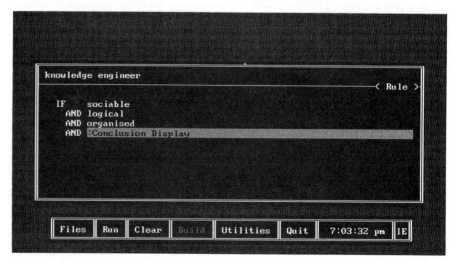

Figure 6.11 *Conclusion display.*

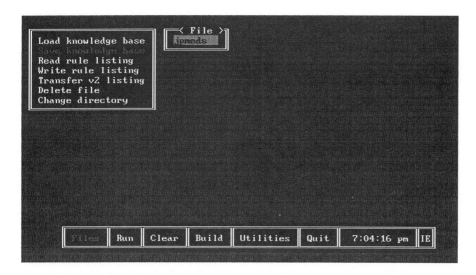

Figure 6.12 *Saving JPMEDS.*

We will now try to load and run JPMEDS. First select **Files** from the main menu and then **Load knowledge base**. A list of existing files is put on the screen. To choose one, use the arrow key to highlight its name, and press ENTER. Choose **JPMEDS**, as shown in Figure 6.13.

You could now run JPMEDS, using the **Run** command from the main menu.

CRYSTAL will now ask the user whether they are sociable, logical and organized. Each question will appear on a screen of its own as shown in Figure 6.14.

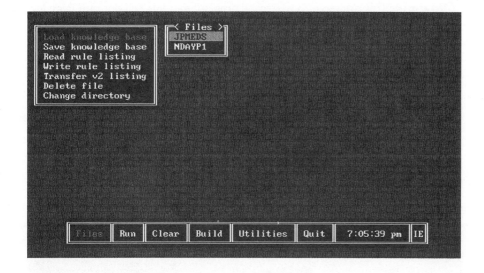

Figure 6.13 *Loading JPEDMS.*

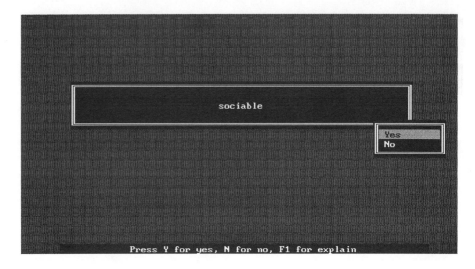

Figure 6.14 *The question screen.*

Answer all the questions with 'Yes', by highlighting **Yes** and pressing ENTER.

Notice that CRYSTAL goes through all three questions, then gives the conclusion display as shown in Figure 6.15.

Notice that the message:

```
Press F1 for explain or any other key to continue
```

appears at the bottom of the screen.

Press Fl and you will see an explanation of CRYSTAL's conclusion, as shown in Figure 6.16.

Now press ESC to leave **Explain** and then another key to continue. You are now back at the main menu.

Figure 6.15 *Conclusion display.*

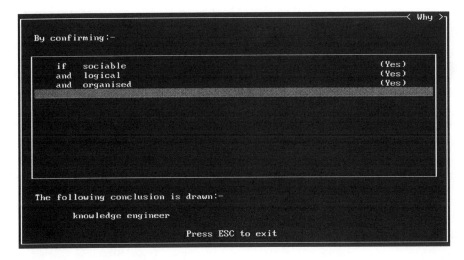

By confirming:-

	if	sociable	(Yes)
	and	logical	(Yes)
	and	organised	(Yes)

The following conclusion is drawn:-

knowledge engineer

Press ESC to exit

Figure 6.16 *Explanation facilities.*

Run JPMEDS again, but this time answer '**No**' to the first question. You will see that CRYSTAL takes you out of the system and back to the main menu. You answered '**No**' to the first condition, to cause it to fail. Therefore the next two questions were missed out. This is because all three conditions need to succeed in order for CRYSTAL to display the conclusion: **knowledge engineer**.

JPMEDS gives an answer when all the conditions are true. We are now going to add to the rule so that it will also provide an answer when one of the conditions is false.

Select **Build** and **Rules** from the main menu and press F10 to expand the rule. Now move two lines below the last condition in the knowledge engineer rule and the word '**OR**' appears. Moving two lines below the last condition will always allow you to add an OR to the rule.

Type the following:

```
no match found
```

We are now saying that the rule is:

```
knowledge engineer
IF      sociable
AND     logical
AND     organized
OR      no match found
```

In other words, if **knowledge engineer** is not proven, then the alternative is **no match found**. The rule is shown in Figure 6.17.

Press F10 to expand the **no match found** condition. We will now tell CRYSTAL to display a message to the user. Press the F6 (**Command**) key

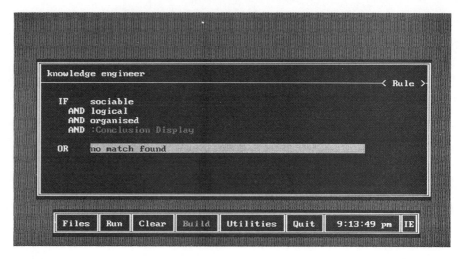

Figure 6.17 *Adding `no match found'.*

to display the list of CRYSTAL commands, as shown in Figure 6.18. Select
Display Form.

A box appears, where you can type text to be displayed when no match is
found. In the box, type:

```
Your skills do not match those of a knowledge engineer
```

as shown in Figure 6.19.

Press ESC twice, to go to the main menu. Select **Files** and **Save knowledge
base**. You are prompted with the name which you have already given to this

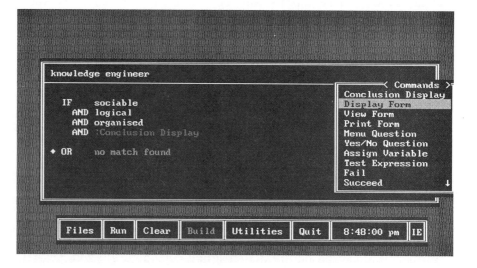

Figure 6.18 *Choosing `display form'.*

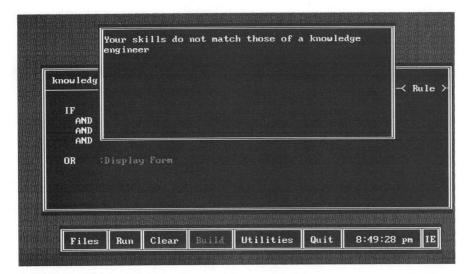

Figure 6.19 *Completing a form.*

knowledge base, JPMEDS. To overwrite the old version of the file with this new one, press ENTER. The screen shown in Figure 6.20 appears:

Press 'Y' for yes, to save the new version of your file.

Now run JPMEDS again, answering '**No**' to the first question. Notice that the form appears, as shown in Figure 6.21.

Now we will leave CRYSTAL, so make sure you are at the main menu by pressing ESC.

Don't forget that you will normally need to save your work before quitting from CRYSTAL. We have not made any changes to JPMEDS since we last

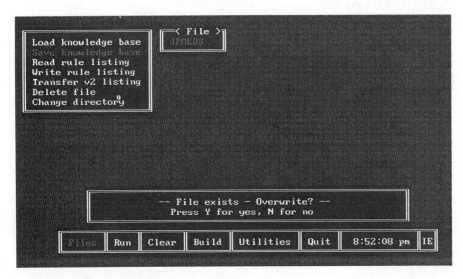

Figure 6.20 *Saving JPMEDS.*

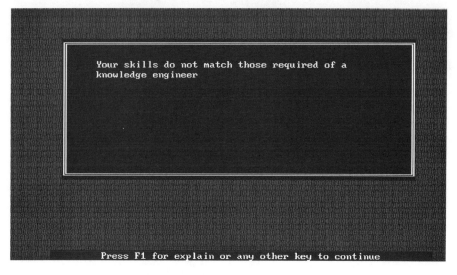

Figure 6.21 *JPMEDS showing a form.*

saved it, so we can quit from CRYSTAL without saving the file again by selecting **Quit**, then **Quit without saving** from the next menu.

You have now created a very basic version of the JPMEDS expert system. To do so you have used the following:

- the main menu
- **Build**
- **Rules**
- CRYSTAL master rule screen
- F10 (**Expand**) key
- F8 (**Reference**) key
- ESC key
- F6 (**Command**) key
- **Conclusion Display**
- **Display Form**
- **Files**
- **Save knowledge base**
- **Load knowledge base**
- **Run**
- Fl (**Explain**) key
- **Quit**

6.3.3 An extract of CRYSTAL code from the forecasting system

This section of code will give a feel for the structure of the rules in this system.

```
[    1]   adjust base for day, wind, and precipitation
         + IF   [   30]  test for regression day type
         +  AND [   32]  test for regression wind
         +  AND [   31]  test for regression precipitation
```

The rule below calls later rules in the KB (27, 28, 29, 30, etc.). It takes into account the affect of today's and tomorrow's weather on tomorrow's gas usage.

```
[    2]   adjust dailydiff for precipitation
         + IF   [   27]   test for mild weather today morning
         +  AND [   26]   test for mild weather today afternoon
         +  AND [   29]   test for mild weather tomorrow morning
         +  AND [   28]   test for mild weather tomorrow afternoon
            AND DO: Assign Variable
                base3:=base3
         + OR   [   27]   test for mild weather today morning
         +  AND [   26]   test for mild weather today afternoon
         +  AND [   29]   test for mild weather tomorrow morning
         +  AND [   35]   test for severe weather tomorrow afternoon
            AND DO: Assign Variable
                base3:=base3*1.03
         + OR   [   27]   test for mild weather today morning
         +  AND [   26]   test for mild weather today afternoon
         +  AND [   36]   test for severe weather tomorrow morning
         +  AND [   35]   test for severe weather tomorrow afternoon
            AND DO: Assign Variable
                base3:=base3*1.05
         + OR   [   34]   test for severe weather today morning
         +  AND [   33]   test for severe weather today afternoon
         +  AND [   36]   test for severe weather tomorrow morning
         +  AND [   35]   test for severe weather tomorrow afternoon
            AND DO: Assign Variable
                base3:=base3
         + OR   [   34]   test for severe weather today morning
         +  AND [   33]   test for severe weather today afternoon
         +  AND [   29]   test for mild weather tomorrow morning
         +  AND [   28]   test for mild weather tomorrow afternoon
            AND DO: Assign Variable
                base3:=base3*0.98
         + OR   ........................................................

[    4]   assign variables
         IF DO: Assign Variable
                 tediff:=2
            AND DO: Assign Variable
                 tewind:=10
            AND DO: Assign Variable
                 minte:=10
            AND DO: Assign Variable
                 windper:=0.02
            AND DO: Assign Variable
                 tevalue:=23
            AND DO: Assign Variable
                 friper:=0.975
            AND DO: Assign Variable
                 satper:=0.91
            AND DO: Assign Variable
                 sunper:=1.03
```

```
                      AND DO: Assign Variable
                             monper:=1.105
                      AND DO: Assign Variable
                             friregper:=0.975
                      AND DO: Assign Variable
                             satregper:=0.885
                      AND DO: Assign Variable
                             sunregper:=0.91

   [   30]    test for regression day type
              IF DO: Test Expression
                     daytype=2
                 AND DO: Assign Variable
                        base1:=base1*friregper
                 OR DO: Test Expression
                        daytype=3
                 AND DO: Assign Variable
                        base1:=base1*satregper
                 OR DO: Test Expression
                        daytype=4
                 AND DO: Assign Variable
                        base1:=base1*sunregper
                 OR DO: Test Expression
                        daytype=5
                 AND DO: Assign Variable
                        base1:=base1
                 OR DO: Test Expression
                        daytype=1
                 AND DO: Assign Variable
                        base1:=base1

   [   31]    test for regression precipitation
              + IF   [   27]    test for mild weather today morning
              +   AND [   26]    test for mild weather today afternoon
              +   AND [   29]    test for mild weather tomorrow morning
              +   AND [   28]    test for mild weather tomorrow afternoon
                 AND DO: Assign Variable
                        base1:=base1
              + OR   [   27]    test for mild weather today morning
              +   AND [   26]    test for mild weather today afternoon
              +   AND [   29]    test for mild weather tomorrow morning
              +   AND [   35]    test for severe weather tomorrow afternoon
                 AND DO: Assign Variable
                        base1:=base1*1.03
              + OR   [   27]    test for mild weather today morning
              +   AND [   26]    test for mild weather today afternoon
              +   AND [   36]    test for severe weather tomorrow morning
              +   AND [   35]    test for severe weather tomorrow afternoon
              AND DO: Assign Variable
                        base1:=base1*1.05
              + OR    .........................................

   [   32]    test for regression wind
              IF DO: Test Expression
                  todte<minte
                 AND DO: Test Expression
                        tomte<minte
                 AND DO: Test Expression
                     wintod>tewind
                 AND DO: Test Expression
```

```
                    wintom>tewind
        AND DO: Assign Variable
              diff:=(wintom-wintod)
        AND DO: Assign Variable
              base1:=base1+((diff*windper)*base1)
    OR DO: Test Expression
       todte<minte
        AND DO: Test Expression
              wintod>tewind
        AND DO: Test Expression
              wintom<=tewind
        AND DO: Assign Variable
              diff:=(wintod-tewind)
        AND DO: Assign Variable
              base1:=base1-((diff*windper)*base1)
    OR .......................................
```

```
[   37]   test for wind strengths
        IF DO: Test Expression
            todte<minte
        AND DO: Test Expression
              tomte<minte
        AND DO: Test Expression
              wintod>tewind
        AND DO: Test Expression
              wintom>tewind
        AND DO: Assign Variable
              diff:=(wintom-wintod)
        AND DO: Assign Variable
              base:=base+((diff*windper)*base)
    OR DO: Test Expression
            todte<minte
        AND DO: Test Expression
              wintod>tewind
        AND DO: Test Expression
              wintom<=tewind
        AND DO: Assign Variable
              diff:=(wintod-tewind)
        AND DO: Assign Variable
              base:=base-((diff*windper)*base)
    OR .......................................
```

6.3.4 An extract of CRYSTAL code from the integrated system

The rule below reads a database (with the DB commands) and store the values in the knowledge base.

```
[    1]    assign pskill variables to arrays
        IF DO: Test Expression
            psttl>=pscurr
        AND DO: Test Expression
              DBreadrec(pskill$[#])
        AND DO: Test Expression
              DBreadrec(pskill[#])
        AND DO: Test Expression
              pskill$[0]=g1staff$[d]
        AND DO: Assign Variable
              psrec_no:=psrec_no+1
        AND DO: Assign Variable
```

```
                           pskill_code$[psrec_no]:=pskill$[1]
                AND DO: Assign Variable
                           pskill_levl$[psrec_no]:=pskill$[2]
              + AND    [ 182]   whether ps-end of file
                AND DO: Assign Variable
                     pscurr:=pscurr+1
                AND DO: Restart Rule
           OR DO: Succeed


[    2]   assign variables to arrays
          IF DO: Test Expression
              vsttl>=vscurr
             AND DO: Test Expression
                   DBreadrec(vskill[#])
             AND DO: Test Expression
                   DBreadrec(vskill$[#])
             AND DO: Test Expression
                   vskill[0]=vac_no
             AND DO: Assign Variable
                   srec_no:=srec_no+1
             AND DO: Assign Variable
                   vskill_code$[srec_no]:=vskill$[1]
             AND DO: Assign Variable
                   vskill_levl$[srec_no]:=vskill$[2]
             AND DO: Assign Variable
                   arraysize:=arrsize(vskill_code$[#],0)
           + AND    [  91]   if vs-not last record
             AND DO: Assign Variable
                   vscurr:=vscurr+1
             AND DO: Restart Rule
          OR DO: Succeed


[    3]   availability consideration
          IF DO: Test Expression
              DBselect(aptmntf)
             AND DO: Test Expression
                   DBfirst()
             AND DO: Test Expression
                   DBfsearch("STAFF_NO",person$[0])
             AND DO: Test Expression
                   DBreadrec(apt$[#])
             AND DO: Test Expression
                   DBreadrec(apt[#])
             AND DO: Test Expression
                   person$[5]=apt$[1]
             AND DO: Assign Variable
                   vdate:=date(v_s_date$)
             AND DO: Assign Variable
                   pdate:=apt[4]
             AND DO: Assign Variable
                   date_num:=vdate-pdate
             AND DO: Assign Variable
                   av_success:=2
           + AND    [  21]   check availability
             AND DO: Test Expression
                   DBselect(personf)
             AND  DO: Test Expression
                   DBgoto(pecurr)
```

```
[   10]   avsell-qualifies
          IF DO: Test Expression
              find(site_code$,person$[8])
            AND DO: Test Expression
             find("CS",person$[4])
      +  AND   [  86]   grade consideration
      +  AND   [   3]   availability consideration

[   12]   avsell-skills qualified
          IF DO: Test Expression
              DBselect(pskillf)
            AND DO: Assign Variable
                ipskillf:=DBiopen("ipskill.crx")
            AND DO: Test Expression
                DBreindex(ipskillf)
            AND DO: Test Expression
                DBorder(ipskillf)
      +  AND   [   7]   avsell staff skills consideration

[   20]   avsel2-skills qualified
          IF DO: Test Expression
              DBselect(pskillf)
            AND DO: Assign Variable
                ipskillf:=DBiopen("ipskill.crx")
            AND DO: Test Expression
                DBreindex(ipskillf)
            AND DO: Test Expression
                DBorder(ipskillf)
      +  AND   [  16]   avsel2 staff skills consideration

[   22]   check avsell criteria
          IF DO: Test Expression
              pecurr<=ttlrec
            AND DO: Test Expression
                DBreadrec(person$[#])
            AND DO: Test Expression
                DBreadrec(person[#])
            AND DO: Assign Variable
                av_success:=0
      +  AND   [  23]   check avsell record
      +  AND   [  68]   g1-wether end of file
            AND DO: Assign Variable
                pecurr:=pecurr+1
            AND DO: Restart Rule
          OR DO: Succeed
```

6.4 ESTA

The author wishes to thank Finn Gronskov for his contributions to this section.

6.4.1 Introduction

ESTA is an easy-to-use shell for constructing advisory and decision support systems (Figure 6.22). Building knowledge bases with ESTA requires no previous programming experience and it is suitable for many problem do-

Figure 6.22 *ESTA.*

mains. ESTA is produced by the Prolog Development Center who are based in Copenhagen, Denmark. It is marketed by PDC-UK within the UK.

You can use ESTA to build advisory systems that:

- make knowledge more accessible;
- help with decision making;
- preserve valuable knowledge.

You can also interface ESTA systems to external applications such as spreadsheets, databases and word processors. ESTA includes an interface to Prolog (section 6.6). This means that you can go beyond the built-in functionality which is provided by ESTA and you can build your own extensions to ESTA or integrate ESTA into an existing Prolog application. This, however, requires some Prolog programming experience.

In addition to advisory systems, ESTA is a powerful prototyping tool. A knowledge base in ESTA has a hierarchical structure from which a tree display is automatically drawn. You can edit or expand your knowledge base directly from the tree. In this way you can easily get an overview of your knowledge. A display of the structure from a car problem diagnostic system is shown in Figure 6.23.

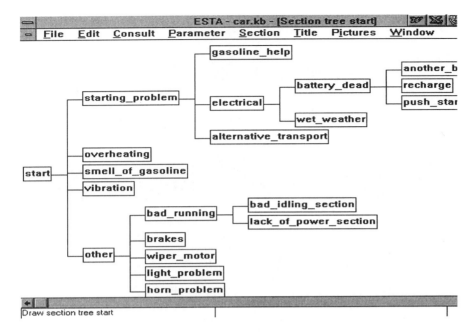

Figure 6.23 *An ESTA section tree.*

6.4.2 Interacting with ESTA

ESTA is designed so that a dialogue with an expert system running under the shell resembles having a conversation with an actual expert in the subject area. The user initially provides some information in the form of replies to questions posed by the system. Then he or she receives the appropriate advice. A record of the dialogue can be logged in a window and it can be stored in a file for later reference. A sample dialogue screen is shown in Figure 6.24.

For some questions, the user responds by selecting from a menu. For example: **What is the problem with your car?**

In other cases, the user can click with the mouse on some part of a picture. For example: **Point to the place where the noise comes from.**

And in some cases it is necessary to type in the answer. For example: **What is your name?**

If requested by the user, the system will elaborate on questions that have not been fully understood, as well as provide a more general explanation of how conclusions have been reached.

6.4.3 ESTA features and functionality

ESTA uses the facilities of Microsoft Windows. The result is a pleasant, user-friendly interface. ESTA includes provisions for generating executable versions of the system, which may then be distributed to end users.

In addition to knowledge representation, ESTA includes useful features from traditional programming languages, such as procedure calls and math-

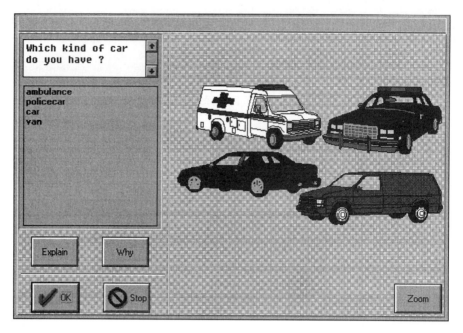

Figure 6.24 *A sample ESTA screen.*

ematical functions. ESTA is configurable. Menus, start-up pictures and other user interface functionality can be customized to match the specific needs of an application.

ESTA includes facilities for the knowledge base to call general-purpose routines written in Prolog, C or other languages. It also has facilities to explain why a question is being asked or why an answer has been given, or to repeat advice given earlier in a consultation. ESTA also enables the user to break off a dialogue, change the answer to a previously asked question or bring up new questions.

ESTA provides the knowledge engineer with a number of views of the knowledge, including the hierarchical tree representation (Figure 6.23). Clicking on a node in the tree brings up an edit window containing the corresponding rules. The knowledge entered into ESTA is automatically translated and syntax checked, and errors are pointed out directly to the user.

6.4.4 Knowledge representation in ESTA

In ESTA, knowledge is represented in an intuitive way. Rules are written in English-like statements such as:

```
if its_raining and person_has_umbrella advice 'You can go
out'
```

A knowledge base in ESTA consists of **sections** and **parameters**. The sections contain the rules (the logic) that directs the user to the right place in the knowledge base and gives the appropriate advice.

Parameters are the variables that can obtain values: 'its_raining' or 'person_has_umbrella' are examples of parameters that can either be true, false or unknown. Other parameter types are text, numbers and categories. Parameter definitions can themselves contain rules and thus their values can be based on other parameters.

6.4.4.1 Sections
Sections contain the rules that tell ESTA how to solve a problem and which actions to perform, such as giving advice, going to other sections, calling special routines and linking with other knowledge bases.

Each section can be edited individually in a text window. The first section in a knowledge base must be called 'start', and this is the place where ESTA begins the consultation. The example below shows a small section of knowledge base for diagnosing car problems.

```
section   start : 'main section'
if (problem='starting_problem') do starting_problem
if (problem='overheating') do overheating
if (problem='smell_of_gasoline') do smell_of_gasoline
if (problem='vibration') do vibration
do other
```

The 'do' command executes another section, thus 'do overheating' will execute the overheating section shown below.

```
section  overheating 'the engine gets overheated'
advice 'Overheating is normally caused by problems in the
cooling system'
if not(water_ok) advice
'Top up your radiator but keep an eye on the water level
as there might be a leak in the system'
if water_ok and acceleration_noise advice
'The fan belt may be slipping. Tighten it up.'
if water_ok and not(acceleration_noise) and not(oil_ok)
advice
'Top up the oil in your ' car '. In future, watch the oil
level carefully as it is cheaper to buy new oil than a
new engine'
```

Should you wish to know how the system reached a certain conclusion or why a certain piece of advice is given, you can click on the **Why** button. The system will tell you why the conclusion was reached and which rules were used to reach the conclusion, as shown in Figure 6.25.

6.4.4.2 Parameters
A parameter is a variable that can have a value (text, number, true/false or one of a number of options). The value can be calculated from other parameters or specified by the end user.

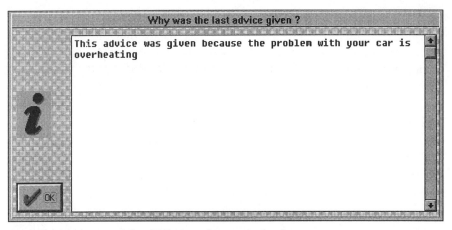

Figure 6.25 *Use of the `Why' explanation facility.*

A typical parameter might be defined as shown below, with entries to specify the question to be asked, an explanation to give if the user presses the **Explain** button, the possible values and links to a graphic representation.

```
parameter car    'the kind of car'
type category
explanation
        'identify your car with one of the listed
        types as closely as you can.'
option
        ambulance
        policecar
        sedan - 'car'
        van.
question 'Which kind of car do you have ?'
picture 'cars'
```

When a parameter is declared, it is necessary to specify the name of the parameter (e.g. 'car'). This name is used when the parameter is referred to in rules. A parameter has one of the following four types:

- boolean (true, false or unknown)
- number (integers or reals)
- text
- category (used when the parameter is known to take one value from a set of values)

ESTA determines if and when it needs the value of a parameter. If the value depends on other parameters it will calculate the value, otherwise it will prompt the user for the value. ESTA generates a dialogue box and asks the question given in the parameter definition under the 'question' heading.

When a question is given during a consultation, the user will have the option to ask ESTA to 'explain the question'. This explanation can be provided by the knowledge engineer in the 'explanation' field of a parameter declaration. In the dialogue it will appear as shown in Figure 6.26.

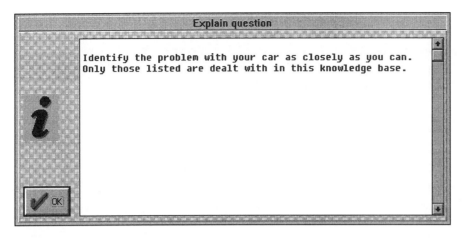

Figure 6.26 *Use of `Explain'.*

You can also answer '**Unknown**' to a question posed by ESTA if you are unaware of the value of the parameter. This can either lead to special advice or to a dialogue which will establish the value by using other rules.

Pictures can be included as part of advice, questions or explanations. It is possible to define links between areas of a picture and the parameters. The user can then answer a query by pointing at regions of a picture and clicking the mouse button.

6.4.5 ESTA in action

To show the power and ease of use of ESTA, this section will take you through a small ESTA KBS development. We want to build a financial KBS for use in a bank. Bank customers should be able to use the system to find out what kind of loan the bank can offer them to best suit their needs. We will start out by describing the problem that we want the KBS to solve.

To decide which loan the customer qualifies for, the bank calculates a risk factor for the customer. The bigger this factor is, the bigger is the risk. A negative risk factor is desirable.

- A risk factor of zero is the average risk.

- Below zero is a low risk.

- Above zero is a high risk.

The risk can depend on several criteria such as personal income, age and the amount of disposable income after tax. The risk factor is calculated using this formula:

```
Risk =   (20,000 - gross income)        +
         (500 - available amount)*12    +
         (5 - years employed)*100       +
         agefactor                      +
         15,000 if self employed.
```

The available amount is the amount available after tax, housing, food and other expenses (often called disposable income). Years employed is the number of consecutive years in the current line of work. The variable age factor is calculated based on the formula shown below:

```
10,000 if age<20,
4000 if age>=20 and age<50,
7000 if age>=50
```

The risk factor, together with other variables, is used to determine which loan a customer can have. The bank has these six loan types:

```
The loans
A - The super-duper loan with very low interest (12%)
Risk factor < -20,000
Max amount 10,000
Not for real estate
For customers with at least two other accounts with the
bank

B - The cheap car loan with no down payment (12.5%)
Risk factor < -10,000
Max 7 years pay back
At least one other account with the bank

C - The cheap car loan with a 30% down payment (12.5%)
Risk factor < -5000
Max 7 years

D - The not-so-cheap car loan with no down payment (14.5%)
Risk factor <= 0
Max 8 years

E - The real-estate loan (11.5%)
Risk factor < -5000
not (self employed)

F - The 'normal', pretty-high-interest loan for anything
you wish (16%)
Risk factor < 5000
Max amount: 2500
The loan type F can be used for anything including cars
and real estate.
```

6.4.6 The knowledge base

We will now make a simple ESTA knowledge base that tells the customer what kind of loan he or she can have based on his or her personal data.

For our bank's system, the 'start' section looks like this:

```
section start : 'start'
if risk_factor>= 5000
        advice 'Risk factor is too high - we cannot give
        you any loans',
if loan_amount<=10000 and risk_factor<-20000 and
not(use='real_estate')
        advice 'Congratulations - you qualify for the
        Super-Duper cheap A-loan',
if use='car'  do car_section
if use='real_estate'  do real_estate_section
if use='other'  or not(loan_found)  do other_section
```

If the 'risk_factor' parameter is above 5000 no loans can be given – this 'advice' is given and the start section terminates at the quit statement. The 'risk_factor' parameter has the following definition:

```
parameter risk_factor : 'Risk factor'
type number
rules
        (20000-gross_income) + (500-available_amount)*12 +
(5-years_employed)*100 + agefactor -15000 if self_employed,
        (20000-gross_income) + (500-available_amount)*12 +
(5-years_employed)*100 + agefactor.
```

The first rule deals with the self-employed person and the second one deals with those who are not self employed. The parameters 'gross_income', 'available_amount', 'years_employed' and 'self_employed' are entered by the end user (the bank customer). The parameter definitions look like this:

```
parameter gross_income : 'Gross income'
type number
explanation 'The gross income is the total income before
tax'
question 'What is your gross income per year ?'
```

When ESTA needs the value this question is asked:

```
What is your gross income per year?
```

The 'agefactor' parameter is based on the parameter 'age' which is also typed in by the customer.

When ESTA starts evaluating the start section and gets to the line:

```
if risk_factor>5000
```

The parameter 'risk_factor' has no value – hence it goes to the definition of the parameter to find out how to give it a value. In the definition it finds references to other parameters with no value (yet) and in turn goes to their definitions to find out how they should obtain a value. ESTA starts asking for the values of certain parameters in order to give 'risk_factor' a value. So the beginning of the dialogue could go like this:

```
Are you self employed ?
No
What is your gross income per year ?
30000
What is the available amount per month ?
600
How many years have you been employed ?
7
What is your age ?
27
```

The basic strategy is to find the cheapest loan a customer qualifies for. In the start section, the parameter **use** holds the item the customer wants to use the money for. This can be either 'car', 'real estate' or 'other'. There is a section for each item. If the 'car_section' or the 'real_estate_section' section doesn't yield any results the 'other_section' is tried to see whether any of the non-specific loans can be used. We check for the SuperDuper loan before anything else if the loan isn't for real estate, because the SuperDuper loan is cheaper than any of the other loans.

The 'car_section' looks like this:

```
section car_section : 'The car loans'
if risk_factor<-10000 and min_years<=7 and other_engagements>=1
       advice ' cheap car loan B with no down payment'
if risk_factor<-5000 and min_years<=7 and down_payment_30
       advice 'cheap car loan C with 30 % down payment'
if risk_factor<=0 and min_years>=8 and not(down_payment_30)
       advice 'the not-so-cheap car loan D with no down
       payment'
```

The parameter 'min_years' holds the minimum pay back period acceptable for the customer. The parameter 'down_payment_30' is true if the customer can give a 30% down payment on the car.

We have now made an advisory system that tells customers what loan they can have, based on their personal data.

6.4.7 Interfacing ESTA with other Windows applications

DDE (Dynamic Data Exchange) is a Windows protocol that lets applications talk to each other. ESTA supports DDE which means that you can interface ESTA to all other applications that support DDE. Thus you can have your KBS controlling spreadsheets, word processors and database-systems. You can send data to these applications, you can retrieve information from them and you can execute commands in the applications.

In the following example, a conversation is opened with Excel using the spreadsheet file 'file_a.xls'. The value 546 is sent to the cell R2C4 (D2). The file

'file_b.xls' is opened using the Excel **OPEN** command, and the value of R1C1 (A1) is returned.

```
CH = dde_initiate("excel","file_a.xls")
dde_poke(CH,"R2C4","546")
dde_execute(CH," [OPEN(file_b.xls)]")
VAL = dde_request(CH,"R1C2")
dde_terminate(CH)
```

6.5 Languages

These can be divided into two main types:

- conventional, procedural languages such as C, COBOL, Pascal and FOR-TRAN – these are for use with particular classes of problems, for instance, FORTRAN has features which were specially designed for scientific problem solving and COBOL was specially designed for building commercial data-processing systems;
- declarative languages such as Lisp and Prolog – these are designed for KBS applications; LISP has features to manipulate symbols in the form of list structures and is good for representing complex concepts; there are many versions of LISP and there are also workstations which have been specifically designed as 'LISP machines' for developing large knowledge-based systems.

6.5.1 Declarative languages

A declarative (or non-procedural) language is a language which allows the user to express 'what' a problem is without worrying about 'how' a solution to that problem is to be obtained. That is, the user simply has to express clearly and unambiguously the elements of a problem and the language itself will be able to provide a solution. A declarative language thus allows the user to express the 'what' of a problem without having to figure out 'how' to solve it. Prolog is such a language. The name 'Prolog' comes from the term 'PROgramming in LOGic'.

It is for this reason that Prolog was chosen by the Japanese as the main language for the development of much of the software for their fifth-generation computer system.

6.6 Prolog

This section will give you an introduction to the Prolog language. The examples used throughout the section are based on the monitoring case study. At the end of the section you will be shown a substantial section of Prolog code from the monitoring KBS.

Prolog provides the user with a total environment consisting of facilities for the rapid development of KBS. This environment is interactive and conversational. It allows the user to sit at the computer terminal and take part in a conversation with Prolog. This conversation session will usually begin with the user entering facts and rules about a particular problem area, thus defining a KBS for that area.

Alternatively, the user may ask Prolog to load an existing KBS which he or she wishes to use. The user will then ask Prolog a series of questions (known as queries) relating to the particular problem area from which the KBS draws its expertise. Prolog will then respond by providing answers to these queries.

A Prolog program takes the form of a database of knowledge (a knowledge base) about a particular problem area. The terms database (of knowledge), knowledge base and program are thus (arguably) interchangeable in the context of the Prolog language.

To enter the Prolog environment you must first obtain access to the computer system and then type in the appropriate command to enter the Prolog environment. This command is usually simply

```
prolog
```

You will then receive the standard Prolog 'query' prompt which is instantly recognizable:

```
?
```

The query prompt is simply informing you that Prolog is waiting for you to ask it a question. In fact, Prolog can be thought of as a question-and-answer environment which is continually waiting for you to ask it queries about those subjects for which it has been given knowledge and expertise. The questions which you ask Prolog must always be phrased in lowercase letters. This important point is worth stressing at the earliest possible stage as uppercase (capital) letters have a special meaning in Prolog (this will be explained later).

The query prompt signifies that you are in query mode. This is the mode which allows you to ask questions of the knowledge base which is currently available to Prolog.

The command needed to leave the Prolog environment will depend upon the particular computer on which you are working and the version of Prolog you are using. In general, however, this command will be the standard exit command for your system.

6.6.1 Facts

The simplest way in which we can give knowledge to Prolog is in the form of a collection of facts. These facts must be expressed in the correct manner according to the grammar rules, or syntax, of Prolog. For example, consider the following simple English fact:

```
The expert system monitors the ventilator.
```

This fact consists of two important components:

- a relationship
- objects

In this particular fact the relationship is 'monitor' and it is used to relate together two objects, the expert system and the ventilator. The fact would be expressed in Prolog as:

```
monitors(expert_system,ventilator).
```

Notice that the Prolog fact consists of the name of the relationship followed by the name of the two objects enclosed in brackets. In Prolog terminology the relationship is known as a predicate and the objects are known as arguments. The entire fact is known as a clause.

Notice also that the names of both the relationship and the objects are expressed in lowercase and that the clause is terminated by a full stop. The latter point is a very important one to remember as Prolog uses the full stop to recognize the end of a fact. It is very easy to miss out your full stops from a Prolog program – the results of doing so can be both annoying and disastrous.

The order of the two arguments 'expert_system' and 'ventilator' within the brackets does not have any significance to Prolog. However, it is important that the user is consistent in the way he or she orders arguments within a particular program. For instance, the two facts:

```
The doctor treats the patient
```

and

```
The patient treats the doctor
```

are obviously very different and this must be reflected in their translation into Prolog by using consistent ordering of the arguments as below:

```
treats(doctor,patient). - The doctor treats the patient
treats(patient,doctor). - The patient treats the doctor
```

It should also be noted that the existence of one of the above facts within the knowledge base does not imply the existence of the other fact. That is, the fact that the doctor treats the patient does not imply that the patient treats the doctor!

Here are some more simple Prolog facts relating to a patient:

```
fact                      meaning
surname(smith).           The surname is smith.
age(56).                  The age is 56.
value(pH,7.27).           The pH value is 7.27.
value(pCO₂,46).           The value of pCO₂ is 46.
resp_rate(9).             The respiratory rate is 9.
```

Notice that facts may have any number of arguments, depending upon the number of objects which you wish to relate together. For instance, the predicate 'surname' has one argument; the predicate 'value' has two arguments and the predicate 'initial_set' has five arguments. It should also be stressed that Prolog has no means of knowing whether or not the facts which you give are true.

For example, the fact:

```
bird(pig).— A pig is a kind of bird
```

is perfectly acceptable to Prolog.

Now let us set up a simple knowledge base comprising facts relating to the monitoring case study. Consider the following facts about patients in the Intensive Care Unit:

```
Fred is male.
Tina is female.
Susan is female.
Fred is on a ventilator.
Tina is not on a ventilator.
Susan is on a ventilator.
```

In Prolog these would be:

```
male(fred).
female(tina).
female(susan).
ventilator(fred).
ventilator(susan).
```

You can then use query mode to ask Prolog questions about the patients. For instance, you may wish to ask:

```
Is Fred on a ventilator?
```

This could be done by typing:

```
?- ventilator(fred).
```

In order to respond to the above query Prolog will examine the knowledge base, looking for facts which match the question. A fact matches a question if its predicate and arguments are spelt the same and the arguments are in the same order. As our simple knowledge base does contain such a fact Prolog will find a match and will provide you with the response:

```
yes
```

However, if you were to ask Prolog whether Tina was on the ventilator by typing:

```
?- ventilator(tina).
```

no matching fact would be found in the knowledge base and Prolog would give the response

```
no
```

When we give Prolog a query to answer we are setting it a 'goal' to achieve. The concept of goals and their success or failure is one of the most fundamental and important ideas in Prolog. Indeed, the Prolog system is designed to continually try and satisfy goals in order to provide answers to queries given to it by the user.

6.6.2 Variables

A variable is used when it is possible for a particular structure to have one of several different values. For instance, the knowledge base which was discussed previously in this section contained information about patients in the Intensive Care Unit. We might, therefore, wish to ask a question such as:

```
Which patients are female?
```

The above query would be expressed:

```
?- female(Patient).
```

where 'Patient' is a variable name and begins with an uppercase (capital) letter. In general, variables must begin with a capital letter and consist of letters, digits or underscore characters.

In order to find an answer to the above question Prolog would attempt to find a match in the database. This it would do when it came across the second fact in the knowledge base:

```
female(tina).
```

The result of this match is that the variable 'Patient' would take the value 'tina' and Prolog would thus respond:

```
Patient = tina?
```

This, of course, is not the only answer to the query. Indeed, the question mark is signifying the fact that Prolog is asking us if we wish to search for any further solutions. We can tell Prolog to search for more answers by typing

```
;
```

immediately after Prolog has given us the first answer. The entire question-and-answer session would thus appear:

```
?- female(Patient).
Patient = tina?;
Patient = susan?;
no
```

If you do not wish Prolog to search for any more answers to your question you simply press the return key after you have been given the first answer. The system will then return to query mode as shown below:

```
?- female(Patient).
Patient = tina? < return >
yes
?-
```

In general, matching a variable which does not currently have a value with an object sets the variable to the value of that object. A variable which does not have a value is known as an 'uninstantiated' variable. When it is matched with an object it is 'instantiated' (set) to the value of that object. For example, the result of matching:

```
male(Patient)
```

with

```
male(john)
```

is that the previously uninstantiated variable Patient is instantiated to the object 'john'.

6.6.3 Conjunctions
In this section we will move on to the means of forming more complex goals for Prolog to satisfy. Consider the program below which contains information about patients in the hospital:

```
male(tim).
male(marc).   - male(X) succeeds if X is male.
male(simon).
female(louise).
female(hazel).  - female(X) succeeds if X is female.
female(marie).
ward(tim,4).
```

```
ward(marc,1).
ward(simon,2). - ward(X,Y) succeeds if patient X is in ward Y
ward(louise,3).
ward(hazel,3).
ward(marie,4).
resp(tim,acute).
resp(marc,medium).
resp(simon,acute).- resp(X,Y) succeeds if the patient X
resp(louise,medium). has respiratory condition of state Y
resp(hazel,medium).
resp(marie,acute).
age(tim,56).
age(marc,65).
age(simon,72). - age(X,Y) succeeds if X is Y years old
age(louise,41).
age(hazel,22).
age(marie,18).
```

The sort of question which one might wish to ask Prolog about such a knowledge base could be:

```
Do any male patients have an acute respiratory condition?
```

In order to express the above question in Prolog it is necessary to form a more complex query than those which have been dealt with so far in this section. This is because the question involves the use of two forms of fact from the knowledge base:

- those facts which state which patients are male;
- those facts which state which respiratory condition a patient has.

We have, therefore, to join two simple queries together with the 'and' symbol, which is denoted by a comma. The correct form for this particular query would thus be:

```
?- male(X),resp(X,acute).
```

which translates literally to:

```
Is there an X who is male and has a respiratory condition
which is acute?
```

This is what is known as a conjunction of goals. We are giving Prolog a goal to satisfy which consists of a conjunction (joining) of two goals, namely:

```
male(X)
```

and

```
resp(X,acute).
```

In order to satisfy the complete goal Prolog must first satisfy these two subgoals. If it cannot find a value for X which will satisfy both subgoals the complete goal will fail (and Prolog will answer '**no**'). Of course, in this particular case the response would be:

```
X = tim ?
```

An even more complex query of this knowledge base might be:

```
Does any patient in ward 3 who is older than 40 have a
medium respiratory condition?
```

which is expressed as a conjunction of subgoals in the form:

```
?- ward(X,3),age(X,Y),Y > 40,resp(X,medium).
```

and produces the response:

```
X = louise ?
```

Notice that we have introduced the greater-than symbol in the goal 'Y > 40'. This goal succeeds if the value of Y is greater than 40.

6.6.4 Syntax rules

Syntax rules are those rules relating to punctuation, spelling, etc. that we are forced to adhere to in order to produce correct Prolog programs. The use of incorrect syntax in our Prolog programs will result in error messages and programs that will not work. It will then be necessary to use the editor to correct the errors. The following points concerning Prolog syntax are worth stating as they provide some of the commonest mistakes in Prolog programming.

The full stop
The full stop is used to denote the end of a clause. Prolog will take everything between two full stops as a single clause. Thus, if you do forget a full stop after a clause, Prolog will run that clause into the next and will continue to do so until it does encounter a full stop. It will then become confused as to what this strange new clause means and signal its displeasure by giving you an error message.

Lowercase letters
These must be used as the first character of the names of objects and predicates. For example: apple, pear, likes, male, female.

Uppercase (capital) letters
These are used as the first character of variable names. For example: Mother, Father.

Arguments

The arguments of a predicate must be enclosed in round brackets and separated by commas. For example: patients(dr_thomas,smith,jones,thompson).

The comma (,)

This means 'and' and is used to join two or more goals to form a conjunction of goals.

The semicolon (;)

This means 'or' and, during a question-and-answer session, is used to ask Prolog to search for another answer to your question. It can, however, also be used to form what is known as a 'disjunction' of goals. For instance, the query:

```
?- age(tim,56);ward(tim,4).
```

means

```
Is the age of tim 56 OR is tim in ward 4?
```

This goal will succeed if either of the two subgoals age(tim,56) or ward(tim,4) succeed. In general, however, it is not considered good practice to use the ';' symbol too frequently within your Prolog programs as it can make the logic of them unclear and difficult to follow.

The underscore symbol (_)

This can be used within object, variable or predicate names to join together two or more words. For example: red_car, ginger_beer, Mother_in_law, dr_simpson, respiratory_rate.

6.6.5 Rules

So far in this section we have considered knowledge bases which consist solely of one form of clause, namely the fact. In order to develop Prolog programs which are of any real practical use it is necessary to use rules.

In our programs so far Prolog has had a comparatively easy task to perform in finding answers to our queries. This is because our programs have consisted of nothing more complicated than a collection of facts. In order to answer a question, therefore, Prolog has simply had to find a fact which provides an exact match to the query. But the language also has very powerful facilities for making inferences from rules expressed in the knowledge base. It is the structure of rules and the method which Prolog uses when searching them that we will explore next.

Let us start by considering a simple rule:

```
state(X,dangerous)  :-    value(X,pO₂,Y),
                          Y < 50.
```

which states X is in a dangerous state if their value of pO_2 is Y and Y is lower than 50. The above rule consists of three important elements (as do all Prolog rules):

- the head of the rule (in this case 'state(X,dangerous)');
- the ':-' symbol (which can be read as 'provided' or 'if');
- the body of the rule (in this case 'value(X,pO_2,Y), Y < 50.').

Prolog uses rules in the following manner. When we give Prolog a query we are, as we know, setting it a goal which can either succeed (if a match for the query is found), or fail (if no match is found within the knowledge base). If a fact which matches the query exactly (that is its predicate and arguments match and its arguments are in the same order) is found then Prolog immediately records a success and returns the appropriate answer(s). If, during its search of the knowledge base, Prolog comes upon a rule which may provide a match it proceeds in the manner described below.

First it attempts to match the query with the head of the rule. If such a match is achieved, then the goal will succeed if the goals which form the body of the rule succeed. The goals which form the body of the rule are known as subgoals and, in the example above, the body of the rule consists of a conjunction of two subgoals 'value(X,pO_2,Y)' and 'Y < 50'.

Prolog has thus reduced the task of trying to satisfy a query such as:

```
?-  state(X,dangerous).
```

to that of satisfying two subgoals:

```
value(X,pO₂,Y).
```

and

```
Y < 50.
```

Prolog will thus search the knowledge base in an attempt to satisfy these two subgoals. If it does so (that is, the two subgoals succeed) then the goal which forms the head of the rule will also, by inference, succeed and hence Prolog will provide us with an answer to our query.

Now let's examine a complete program which includes a version of the state rule which we have just considered.

```
state(X,dangerous)   :-    value(X,pO₂,Y),
                           Y < 50.
value(john,pO₂,60).
value(susan,pO₂,75).
value(tina,pO₂,40).
```

Consider how Prolog would deal with the following query:

```
?- state(tina,dangerous).
```

This query sets Prolog the task of proving that Tina's condition is dangerous. In order to satisfy the above goal Prolog would search for a match in the knowledge base. This it would find when it encountered the head of the 'state' rule because the predicate ('state') and the arguments ('tina' and 'dangerous') will match, with the variable X in the head of the state rule being instantiated to the value 'tina'. At the same time all the other occurrences of the variable X within the state rule are also instantiated to 'tina'. This is because the variable X is said to be 'sharing' within that rule. When one occurrence of a shared variable is instantiated to a particular value all other occurrences of that variable within the same clause are also instantiated to the same value.

So the goal has now been reduced to that of satisfying the conjunction of subgoals:

```
value(tina,pO₂,Y),
Y < 50.
```

In order to satisfy this conjunction of subgoals Prolog must find a match to the clause value(tina,pO$_2$,Y) and then prove that Y < 50. It will succeed in doing this as the fact value(tina,pO$_2$,40) is present within the knowledge base and 40 is indeed less than 50. These two subgoals will thus be satisfied and the entire rule will, therefore, also succeed and Prolog will provide a positive response to the query.

Consider, however, the query

```
?- state(john,dangerous).
```

This reduces to the task of satisfying the conjunction of subgoals:

```
value(john,pO₂,Y),
Y < 50.
```

A match would be found for the first subgoal value(john,pO$_2$,Y) and Y would be instantiated to 60. The subgoal Y < 50 would, however, fail. This failure would result in the failure of the entire goal and Prolog would thus reply:

```
no
```

Think carefully about the above question-and-answer session and make sure that you understand how, and why, Prolog arrived at the above answers.

6.6.6 Comments and other points on formatting your programs

When writing your Prolog programs it is worth spending a little extra time to ensure that your programs are both readable and comprehensible. It is easy to convince yourself that, because you understand a program fully when you are designing it, you will also be able to understand it at any time in the future. This is by no means true. It is more likely that, when you return to the program at some point in the future, you will find it exceedingly difficult to figure out the point of the program and how it works. This is even more the case for someone else who wishes to understand what your program is doing and how it does it.

There are a few simple measures which you can take to ensure that your programs are comprehensible to yourself and others. This will mean that, if it is necessary to modify your programs at any time in the future, the task of doing so will be made much more simple and straightforward.

The first measure which you can take to make your Prolog programs more readable and comprehensible to both yourself and other users is to sprinkle it liberally with comments. A comment is enclosed in the symbols '/*' and '*/' as below:

```
/* This is a comment */
/* Comments can stretch over more than one line
if necessary - as long as they are enclosed
in the correct symbols */
```

It is difficult to try and give general rules as to when and where comments should be used within programs. However, the following points are worth mentioning:

A general comment at the beginning of a program is a good idea. Such a comment should explain the purpose of the program and could include other details such as who developed the program, when it was developed and for whose use it was designed.

It is good practice to place a comment beside each set of clauses of a similar form. Remember that, for someone reading a program for the first time, there is no way of knowing whether:

```
likes(terry,linda).
```

expresses the fact that Terry likes Linda or the fact that Linda likes Terry. (Remember also that these are two quite different facts and that one definitely does not imply the other!) It is, therefore, sensible to include comments to prevent such ambiguities.

Whilst we are on the subject of how to make your programs more comprehensible, it is worth mentioning two other measures which can be taken to improve the readability of your programs.

When typing in a rule, it is useful if you structure it in the following format:

```
head :-  subgoal1,
         subgoal2,
         subgoal3,
         subgoal4.
```

That is, place each subgoal on a separate line under each other and indent the subgoals with respect to the head of the rule. This will make your rules easier to pick out and read at first glance.

The readability of your programs can be greatly improved by using meaningful names for your predicates, objects and variables. That is, try not to use variable names such as X and Y, which bear no meaning whatsoever, but choose some names that describe exactly what your variables represent, such as Father and Mother, for example. Remember you can use the underscore character (_) to string words together in names (for instance white_car, bitter_lemon).

6.6.7 Summary of definitions

In this section we have met a number of new terms and concepts, each of which is vital to the understanding of Prolog. We will now review the definitions that we have met so far.

- **Clause** – a clause is a fact or rule within a Prolog knowledge base.
- **Goal** – when we give Prolog a query to answer we are setting it a goal to satisfy. If it can find a match in the knowledge base the goal will succeed, otherwise it fails.
- **Instantiation** – Prolog terminology for setting a variable to a particular value. A variable which is not defined (does not yet have a value) is said to be 'uninstantiated'. A variable which does have a value is said to be 'instantiated'.
- **Matching** – Prolog attempts to find matches in the knowledge base to the queries we set it. Two clauses are said to match if they have the same predicate and arguments and the arguments are in the same order. An uninstantiated variable will match with an object and the variable will become instantiated to the value of that object.
- **Object** – a Prolog constant value. For example: apple, orange and pear are all objects. Object names begin with a lowercase letter. It is, however, possible to begin an object name with an uppercase letter by enclosing the name in single quotes, such as 'Frankenstein', 'Thomas' and 'Danube'. Similarly, special characters (including blanks) may be included in an object name by the use of single quotes; for example, 'New York', 'bye?' and '£5300'.
- **Predicate** – the name of a clause in the knowledge base. A predicate has arguments which must be enclosed in brackets and are separated by commas.
- **Program** – a Prolog program takes the form of a series of clauses (facts and rules). These form a database of knowledge (or knowledge base) about a particular problem area.
- **Rules** – a rule consists of a head and a body. The head is the goal to be satisfied. This is reduced to the satisfaction of a conjunction of subgoals which form the body of the rule.
- **Sharing** – variables within a clause which have the same name are said to be sharing. If one of these variables is instantiated to a particular value then the variables which are sharing with it are also instantiated to the same value.

This section has presented an overview of the important aspects of the Prolog language. It is now up to you, the reader, to try these out in some programming applications. Prolog is, as I hope you have gathered, an extremely powerful language with many potential application areas.

6.6.8 Extracts of code from the monitoring system

Here are some sections of code from the monitoring system. The entire system is too large to include. The code below should, however, give you a feel for the system and for the Prolog language.

```
#################################################################
EXPERT SYSTEM FOR THE DIAGNOSIS AND MANAGEMENT
OF RESPIRATORY FAILURE
#####################################################*/
/* This is the Master Rule which starts the program */
run(y):- nl,
         write("EXPERT SYSTEM FOR THE DIAGNOSIS AND
         MANAGEMENT OF RESPIRATORY FAILURE"),
         write("Ensure all your responses are typed in
         lowercase!"),
         write("What is the patient's unit number ? > "),
         readln(Number),
         inputcond(Condition),
         inputsex(Sex),
         inputwt(Weight),
         inputage(Age),
         write("Enter the patient's height in feet and
         inches"),nl,
         inputft(Feet),
         inputins(Inches),
         diagnose(Condition,Sex,Age,Weight,Feet,Ins).

/* The rules below are used to read in data and check
that they are within the correct ranges */

inputwt(X):-   write("Enter the patient's weight in kilo
               grams"),
               readint(X),
               X > 0,
               X < 175,!.
inputwt(X):-   beep,
               write("You haven't entered an integer or it
               is outside range ").
inputage(X):-  write("Enter the patient's age (range: 0 <
               age < 100) "),
               readreal(X),
               X < 100,
               X > 0,!.
inputage(X):-  beep,
               write("You haven't entered a number or it
               is outside range").
```

```
inputft(X):-     write("Feet (range: 0 < feet < 9) "),
                 readint(X),
                 X > 0,
                 X < 9,!.
inputft(X):-     beep,
                 write("You haven't entered an integer or
                 it is outside range").
inputins(X):-    write("Inches (range: 0 <= inches < 12) "),
                 readint(X),
                 X >= 0,
                 X < 12,!.
inputins(X):-    beep,
                 write("You haven't entered an integer or it
                 is outside range").
inputcond(X):-   write("Is the patient normal or asthmatic?
                 (enter n or a)"),
                 readln(X),
                 member(X,[n,a]),!.
inputcond(X):-   beep,write("You must enter n or a"),
                 inputcond(X).
inputsex(X):-    write("Is the patient male or female ? (m
                 or f) > "),
                 readln(X),
                 member(X,[m,f]),!.
inputsex(X):-    beep,write("You must enter m or f"),
                 inputsex(X).

/* This rule will compute the intial settings */

diagnose(Condition,Sex,Age,Weight,Feet,Ins):-
        oxygen(Condition,Percent),
        tidal(Weight,Value),
        resp(Condition,Rate),nl,nl,
        age(Age,Percent,Value,Rate,New_per,New_val,New_rate),
        print_settings(New_per,New_val,New_rate,Age),
        write("The normal peak inspiratory pressure is
        between 10 and 25 cmH2"),
        write("Is peak inspiratory pressure higher than 40
        cmH2O? (y/n) "),
        readln(Resp),nl,
        get_readings(PIP,PO2,PCO2,PH),
        write("Enter the value of systolic Blood pressure > "),
        readint(BP),nl,
        process1(Resp,PIP,PO2,PCO2,PH,BP,New_per,New_rate,
        New_val),
nl.

/* A rule to compute the new value of po2 */
po2(alter_1,PO2,O2,New_O2,I):- PO2 >= 12,
                               PO2 <= 18,
                               I = 2,
                               New_O2 = O2.
```

```
po2(alter_1,PO2,02,New_02,I):- PO2 > 18,
                                I=3,
                                New_02 = round(02 - (02 * 0.1)).
po2(alter 2,PO2,02,N_02):-      PO2 >= 12,
                                PO2 <= 18,
                                N_02 = 02.
po2(alter_2,PO2,02,N_02):-      PO2 > 18,
                                N_02 = round(02 - (02 * 0.1)).
po2(alter 2,PO2,02,N_02):-      PO2 >=10,
                                PO2 <=18,
                                N_02 = 02.


/* A rule relating to ph */
ph(set L,PH,K):-PH < 7.2,
                K = 1,
                write(" Consider treating the patient with
                bicarbonate").
ph(set_L,PH,K):-PH >= 7.2,
                pH <= 7.4,
                K = 2,
                write("Make no adjustment"),nl.
ph(set_L,PH,K):-PH > 7.4,
                K = 3,
                write("If PCO2 normal then treat the patient
                by metabolite").
ph(input,1,P):- write("Re-enter PH > "),
                readreal(P),nl.
ph(output,PH):- PH >= 7.2,
                PH <= 7.4,
                write("Make no further adjustment "),nl.
ph(output,PH):- PH > 7.4,
                write("Is the patient overventilating? "),nl,
                write(" If PCO2 low then decrease ventila-
                tion"),
                write(" OR decrease tidal volume"),nl.
```

6.7 Knowledge-engineering environments

These are also known as 'multiple-paradigm programming environments'. They allow the skilled programmer to experiment with different problem-solving architectures by combining different software modules, especially when prototyping.

This is required in the design of complex knowledge-based systems, as experience has shown that all representation schemes and reasoning strategies have their weaknesses. These knowledge-engineering environments are mainly concerned with giving the user greater flexibility in knowledge representation and procedural application, rather than imposing an overall framework on developing a KBS. They allow the knowledge engineer to build his or her own architecture for a KBS.

They allow for the development of large, complex KBS. They can, however, be expensive to buy and it can take a considerable time to learn how to program in them. Examples of knowledge engineering environments include:

- **KEE (Knowledge-Engineering Environment)** – KEE is a hybrid system that integrates rule, object and procedural representations. The reasoning facilities include forward and backward chaining, object-oriented programming and a reasoning package called KEE Worlds. KEE also has a powerful graphics-based development environment.
- **ART (Automatic Reasoning Tool)** – ART is a hybrid system that integrates rule, object and procedural representations. Its reasoning facilities include forward and backward chaining, and object-oriented programming. ART also has a sophisticated development environment called the ART Studio.
- **NEXPERT** – NEXPERT is primarily a rule-based system integrated with an object-based representation language. It allows a developer to combine both forward and backward reasoning strategies. NEXPERT has a graphically rich development environment. Editing, tracing and browsing facilities are all window-based and graphically oriented.

6.8 Choosing: a language or a shell?

> Use a shell if you can
> an environment where you should,
> and an AI language when you must.
>
> (Barrett and Beerel, 1988)

For developing an expert system using a PC there are two alternatives:

- a programming language (e.g. Prolog)
- a commercial shell (e.g. CRYSTAL).

Preece and Moseley compared the above choices in their paper in 1992 and drew the following conclusions.

They found that there was not much to choose between Prolog and CRYSTAL in the design and implementation stage of the project. However, CRYSTAL was significantly more effective overall, in terms of rate and speed of development. The most important factor was that of the efficiency in testing and debugging. CRYSTAL was found to be much better in this respect.

In this case, then, the shell appeared to be a better tool for KBS development than the programming language. Table 6.1 is a summary of the findings of Preece and Moseley which shows that they found CRYSTAL to be the best overall choice for system development.

Table 6.1 *Summary of strengths and weaknesses of each approach (from Preece and Moseley, 1992)*

	Prolog	CRYSTAL
Implementation	Good	Good
Debugging	Poor	Good
Maintenance	Poor	Good
Reliability	Poor	Good
Brevity	Good	Poor
Prototyping	Poor	Good
Overall	Poor	Good

There are now available for the knowledge engineer a great variety of PC-based expert system shells. There have been a number of studies which have compared the merits and otherwise of the various commercial shells.

Vedder, in 1989, compared five different PC-based shells and suggested criteria that the knowledge engineer might take into account when choosing a shell. The research project lasted fourteen and a half weeks and all five shells were tested using the same hardware. Each shell was used to develop the same KBS application.

The chosen domain was the business reference activity at the University of North Texas Main Library. The task of the staff in this department is to answer requests for specific business information. Each project team used its tool to build a prototype for advising patrons with business reference questions, regardless of the level of difficulty.

The major conclusions drawn from the study (Vedder, 1989) were as follows:

- A major criterion in choosing a shell must be the developer's prior experience with building expert systems. Expert system shells that have well-designed documentation (with separate paths for novice and experienced expert system builders) and online tutorials are best. These features reduce training time and costs.
- Applications may need access to external software or hardware, therefore only consider shells that can deal with interfacing simply and effortlessly.
- The structure and guidance provided by the development interface can have both positive and negative aspects. While helpful to novice builders, experienced knowledge engineers may find the constraints imposed irritating. Therefore, both the environment of the developer and the user must be considered. The user interface must be easy to learn, if not intuitive. The shell's explanation facility must justify reasoning without confusing the user.

- Unless the domain knowledge remains static, then the user will need the services of a knowledge engineer to maintain and expand the system. All shells can be complicated and need updating by someone with experience in working with the tool's development environment.

In general terms, the following guidelines should be followed when selecting a development tool:

- **Cost** – more features means more expense.
- **Development platform** – more features will require more expensive workstations.
- **Performance** – more features may mean a slower performance than a more modest shell. Therefore it is a good idea to carry out a demonstration on the platform to be used prior to buying the shell.
- **Ease of use** – more features may mean the shell is more difficult to use.

6.9 Summary

Recent years have seen the development of many tools and techniques for the development of knowledge-based systems. The use of shells is widespread, whilst a plethora of other software tools and languages are also available. The 'professional' engineer should be aware of all of these and attempt to appreciate their advantages and disadvantages. What tools can practically provide for the engineer depends upon how much the engineer actually understands the capabilities and limitations of the tool.

As the number of KBS developments increases, so knowledge engineers must master the facilities of reusability and genericity which are now being offered by tools. Without these, knowledge engineering will remain a craft in which every application is built from scratch.

6.10 Exercises

1. An employer is sifting through a large pile of applications which he has received for a recently advertised job vacancy. In order to produce a short list of candidates for interview he applies the following criteria:

In order to be selected for interview an applicant must be able to type and drive and must live in London.

Express the employer's selection criteria as a Prolog rule.

2. Express the following applicant details as Prolog facts:

```
John Smith lives in Cambridge, can drive but can't type.
Charles Brown lives in London, can drive and can type.
Mary Jones lives in Glasgow, can't drive but can type.
Sue Evans lives in London can drive and can type.
Alice Green lives in Luton, can drive and can type.
```

3. Ask Prolog to provide you with a list of applicants for interview.

Chapter 7

Practical considerations in KBS design

OBJECTIVES

In this chapter you will learn:

- ❏ four major lessons from the case studies;
- ❏ that people matter;
- ❏ that dealing with human experts is not easy;
- ❏ that safety-critical systems have their own set of problems;
- ❏ why system integration is a key issue.

7.1 Introduction

This chapter looks at the four case studies, and draws one major lesson from each of them. The four lessons are:

- **People matter** – the people factor is probably the most important factor in any KBS development project. Without the backing and support of the people involved in the project, it will be doomed to failure from the very start.
- **Dealing with human experts is not easy** – the knowledge-acquisition bottleneck is well documented. This section looks at the problems of dealing with multiple experts and discusses whether it is advisable for the domain expert to become a knowledge engineer.
- **Safety-critical systems have their own set of problems** – the more disastrous the results of failure of a KBS, the more important it is to tread very carefully right from the start of the project.
- **System integration is a key issue** – this will become more and more important in the future as hybrid information systems become common-place.

7.2 The quality-control system

7.2.1 Background

As outlined in Chapter 2, the problem in this case study is the manufacture of plastic cups – the sort of cups which are used in vending machines and which we drink our coffee or hot chocolate out of. In this case, the software appears to have exceeded the expectations made of it. The knowledge engineer states:

> Certainly, it is the largest single development that I have undertaken to date, and the response to it has certainly been satisfying. I believe that I was lucky, in that the experts whose knowledge I acquired were keen to assist me. The outcome may well have been otherwise, had I had problems acquiring the knowledge, and for that I am indeed grateful to those who assisted me at the company.
> I believe that the project, as a whole, has been managed tightly, with sufficient leeway built-in to allow for minor difficulties, and changes in plan. Consequently, I have been able to make practical use of the time available, and ensure that each aspect of the development has been balanced, and as rigorous as possible.

This success was largely a result of the way in which the knowledge engineer acted as a 'champion' for the project throughout its life. He convinced senior management of the importance of the work and managed to get the users of the system on his side. This meant that the knowledge acquisition, system design and implementation of the KBS went smoothly and the system was readily accepted within the company. The importance of these people factors is discussed below.

7.2.2 People matter

> Why don't they invent a machine to mind the beastly machines?
> Then all my problems will be over.
>
> (7:84 Theatre Company, *Lay Off*)

People are the most important part of any system. Without the support of the staff, any KBS project is doomed from the beginning. This support must come from all levels, from senior management through to the eventual users of the system.

7.2.2.1 The project champion

The project champion needs to be totally committed to the project. He or she must:

- really care about the project;
- believe in the KBS and the need for it;
- be highly motivated towards the success of the project;
- be prepared to work hard (and long hours);
- present the business benefits to senior management;
- convince the users that the KBS is needed;
- 'get on' with management and the users.

7.2.2.2 Senior management

In any innovation within an organization, the support of senior management is crucial. The introduction of KBS is no exception. Indeed, the very fact that KBS is a relatively new and innovative technology may mean that staff may be quite sceptical, and management support is even more important.

Everyone seems to have worked in an organization where, at some time, an edict has come down from on high, only to be followed by practical experience that shows that it is a case of 'do as I say, not as I do'. Nothing kills an innovation more quickly than this type of senior management hypocrisy.

Only if the support for the new KBS comes right from the top will the organization accept the system. Other managers within the organization may not have the authority to carry things through. In particular, the knowledge engineer must feel that in a crisis he or she will receive the backing of senior management. Otherwise they may not be able to resist the pressures which face any KBS development project.

The level of commitment of senior management must be gauged at the start of the project and any potential problems presented to them. Although it may be tempting to avoid problem issues in presentations to senior management in order to push the project through, this can be counter-productive as their support may then evaporate at the first sign of any problems.

7.2.2.3 Convincing management

In this case study, the knowledge engineer presented the project to senior management at a very early stage. It was crucial that he made such a presentation, for the following reasons:

- It gave an opportunity for management to be aware of the reality of the KBS project.
- It gave the knowledge engineer a chance to gauge the real level of the support which he was likely to get.
- If there was not going to be support for the KBS, it would have been better to give up with the project at an early, rather than at a later, stage.

A summary of the presentation which the knowledge engineer made to the senior management at the company is given in Figure 7.1.

PRESENTATION

26/1/93 9.30 am

The development of a KBS in a real-world setting is influenced by a number of factors. What I intend to talk about this morning is, in general terms, what these factors are, and in what way they are related. Having done that, I will then describe how these will be dealt with in the current development.

It should be remembered that although the use of KBS (expert systems, if you wish) in business and industry is gaining in popularity, many of the advances in the field are still quite new. Whilst their technical excellence is unquestionable, what you need to know is how useful this software is going to be for your company.

The key factors are:

- What are the business benefits?
- Why should you go ahead?
- What happens if you don't go ahead?
- What is the area to be developed?
- Is it suitable for KBS development?
- What do you expect it to do?
- How much time can you spend on its development?
- How much will it cost?
- Are your experts willing to part with their knowledge?
- How will staff react to the system?
- Who is going to use the finished product?

Figure 7.1 *Presentation to senior management.*

7.3 The forecasting system

7.3.1 Background

Forecasting is the practice of estimating, as closely as possible, future trends. This project's aim was to investigate the use of a KBS to improve the accuracy of the short-term forecasting of gas usage that is carried out daily within each region of British Gas, concentrating on one particular region.

Just before four o'clock each afternoon in the gas regions a Shift Control Officer phones London and gives his or her estimation of the amount of gas their region will need the next day. To help them decide they received a forecast of today's and tomorrow's weather at three-thirty. They also know how much gas the region has sold up to present on that day. However, this is less than a third of the day, as the gas day runs from 06:01 in the morning to 06:00 the next morning. The only thing the Shift Control Officer knows for certain is that the estimate will not be correct.

The gas customers have no worries. If they feel cold they turn up the heat or if they feel hot they turn it down. However, they also react to factors that don't directly affect their comfort. For instance, if it is raining and windy then they turn up their heating no matter what the temperature actually is outside, or if the national weather forecast in the evening states that frost is expected, then they will turn up the thermostat before going to bed even if the weather forecast for their region is not too bad.

It is the job of the Shift Control Officer to anticipate these responses and allow for them in the estimate. The aim of this project was to build a KBS system which would assist the estimators in their task. The major lesson learnt from this project was that dealing with human experts can be difficult, particularly when there is more than one expert involved.

7.3.2 Dealing with human experts is not easy!

7.3.2.1 Problems of multiple experts

The problems of dealing with multiple experts have already been discussed in some detail in Chapter 4. To summarize, the issues which must be addressed by the knowledge engineer are:

- How can experts reach an agreement about vocabulary and definitions? The knowledge engineer may use 'voting' to reach a consensus.
- Should the expert system try to model a consensus among a given set of experts when recommending solutions? The knowledge engineer may have to rely on his or her own judgement about when, and in which areas, consensus seems to have been reached.
- Experts in the same area who try to solve the same problem may use different techniques. These differences in technique and solutions make it difficult to use several experts to build a KBS.

7.3.2.2 Using an expert as the knowledge engineer

The knowledge engineer in this project had been a Shift Control Officer for many years and so considered himself to be a domain expert. But is it a good idea for knowledge engineers to themselves be the expert? Should the experts build their own KBS? Certainly current tools allow, and even encourage, this. The shells which are now on the market are very easy to use, and it would not be difficult for a domain expert to learn to us one and then to build a KBS. The situation does, however, present several advantages and disadvantages:

Advantages
- It may be easier to teach an expert about a shell than to give a knowledge engineer the expertise needed to build a KBS in a specialized domain.
- Systems can be built more quickly.
- Expertise is not lost in the translation.

Disadvantages
- Experts may be good at their own jobs but are not necessarily good analysts.
- Personal prejudices and biases have free reign.
- Outsiders can probe more deeply and ask the uncomfortable questions that the experts might like to avoid.
- The time of an expert is precious. It is hard enough to have them give of their expertise let alone build the system themselves.
- Experts can be parochial; outsiders will be more aware of other user needs.

7.4 The monitoring system

7.4.1 Background

This case study discusses the development of a KBS which has been designed to give advice as to how to operate a mechanical ventilator which is used to control the breathing of patients in an intensive care unit. The KBS gives advice on the initial setting up of the ventilator and how (and when) to adjust the equipment in order to maintain the stability of the patient.

The ventilator is used to control the breathing of seriously ill patients who have often been rushed into a hospital. Previous manual systems relied heavily on the intuition of the clinician in order to set up the ventilator. Development of the system involved extensive knowledge-engineering sessions with clinicians from two intensive care units. The system was developed in Prolog to run on an IBM PC.

A ventilator is a mechanical device which ventilates a patient's lungs or in other words 'does the breathing for the patient.' All modern ventilators achieve this by periodically forcing a tidal volume (VT) of gas into the patient's lungs at a positive inflation pressure (PI), then allowing the gas to be passively exhaled. The ventilator tubing is connected to the patient's lungs by a flexible endotracheal tube (ET) which passes through the mouth and is sealed in the trachea by an inflatable cuff.

One of the ventilators used in this project was the ERICA, which is manufactured by Gambro Engstrom of Sweden. It is electrically powered and allows adjustment of all ventilatory parameters. It also allows the use of small positive pressure maintained at the end of the expiratory phase of the ventilation cycle, known as positive end expiratory pressure (PEEP). Use of PEEP can, in some circumstances, prevent collapse of small functional lung units during expiration. The ventilators which were used in this study allowed the measurement and display of a number of important functional parameters such as minute volume (V), airway pressure (AP) and oxygen concentration (FIO2). In addition, the equipment would activate an audible and visual alarm if any important measured parameters exceeded limits set by the user.

Patients in intensive care may require artificial breathing support. Such therapeutic interventions are instituted for many different reasons, but usually for actual, impending or expected respiratory failure. This can include the post-operative period immediately following major anaesthesia and surgery.

In normal clinical practice, the initial setting of the ventilator is decided by the clinician on the basis of a number of known or estimated physiological factors relating to a particular patient. Such factors include weight, height, age, lung condition, disease, etc. Such an initial setting is inevitably somewhat arbitrary. Subsequent readjustments are made mainly according to the values of arterial blood gas levels, but in addition taking into account any improvement or deterioration in the patient's respiratory, cardiovascular or general condition. These adjustments are made in order to stabilize the patient's condition and to achieve a satisfactory overall clinical state.

Ventilator adjustments which are made by the clinician tend to be only semi-quantitative in nature; that is, the rules that are applied are by no means 'hard and fast' and there always exists an element of inspired guesswork in the manipulations.

In order to maintain patient stability measurement of blood gases, observation of patient condition and continual readjustment of the ventilator are all required. When the patient's state improves, attempts may be made to disconnect him or her from the ventilator. In particular, when the patient can demonstrate adequate spontaneous ventilation, the endotracheal tube can be removed.

The goal of the KBS was to assist the clinician in the intensive care unit (ICU) by adding a computerized measurement, interpretation and evaluation capability to the existing manual monitoring system. The system addressed the following problems of patient monitoring:

- the inability to form a concise presentation of important measurements;
- the need for interpretation of measurement values with respect to historical information about changes in patient status and therapy;
- the difficulty of directly relating measurement values to therapeutic recommendation.

The KBS was designed to perform several tasks in the ICU:

- to predict the initial setting of the mechanical ventilator;
- to suggest adjustments to treatment by continuous reassessment of the patient's condition;
- to summarize the patient's physiological status;

- to maintain a set of patient-specific expectations and goals for future evaluation;
- to aid in stabilization of the patient's condition.

The system provides advice based on a series of physiological measurements taken over a period of time, using a model of respiratory failure and clinical knowledge about the diagnostic implications of the data.

Although the system prototype was a success in that it satisfied the requirements of the clinicians in the ICU, it never went into day-to-day use. You could, therefore, say that this KBS development project was a failure. It is the reasons for this 'failure' that constitute the lesson here.

7.4.2 Safety-critical systems have their own set of problems

The KBS described in this case study was developed as the result of a lengthy series of knowledge-elicitation sessions with several clinicians from two intensive care units. The knowledge-engineering sessions took the form of in-depth, structured interviews during which the clinician concerned attempted to describe the way in which he or she would set and adjust the ventilator for a set of typical patient cases. This was often a difficult task for the clinician because much of their knowledge was based on past experience and, in many cases, included a significant amount of guesswork. Also, the experts would sometimes disagree on the best settings and/or adjustments for the ventilator.

This was perhaps the first danger sign. If the experts can't agree, will they ever believe the results of a computer system?

The results of these knowledge-elicitation sessions was a list of rules, expressed in English. This rule set was shown to each of the clinicians for their amendment. Once the rule set was complete, the knowledge engineer began work on a series of prototype systems.

Each of the prototype systems was also shown to the clinicians for comment. This resulted in refinements to both the system and the rule set. A number of iterations of this form were performed until the current version of the system was obtained.

The expert system was tested on over fifty patients from the ICU and the results compared with the evaluations made by the consultants concerned. During this period, the majority of tests were in close agreement with the consultant's evaluations.

So the system appeared to be a success. Yet it was never fully accepted and is not in use. Why? Let us examine the reasons.

Knowledge-based systems are increasingly being used in situations where lives literally depend on the correct functioning of the software: such systems are known as safety-critical systems. This was the case here – the KBS was to be used within an ICU on critically ill patients.

The failure of the computerization of the London Ambulance System in Autumn 1992 dramatically brought to light the need for standards to ensure software quality in safety-critical systems.

The London Ambulance System aimed to provide a computerized emergency call answering system that would greatly increase the efficiency of ambulance dispatch. In reality, quite the opposite was true. For a number of hours, London was effectively left without any ambulance cover. As a result, two senior managers resigned and public confidence in computer systems was severely dented (the ambulance service returned to a manual system).

The resultant report criticized senior management for being overzealous, not winning the confidence of staff involved in running the system and for failing to provide an adequate level of training. The computerized system itself had not been adequately tested and was obviously of questionable quality.

Such was the situation here. The KBS development project had been treated as a sort of experiment, a research project if you like. Ultimately it was a nice idea, but no one was willing to put it into real operation. Unfortunately, this has been the fate of many KBS. They have been nice research experiments but have not seen real use at the end of the day.

This can be because of questions such as:

- There are too many unknowns. Whose fault is it if the system fails?
- Has the system been developed to quality standards?
- Do we really know if it is correct?

Knowledge-based systems are being given an increasing role to play in safety-critical situations: a recent British Computer Society conference on 'Intelligent Systems Engineering' (BCS, 1990) contained articles on KBS that were being developed for:

- railway signalling
- alarm systems
- gas leaks
- nuclear power station process monitoring

At one time the term safety-critical systems was associated only with military systems. Now experts field agree that the term should apply not only to the type of intelligent system mentioned above but also to the software in everyday electrical appliances such as sandwich toasters and washing machines where a fault could prove potentially fatal, and to the use of any other software which is placed in potentially life-critical circumstances.

No good company wants to put faulty software onto the market which could cause injury or death to a user. But at the same time, the existence of examples of bad software design has demonstrated that it is not possible to simply rely on the good-will of software houses. Legislation is necessary to regulate the production of software, as is the case with other goods.

Under British law the consumer is protected against the supply of faulty goods by the Consumer Protection Act 1987. With regard to the production and supply of computer software, the Act means that if a plaintiff can prove that the software is faulty, then the software supplier will be liable to pay compensation for death, personal injury or damage to property.

The supplier of the software to the end user is not necessarily the designer of the software. In such a case, the supplier can take the company that supplied the software to them to court, until liability is passed down the line to the company who originally developed the software.

Since 1 January 1993, a new law developed by the European Commission has also applied to software. This law is known as the Machine Safety Directive. It states that if a plaintiff can prove negligence on the part of a manufacturer, then the manufacturer may face criminal, not just civil proceedings. It therefore falls to the software 'manufacturer' to ensure software quality and to put into place QA standards for software design and development.

If a software manufacturer is taken to court, then under the Consumer Protection Act 1987, one of the primary defences against a charge of negligence will rely on proof 'that the defendant has taken all reasonable care in making the product'. Since the standards that are currently applied to KBS development cannot guarantee the reliability of the system, this could cause considerable difficulties for knowledge engineers.

In practice, this means that knowledge engineers should comply to recognized international standards for quality control in project management and software development.

7.5 The integrated system

7.5.1 Background

This case study concerns an application where a KBS is integrated with a conventional software system. This situation is becoming more and more common as knowledge-based systmes are accepted in the everyday business world. The system in this case study is a human-resource management system which was developed for a large organization. A human-resource management (HRM) system is a software system which is designed to make the best use of the people in the organization. In this case the main aim of the system was to identify which staff were best suited for particular projects and to the identify the training needs of those staff.

The company involved employs approximately 4000 staff, which are subdivided into a number of departments each responsible for specific services. Each department has a resource manager who is responsible for a number of projects. The duty of the resource manager is to fit suitably qualified staff to specific projects within their departments. Any vacancy which cannot be filled from within the department is then considered across departments. This will involve staff being transferred between departments. If the resource manager can not find anyone suitable in any of the departments, he or she must then hire external consultants. These are usually employed on high-priority, short-term projects.

The aim in developing the Integrated Human-Resource System (IHRS) was to have a corporate pool of staff. All projects across departments would then employ staff from the pool and all human-resource data would be held and controlled centrally.

7.5.2 System integration is a key issue

Among all the major functional areas in modern organizations, human-resources administration has probably gained least benefit from recent advances in computer technology. There are several reasons for this.

To begin with, many managers believe that personnel work is largely of a house-keeping nature. They may feel that if this work has been done well manually, there is no need to invest sizeable resource in its computerization. Secondly, and probably more importantly, most managers agree that there are major practical problems in using information systems to implement HRM planning functions.

These problems mainly centre on the difficulty of categorizing human resources. The complicated trade-offs involved when attempting to categorize the strengths and weaknesses of individual employees makes decision making extremely difficult. If knowledge about HRM could be automated, managers

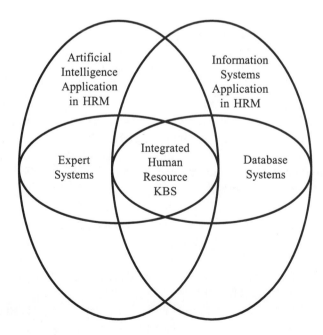

Figure 7.2 *Integrated systems are a key issue.*
(Adapted from Beynon-Davies, 1991)

could not only reduce the burden of information processing but also gain valuable expertise which would help in the process of decision making.

An ideal HRM system can be identified as lying at the intersection of two areas of computing:

- traditional information systems for managing and processing large amounts of HRM data;
- artificial intelligence for dealing with complex HRM knowledge.

Database systems provide a very powerful way to handle large amounts of data. Knowledge-based systems can attempt to model HRM knowledge. Thus a hybrid system which integrates both technologies would be an ideal solution (Beynon-Davies, 1991) as shown in Figure 7.2.

Over the past three decades, there has been a tremendous investment made in information systems. Such systems have evolved from file systems, through database systems to the current knowledge-based systems. With the advent of each new form of technology, there has been a need to integrate with existing information systems.

In recent years, much resource has been put into the area of integration, reuse and re-engineering. Re-engineering involves the redesign of existing information systems, while using as much of the existing system as possible. That is, the approach taken is to transform the existing information system into the format needed for the new technology, rather than to throw away the old system. Re-engineering is not a luxury, but a necessity for effective working in modern times.

The importance of re-engineering is that most systems in use in organizations were written before the advent of current methods and tools. Unless these systems can be brought up to date, the benefits to the organization will be small for a long time to come.

At the last count, the USA alone spends $30 billion a year simply supporting old systems. One estimate even goes so far as to indicate that total US spending on system maintenance amounts to no less than 2% of the country's total gross national product (Gillies and Smith, 1994).

Furthermore, the problem is getting worse. The US Air Force, for example, recently announced that it costs between $2500 and $3000 to change just one line of application code. From this figure, it projected that, unless it could alter in some fundamental way the software maintenance equation, it would require 45% of the country's 18–25 year olds to maintain its software by the year 2000. Figures for the UK are equally grim. Durham University's Centre for Software Maintenance estimates that the UK spends more than £1 billion each year on maintaining software.

System integration, and re-engineering, is thus a key issue. The success of the HRM KBS lay in the way that it integrated the intelligent components with the existing personnel database as shown in Figure 7.3.

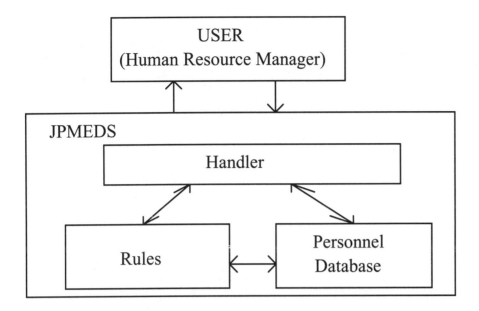

Figure 7.3 *Structure of the intelligent HRM KBS.*

7.6 Summary

This chapter has focused on the major lessons learnt from the four case studies. To summarize, these are:

- The people factor can be the most important factor in any KBS development project. Without the backing of everyone, and in particular senior management, a KBS project may be doomed to failure.
- Dealing with human experts may not be easy, particularly if there are several of them and they don't (or won't) agree!
- Safety-critical systems have their own set of problems, and these must be taken account of. Tread very carefully when dealing with such applications.
- System integration is a key issue. You can't afford to throw away old systems.

Chapter 8

Management issues

OBJECTIVES

In this chapter you will learn:

- ❏ the importance of quality assurance;

- ❏ the role of standards in KBS design;

- ❏ about system maintenance;

- ❏ the importance of project management;

- ❏ what it means to be a 'professional'.

8.1 Introduction

The developers of real-world knowledge-based systems must adopt good quality practice if they are to be taken seriously by the rest of the software community and the business community and if their systems are to stand any chance of survival. This chapter discusses the management issues which relate to the design and delivery of a KBS.

8.2 Quality assurance and validation

An engineer, no matter what his or her discipline, must strive for the development of the highest quality product that is possible. A knowledge engineer should be no different in this respect; he or she should be trying to ensure that the KBS which they produce is of the highest possible quality and provides the user with the best possible level of service and reliability. In order to do so the knowledge engineer must be continually adhering to quality standards and validating every product which results from his or her work, whether it be a piece of software or an item of documentation.

8.2.1 The need for knowledge validation

Knowledge-based systems do have one very specific validation problem. This is the problem of knowledge validation. This arises because in many KBS domains there is no 'correct' answer or gold standard against which the system may be used. Human experts often disagree as to the 'correct' answer. Effectively, the KBS developer faces the situation where the answer to 2 plus 2 is probably 4 but could be 3 or 5 – or even 6 in exceptional cases!

Measuring the quality of a KBS is very difficult. O'Keefe says validation is 'the assessment of the accuracy, utility and dependability of a system' (O'Keefe and Lee, 1990); Smith calls it 'building the right system' (Smith, P., 1990) and Myers defines it as 'trying to find bugs in the system' (Myers, 1979).

The quality of many knowledge-based systems is disappointing. They have a poor record in terms of traditional quality virtues such as maintainability and usability. For example, however clever the classic MYCIN medical system was, it was doomed to failure because of the time taken to enter the required data. This usability limitation will apply to many diagnostic applications unless most of the data can be gleaned from a database or the results are of sufficient significance and value to justify the effort of data input.

The history of KBS validation goes back as far as when the first expert system was built. This section discusses some important milestones in this field.

8.2.1.1 Teiresias

In 1976, Davis and Shortliffe both pioneered the idea of automated knowledge-base debugging. They produced a knowledge-base debugging tool called the Teiresias program. Teiresias worked in the context of the MYCIN infectious disease consultation system. Teiresias examined the completed MYCIN rule set. It then built models showing a number of factors, including which attributes were used to conclude other attributes. Thus, when a new rule was added to MYCIN, it was compared with the rule model for the attribute found in the IF condition. The program then proposed missing clauses that should appear in the new rule. Teiresias did not check the rules as they were initially entered into the knowledge base. Rather, it assumed the knowledge base was 'complete' with the knowledge transfer occurring in the setting of a problem-solving session.

Later, in 1980, van Melle improved EMYCIN, the enhanced version of MYCIN, with a knowledge-acquisition and debugging facility. This knowledge-acquisition program fixed spelling errors and checked that rules are semantically and syntactically correct. It also pointed out the interaction between rules.

8.2.1.2 ONCOCIN rule checker

In 1982, Suwa (Suwa, Scott and Shortliffe, 1982) produced a program for verifying completeness and consistency in the rule-based system ONCOCIN.

The ONCOCIN rule checker detects certain logical problems within rule bases. To check a set of rules, the rule checker firstly finds all parameters used in the conditions of these rules. Secondly, it creates a table displaying all possible combinations of condition parameter values and the corresponding values which will be concluded for the action parameters. It then produces a table for confliction, redundancy, subsumption and missing rules. Lastly a table displaying a summary of errors found is generated. The idea of missing rules is based on the assumption that there should be a rule for each possible combination of values of conditions.

8.2.1.3 EVA

EVA stands for Expert-system Validation Associate. EVA is a research project on the validation of expert systems and a validation system which has been under development at the Lockheed Artificial Intelligence Center since 1986. The goal of EVA is to produce an integrated set of generic tools to validate any expert system written in an environment such as ART, CLIPS, and KEE.

As more and more rules and constraints are added incrementally to an expert system, the system may exhibit inconsistency, redundancy and incompleteness. EVA believes it is necessary to check for the above properties and aims to address the validation needs and objectives of expert-system applications developed under any environment or shell for any application domain.

EVA contains a set of tools that help users to check for redundancy, consistency and completeness of expert systems. EVA is uniform, extensible and, most importantly, independent of a specific shell.

The entire EVA toolset is implemented in Prolog. The validation tools operate on knowledge in terms of both the application knowledge and metaknowledge in order to validate the application knowledge. The architecture of EVA is independent of any particular expert system shell. If a new shell is used, a new translator is the only requirement that needs to be implemented. The translator needs to translate the application knowledge and metaknowledge in the shell into the EVA database format. The advantage of using this metalanguage is that it permits the formulation of constraints which the expert system must meet and not violate.

8.2.1.4 VALID

Another similar project to EVA is VALID. VALID was a European project (VALID, 1991) whose aim was to construct validation methods and tools for expert systems. The project aimed to develop methods and software tools for the validation, verification and refinement of expert systems. The scale of the project was approximately 29 person years of effort. It started in January 1989 and finished in early 1992. The total budget was 4000 KECU (approximately £2.9 million).

The VALID project consortium consists of four partners from Denmark, Spain and France. VALID aimed to provide a way to control expert-system quality in terms of validation methods and tools. Moreover, the methods and tools produced aimed to be applicable to different application areas.

Validation is defined within VALID as attempting to guarantee that the knowledge-base model has the same behaviour as the real world. Validation consists of verification and evaluation in the VALID project. Verification is defined as checking that the knowledge representation and structure is coherent with respect to the formal model design. In other words, verification checks the expert system against its formal specification. The goal of evaluation in VALID is to measure expert-system characteristics. Expert-system characteristics are requirements in time and memory, explanation facilities, reliability and maintainability.

The VALID project provides the following software products:

- implementation of a validation metalanguage;
- a set of validation tools;
- interface to a set of existing shells.

8.2.2 Standards

Standards have now become an accepted tool for many in software engineering. When standards are adopted correctly they can be of great benefit to both individuals and the organization alike, and can help to ensure that software products are of the highest possible quality.

A standard can be defined as 'an accepted or approved example of something against which others are judged or measured', 'a level of excellence or quality' (Smith, R., 1991).

It has furthermore been suggested that because most large institutions have now passed through the stage of integrating information technology into the structure of the organization, into a phase where the organization is totally dependent on the technology, the need for quality-assured software has never been greater: the 1990s have therefore been characterized as the 'quality era' by experts such as Gorney.

Standards can address all facets of project development, and, according to Gorney: 'force a developer to carefully consider all aspects of a topic and to have a written method for carrying out the development' (Gorney and Coleman, 1991).

The UK National Computing Centre recognized the need for standards to regulate the production of data-processing software and, as early as 1972, produced a two-part reference manual entitled 'Programming Standards'. The 1981 revision of this document provides some useful insights into a number of the major issues in standardization. The first chapter is entitled 'Producing Quality Programs', which is really the crux of the matter, for it is through the use of standards that management can ensure the production of quality software.

The NCC point to several factors which have encouraged the adoption of standards for the software-development process:

- The organization producing the software needs to provide users with quality software that operates satisfactorily.
- Management need sufficient information to be able to control and manage the software-development process within the constraints of time, money and available staff.
- The finished product must be at an acceptable level of quality (i.e. display the characteristics of engineered software).
- The product should be easy to maintain, thus documentation is an important area which must be addressed by any standards.

The use of design methods is very important in the production of quality software. Standards allow management to place design methods within an overall framework that provides regular checkpoints for quality assurance at all stages within the software-development process. Standards need to be enforced consistently for them to succeed. But standards should also be dynamic and responsive to change over time.

Standards provide a framework for quality, planning, measurement and control. This exerts a level of discipline on staff, ensures regular progress reviews and establishes performance levels. They also help the organization to make more effective use of its staff. Standards can help inexperienced software or knowledge engineers to develop their skills, increase the level of communication between staff members and make the task of software maintenance that much easier.

A possible problem with standards can arise when it is necessary to establish general agreement within the organization that there is a real need for standards. Longworth points out that without such a consensus it will be very difficult to enforce the usage of any standards (Longworth, 1991).

Longworth also points out that some software developers can see standards as being restrictive. Standards are really only a collection of rules and techniques that ensure good engineering practice and pose no more constraints than the type of hardware or the programming language in use (Longworth, 1981). A further problem is the cost to the organization of adopting standards, in terms of both money and staff time. However, many organizations have now realized that the cost of not having standards can be much greater (in terms of user dissatisfaction, increased maintenance time, greater incidence of errors, etc.).

Some organizations have developed their own standards in-house. Recent figures from a survey by Carol Davis show, however, that only a small number of UK organizations involved in software development have been accredited by the British Standards Institute, with certification to quality assurance standard BS5750 Part 1 (Davis *et al.*, 1993).

The link between standards and quality is clear. While defining standards is straightforward, many attempts to quantify 'quality' have been made. This is unsurprising given the subjective nature of the word. Some would argue, for example, that a quality product is linked to both cost and functionality.

Another view is one of a quality system being one that simply meets a specification dictated by the user.

The formal definition of quality provided by the International Standards Organisation is: 'the totality of features and characteristics of a product that bear on its ability to satisfy specified or implied needs'

This book is about knowledge engineering and the development of KBS. Undoubtedly the most successful KBS projects, in terms of the delivery of quality KBS, are those in which standards and methods are applied.

8.2.2.1 Current practice in the UK

A survey by Stephen Ng of the use of expert-system development methods in UK industry has highlighted the lack of formalism and standardization in the area (Ng et al., 1991). The survey was undertaken by mailing a questionnaire to 360 UK organizations involved in the development of KBS. Of these, 66 organizations responded to the questionnaire. Although this return is not high (18%), the results obtained give a feel for recent trends in the development and validation of KBS in the UK.

The survey revealed that the majority (56%) of organizations had only started to develop KBS in the last five years. Thirty-three per cent of organizations had been developing KBS for up to ten years while only 11% of organizations had been developing KBS for more than ten years (Figure 8.1). These figures are probably not surprising, as KBS are a relatively new concept. However, they do highlight the immaturity of the field in which knowledge engineers are currently working.

Only 22% of expert-system developers claimed to use any methodology to build their knowledge-based systems. The methodologies used by respondents were mainly in-house methodologies (12%). Some respondents used rapid prototyping (5%), while a very small proportion used more formal approaches such as KADS (3%) and GEMINI (2%). This left 78% of existing knowledge-based systems which were not built according to any specific methodology (Figure 8.2). The reality is that many of these will also use

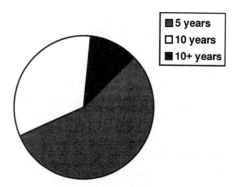

Figure 8.1 *Level of experience in KBS development in UK (Ng, 1991).*

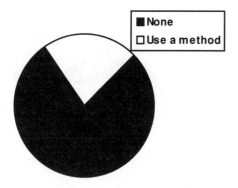

Figure 8.2 *Use of KBS methods in UK (Ng, 1991).*

prototyping as an approach, but that they probably do not recognize this as a methodology.

Only 13% of organizations claimed to use any formal or semi-formal method to validate their knowledge-based systems. The methods quoted as used were:

- qualitative modelling
- induction
- customer satisfaction
- structured walkthroughs
- regression testing
- conventional testing methods
- in-house methods

The results also showed that only 38% of knowledge-based systems were live working systems while 62% of systems were prototypes.

To summarize, this survey revealed that the state of the art of KBS development in the UK is, quite worryingly (but not surprisingly), very low technologically. That is, there are very few methods to apply (and very few people are applying these methods!).

The growth in the use of tools and methodologies available to the knowledge engineer, to assist in developing quality systems, is becoming significant and these can only move us closer to the goal of KBS quality. However, it is up to the individual knowledge engineer to use these tools and so act in a professional manner, because whilst it is possible to build 'bad' systems whilst sticking to a defined procedure, it is impossible to build consistently 'good' systems without them. This underlines the importance of project management.

8.2.2.2 Application of external standards in KBS

The survey of Carol Davis (Davis, 1993) revealed that most companies do not adhere to any real quality standards. The results are shown in Figure 8.3.

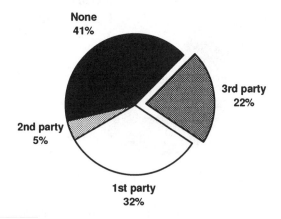

Figure 8.3 *Current QA practice in the UK.*

First-party accreditation refers to internal monitoring only. Second party refers to monitoring by an external customer and third party to accreditation to an internationally accepted quality standard by an approved accreditation body. Thus approximately only one in five companies could claim to have rigorous QA practices which have been validated against international standards, and only one in four have permitted any external scrutiny at all. Many practitioners of quality assurance claim that international standards such as ISO9000 (see next section) represent an acceptable minimum rather than 'best practice'.

The nature of knowledge-based systems with their ill-defined problems, fuzzy knowledge and less structured development methods means that the uptake of rigorous QA practice is certain to be considerably less than for software development in general. As more customers require third-party accreditation of all their suppliers, knowledge-based systems are likely to face a further barrier to their acceptance in the commercial world.

8.2.2.3 The ISO9000-3 standard

ISO9000-3 is a set of notes for guidance for the application of ISO9001 to software development (ISO, 1991). ISO9001 is a general quality standard. The number of potential clients for KBS developers insisting upon accreditation as a prerequisite for supplying systems is increasing, particularly in Europe. The standard lays down procedures in twenty-two areas under three headings, shown in Table 8.1.

Many of the topics relate to project management rather than specific development activities. There are areas where implementation of the standard will need special care within KBS development. These are:

• KBS development has often taken place in a creative environment, without the user of standards and procedures. Careful change is required if stand-

Table 8.1 *ISO9000-3: the application of ISO9001 to software development*

Quality system framework	Quality system life cycle	Quality system support
1. Management responsibility	5. Contract reviews	14. Configuration management
2. Quality system	6. Purchaser requirements	15. Document control
3. Internal quality audits	7. Development planning	16. Quality records
4. Corrective action	8. Quality planning	17. Measurement
	9. Design and implementation	18. Rules, practices and conventions
	10. Testing and validation	19. Tools and techniques
	11. Acceptance	20. Purchasing
	12. Replication, delivery and installation	21. Included software product
	13. Maintenance	22. Training

ards, QA systems and methods are to be accepted without destroying the creativity often required for KBS development.

- The evolutionary or prototyping methods often employed in developing knowledge-based systems do not suit the adoption of quality management practices as well as more structured traditional approaches.
- If a quality system is to be introduced based around a prototyping approach, the tasks concerned with managing different versions of a KBS become crucial. In terms of the standard, this includes configuration management to ensure that different KBS versions are correctly and consistently identified and that the current version is clearly shown as such and document control to ensure the same for the accompanying documentation. It must also be ensured that only the final versions of software are ever released to customers.

The last few years have seen a large increase in companies gaining accreditation to ISO9000. This has been driven by customer demand. A few large customers are now insisting on ISO9000 accreditation as a prerequisite for bidding for contracts. This has effectively forced suppliers to gain accreditation.

As many of these customers are the potential customers for KBS applications, it seems inevitable that KBS development will be forced to change and move more towards standards if it is to survive as a commercial activity.

Indeed, as KBS applications are used in more and more life-critical situations, the need for reliable systems become even more important. A study by Gorney and Coleman (Gorney and Coleman, 1991) into expert-system failure in the USA found many similarities with traditional software. It is importantly the users, who normally pay the price for poor quality software, who are leading the demands for developers to follow quality standards.

One problem for the knowledge engineer is confusion as to the actual standards to follow. The high-level, generic nature of standards often leads to much confusion and misunderstanding for both software and knowledge engineers. The British Computer Society introduced the TickIT (DTI, 1990) guide in 1990 to help software developers apply standards relating to ISO9000-3. As far as specialist KBS standards for quality assurance, there are as yet no acknowledged standards to follow. This is, however, likely to change in the not-too-distant future.

8.3 Operation and maintenance

When a system is delivered to a customer, it is vital that it is accompanied by sufficient and appropriate documentation. In particular, it will be almost impossible to operate and maintain a KBS if it doesn't have:

- a user guide which clearly explains to a user (who may be very inexperienced) how to operate the software;
- a technical manual which will enable software engineers or knowledge engineers to maintain and adapt the software in the future.

Sections from the user guide and the technical manual for the quality-control system are shown in the following section. These are shown merely as an example and should not be taken as ideal models. For instance, it is probably true to say that the user guide in particular could be improved by the inclusion of some screen shots of the software during operation.

User Guide

1 Introduction

This guide provides the user with all the information necessary to run the program. For further details associated with installation, maintenance and troubleshooting, you should refer to the reference manual.

The Fault Diagnosis Program will not solve every problem you might face. It is limited in a number of respects, and consequently is only suitable in the following circumstances:

Rimmed vending cups; PV7 SQUAT, PV7 TALL, 7OZ SQUAT, 7OZ TALL.

The machine has been running.

It has been producing stable product up until the occurence of the problem.

Attempting to apply this program in circumstances, or with products other than those named, will result in meaningless answers.

Given the above, all efforts have been made to provide solutions to the problems you may face. If, having run the program, you are advised that the solution is not currently available (this happens rarely), you should remember, that following the program to that point has, at the very least, stabilised your product, and made checks on all the key factors associouated with the problem. In addition, you have a printout of the problem, adjustments made, and machine parameters, which will make the work of others a lot easier.

Unless stated otherwise, you should assume that each instruction requesting a key to be pressed, will require the Return key to be pressed after it.

2 Running the program
2.1 Program run from the hard disk
1 At the operating system prompt (probably C:\), you should change to the directory which contains Crystal (assuming the directory is called CRYSTAL (you can check this by typing DIR), type "cd crystal").
2 If the program is being used for demonstration purposes, you should now type RUN2.
3 If the program is being run for maintenance or development purposes, you should run Crystal and the knowledge base containing the Fault Diagnosis Progam. To do this, you should type "cr #2".

2.2 Program run from floppy disk/s
Install Crystal as described in the Crystal Manual, and ensuring that the disk containing the "overlay" file (called CRYSTAL.OVL) remains in the drive, you can follow either option 2 or 3, outlined above.

2.3 Using Crystal
When you first enter Crystal, you are provided with a series of options along the bottom of the screen. If you want to run the Fault Diagnosis Program, you should type the letter "R" for `run' to see the full effect. It is possible to move the cursor to the Run option; however, by doing so, the animation

sequence at the beginning of the sequence will not work properly.

2.4 Using the program

When you run the program, you are initially presented with an animation of the forming process. This animation will continue until a choice is made. When you have completed a program run, you will be returned to this animation, and consequently it provides a familiar starting point for the operator. In order to quit from the program altogether, you should use the "X" for exit option.

There are three types of screen used in this program:

- **Menus** - These provide the user with a number of options which, in general, allow for a single choice of answer. These choices are made either by moving the cursor up or down to the relevant choice followed by Return, or by typing the initial letter.

- **Input screens** - These ask you to input particular values at the keyboard. If the values are numbers, you can use either the row of numbers near the top of the keyboard, or the numeric keypad at the side of the keyboard. If you need to include decimal points, you should either use the full-stop (located towards the bottom-right of the typewriter section of the keyboard) or the decimal point on the numeric keypad.

- **Display screens** - From time to time, you will be presented with screens that describe the current state of the program. They may also include instructions as to what to do next. In either event, you will be told to press a particular key in order to proceed.

Regardless of the type of screen, you should make your choice with care, since it is not possible for you to undo such decisions. It is wise for the user to refer to the printout at regular intervals, in order to be assured that the correct decisions are being made.

In the event of error, it is recommended that you quit the program at the first offered ooportunity and re-run the program. Failure to quit will result in the generation of solutions which do not match your current problem.

Remember it is better to waste a little time and paper, than to make adjustments that make the problem worse.

Instructions are provided for the user throughout the program, and consequently there should not be an occasion where you wwill not know what to do next. These instructions are either included in the main text on the screen, or are provided at the bottom left hand side of the screen.

It is recommended, that even if you think you know how to make the correct decisions, you should check these two locations for confirmation.

If the program stops for any reason, you should refer to the Troubleshoooting section in the Technical Manual.

The Fault Diagnosis Program has been designed to be as easy to use and as attractive as possible. It is hoped that it will increase your interest in the potential for computers in general, and expert systems in particular.

Technical manual

1 Installation

1.1 Configuration

The minimum requirement for this product is an IBM or IBM-compatible personal computer, running under MS-DOS 4.1 (or later). It is also necessary to have an Expanded Memory Manager installed prior to use. Expanded memeory is one method of making more than the 512K of working memory available at any one time.

On 386 machines (or larger), Expanded Memeory is no longer provided; however, it can be emulated by a program that should be present in your DOS directory. This file is called EMM386.EXE, and needs to be added to your CONFIG.SYS file after the line relating to HIMEM.SYS. It is advisable that you refer to your operating System manual for more details.

1.2 Installing the program

With the current version of the program, it requires that Crystal be running before this program is loaded. It is possible to run this program from either floppy disks, or from the hard disk (if present). It is recommended that you use the hard disk if possible, as this provides the most efficient running of the program.

1.2.1 Running from floppy disks

If you decide to run the program from floppy disks, it is necessary for you to do some disk maintenance. You should copy the files that make up the Fault Diagnosis Program to the Crystal disk. If there is insuffient room on the disk, you will have to remove some of the demonstration programs provided with Crystal. The key Crystal files, which should not be removed, are CR.EXE and CRYSTAL.OVL.

1.2.2 Running from the hard disk

You should copy the files that make up the Fault Diagnosis Program to your Crystal directory. Once there, the program can either be run from within Crystal, or from the DOS prompt using the command RUN2 (this runs the Batch program RUN2.BAT, which runs Crystal and then overlays the Fault Diagnosis Program).

1.2.3 Installation problems

    EMM386.EXE file not found

You should check that you are running a sufficiently recent version of DOS. This can be done by typing VER at the DOS prompt. If the file is not present in any of the DOS directories, you should contact the software supplier of your Operating System.

```
EMM386.EXE does not load
```

You should ensure that this file follows HIMEM.SYS in the CONFIG.SYS file. If you have attempted to load this file by using the Ctrl-Alt-Del combination, and you machine has a re-set button, it is advisable that you use this button instead.

```
There is not enough space for the program
```

If you are running the Fault Diagnosis Program from floppy, you should obtain a licensing agreement from Crystal, which would allow you to copy the key files to a 3½" High Density disk, where there would be more than sufficient space to store and run both Crystal and the Fault Diagnosis Program.

2 Maintenance

2.1 Introduction

This section is not intended to replace the use of your Crystal manual, which will prove invaluable if you intend to make major changes to the program. What it does offer are the key facilities provided by Crystal, which have been utilised by this program, and which you are going to need, in order to navigate the program effectively.

The Fault Diagnosis Program, like all such Crystal-based programs, was developed inside the Crystal environment. Consequently, in order to maintain the program you will need to run Crystal first, and then load the relevant knowledge base.

If Crystal is not always available at the time of mainte-nance, it might be worthwhile utilising one of Crystal's options, which allows you to save and load knowledge bases from files saved in ASCII format. It should be stressed, however, that modifications made using this approach are not passed through Crystal's validation procedures, and errors may result in a program crash.

The program currently consists of five knowledge bases, of which #2.kb is the most important. The other four are there for maintenance purposes, as they contain the specification weights of the products currently offered by the program.

The remaining files (with the exception of the RUN2.BAT batch file) are those called by the program for particular purpose. They will be discussed in more depth in later sections.

2.2 Modification of products offered by the pro-gram

The Fault Diagnosis Program has been designed so that (providing the diagnostic process remains constant) the addition, deletion or modification of products can be done with relative ease.

Each product specification has been established in its own knowledge base. When run, this exports the specification into a product file. When the Fault Diagnostic Program is run, the user is asked which product is currently running, and then the program calls the relevant product file.

2.2.1 Addition of products
In order to add products to those currently on offer, it would be easiest to modify an existing product knowledge base, and then save it under a new name. Having done so, the knowledge base should be run, in order to generate the associated product file. It would then be necessary to amend the "Product" rule in #2.kb to allow for this option.

2.2.2 Removal of products
In order to remove products from those currently on offer, you should delete the relevant knowledge base and product file from the Crystal directory. In addition, you will need to adjust the "Product" rule in #2.kb.

2.2.3 Modification of products
Modifications to these specifications require that the relevant knowledge base be amended and then run. This will then over-write the product file.

3 Troubleshooting

Installation problems were dealt with in an earlier section; consequently, this section will deal with problem solving at run-time.

This product has been extensively tested throughout it's development, therefore it should respond appropriately, regardless of the input. However, it is acknowledged that some errors may slip through the net.

3.1 The program stops and then says "out of memory"
This is caused by the program attempting to access something that it cannot find. The most common instance of this problem, is when the printer has not been switched on.

The program has been written to output details to a printer connected to LPT1. If the output differs from this, you should change the relevant command in the Crystal Master Rule. If you have not got a printer attached to the computer, you should remove the "output" command. This will send the output to a file on disk, which if un-named by the user will be labelled CR.PRN.

3.2 The program provides an incorrect response
This may well be an editing problem, and as such can be altered by using the instructions offered in earlier sections.

If the problem is not related to editing, this suggests that a rule has failed inappropriately, and the program is following a spurious line of reasoning. If this is the case, you should re-run the session, following the options suggested by the print-out. At the screen before the error, activate the Trace facility (Ctrl-T). You should then step through the process using F5 to isolate where the problem lies. Once found you should press "Escape" "F10" to go to the relevant rule, and make the necessary adjustments. It could be that the rule does not prevent spurious input.

3.3 The program gets stuck

The program is obviously searching for a value, and cannot find it. Consequently, if you press "Escape" "F10" you will be located at the relevant rule, and you should check that the value chosen is actually tested against a particular variable. If this is not the case, then you should include the relevant condition, taking advantage of the format of the current rule, and the Crystal manual.

8.4 Project management

8.4.1 Introduction

One area of work which is often overlooked by the knowledge engineer is project management. Project management is the organization of resources including people, time, money and equipment. It therefore requires skills of planning and motivation. Some of these can be taught, but most of them arrive through experience.

8.4.2 Gathering the project team

For a KBS project, management will assemble a group of people that will include a knowledge engineer, the domain expert(s) and a project manager. It is important to point out that any of these roles can be filled by several people depending on the size and complexity of the project and that one person, given the correct technical skill could fill more than one role. An experienced knowledge engineer could fulfil many (or even all) of the roles within the team.

The project manager has perhaps the most difficult job of all. He or she has to balance the pressures from all sides without having the overall authority of more senior management colleagues. The project manager will carry much of the responsibility but may have little ultimate authority. The project manager's dilemma is summarized in Table 8.2.

The role of the project manager is to try to ensure that all interests are represented and that a proper balance is achieved between the different factors. They must balance the short and the longer term view.

The short-term view says that the project must be completed on time and that this must take priority over all other factors. The longer term view says that the KBS must be properly integrated into working practices in the longer term.

They must balance the need to keep the members of their project team happy and motivated whilst ensuring that the required level of change is introduced. Further, they must endeavour to ensure continuity of staff so that expertise gained is retained. If they fail, there are plenty of people waiting to pounce. The project manager must be absolutely convinced of the merits and benefits of the KBS to be adopted otherwise they will find it impossible to convince others.

Prior to the project, the project manager will have to select the appropriate expert(s) based on initial interviews with the client and act as an administrator organizing the first very important meeting between the domain expert and the knowledge engineer. This is very important. If the domain expert and the knowledge engineer do not get along the development of any prototype would be pointless. Figure 8.5 gives a high-level overview of the organization of a project team.

As can be seen, project management acts as a link between the client and the project, informing the client about the progress of the project and assisting in solving any problems that may arise. Constant communication is essential, as the management team must take into consideration all implications of a change in the client's requirements, to ensure that if they can be accomplished, they are done so with minimum disruption.

Once the necessary personnel have been recruited the team have to produce a project plan and schedule, establishing milestones throughout the course of the project to enable measurement of progress made. A schedule for the quality-control case study is shown in Figure 8.6.

It is vital that such schedules are produced for each major KBS development project. The schedule can then be used to observe and measure progress by the user, the knowledge engineer and the project manager. Schedules are important but should not be seen to be 'cast in stone'. Indeed, it is important to regularly review project schedules and to revise them if necessary. Any revisions must be agreed by the project manager. Obviously the manager will not want schedules to slip back too far, but some slippage often happens and there may be quite valid reasons for this. Reasons for slippage might include late delivery of hardware or software, difficulty in gaining access to experts, staff illness, etc.

8.5 Professionalism

A 'profession' can be defined as: 'an employment not mechanical and requiring some degree of learning; a calling, habitual employment; the collective body of persons engaged in any profession;' (Chambers Dictionary, 1991).

Professions have several characteristics:

- They are established by a Royal Charter.
- They control entry to that profession.
- They act as a self-governing and self-regulatory committee and enforce discipline upon members.
- They have a Code of Practice and Code of Conduct which members must adhere to.

8.5.1 What are the grounds for granting a Royal Charter?

These can be summed up as follows:

- that it should be in the public interest to regulate members within that body;
- that the members should represent a coherent group.

One of the most recent UK bodies to gain a Royal Charter highlights these grounds. On 30 June 1993: 'The Queen gave Royal Assent to a Bill that will

Table 8.2 *The project manager's dilemma*

Stakeholder	Expectation
Users	They want a system which meets their needs
Knowledge engineers	They want to be left to do their job
Quality manager	They wants the system to conform to their quality procedures
Senior management	They want the introduction of the KBS to go smoothly. They also want the project on time, in budget and working

turn practitioners of osteopathy, once a fringe group derided by conventional medicine, into a fully-fledged profession' (*The Independent*, 4 July 1993).

Put simply, the idea is to protect the 'public interest'. This provides the public with safeguards from 'cowboys'; for instance, it is illegal to claim to be a Chartered Engineer. However, it is not illegal to claim to be an 'engineer'.

Professions are usually represented by a federal system. In the UK there are two types of body: an individual body and an umbrella body.

- **Individual bodies** – these include the Institute of Electrical Engineers, the Institute of Mechanical Engineers and the British Computer Society (BCS). Many of these bodies themselves provide a meeting point for interested parties who may or may not be members of that body. For example the BCS Specialist Group on Expert Systems is a forum aimed at the professional knowledge engineer to provide 'information to the growing community of developers and users of expert systems'. Individual bodies are often used as a source of independent advice by the government. For example, the BCS has given advice on subjects such as software law. A further role is in the dissemination of information via journals and conferences.
- **Umbrella organizations** – these organizations are chartered and tend to represent the interests of an entire profession (combined individual bodies). They give advice to central government on issues which affect the profession. Their other main role is to ensure that membership of the individual bodies meet the standards of the chartered body. For example the Engineering Council registers Chartered Engineers, Incorporated Engineers and Engineering Technicians. For the individual member in any type of business this is the most important requirement in that registration is the ultimate recognition of their professional status.

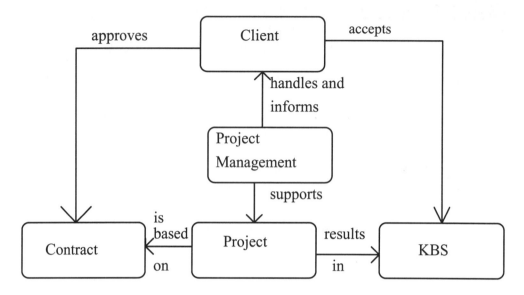

Figure 8.5 *The organisation of a project team.*

8.5.2 Code of conduct

This covers areas of ethics including honesty and impartiality. For example, a member cannot claim to have technical competence which he or she does not possess. If the Code of Conduct is breached then the member can be found guilty by the disciplinary Committee of Professional Misconduct and be expelled from the body.

8.5.3 Code of practice

This concerns areas of a more technical nature. It is not a textbook of how to specifically carry out an operation but concerns itself with approaches members should use in developing a system such as: 'Actively seek opportunities for increasing efficiency and effectiveness to the benefit of the user and of the ultimate recipient' (extract from the British Computer Society Code of Practice).

To some the idea of a Code of Practice may seem an interference with innovation. However, practices which have been standardized are tried and tested and thus can be relied upon by the practitioner and the public. Thus the outward signs of a profession, that is the promotion of standards, quality, methodologies, tools and project management should all be expressed in the Code of Practice.

8.5.4 Entry to professions

The two prerequisites for entry to any profession are normally education and work experience, the balance of which is determined by the individual body. The main way of entry into a chosen profession is through an accredited

PROJECT SCHEDULE

TASK		Hours	Planned Finish Date	Actual Finish Date	Task Deliverable
No	Description				
1	Provision of Terms of Reference and Task Schedule	20	2/11/92	26/10	Terms of Reference Task Schedule
2	Evaluation of available software	40	11/11/92	6/11	Evaluation report on Crystal and Prolog
3	Investigation of the work practices Isolate domain for project	40	17/11/92	16/11	Reports on the sessions used to determine the domain. Orientation of the experts to Expert System practice. Acquisition of the domain expert/s.
4	Knowledge Acquisition sessions. Three one-hour sessions per week on a Monday, Wednesday and Friday.	26	31/1/93	15/1	Each session will generate a Knowledge Acquisition form.
5	Knowledge Acquisition transcription. These are transcriptions for each of the KA sessions, to be generated following each meeting.	60	31/1/93	15/1	Each session will result in the generation of one transcript.
6	Representation of the KA sessions in Crystal. This is to be generated on a Saturday and Sunday, for the previous week.	144	31/1/93	26/1	Generation of a prototype / demo fault diagnosis KBS.
7	Generation of interim report on the current state of the project.	16	16/12/92	17/12	Interim report.
8	System Testing	80	31/1/93	26/1	Report on testing problems, trouble-shooting typical results etc.
9	Production of User guide.	8	31/1/93	31/1	User guide.

Figure 8.6 *Project schedule for quality-control case study.*

course at a university or equivalent institution. There may also be a requirement to sit the professional body's own internal examinations.

Work experience is just as important but may be more difficult to assess
than academic qualifications. One way of doing so is via a Professional
Development Scheme (PDS) such as that used by the BCS. The scheme
involves completing a period of accredited training which relates to an
'Industry Structure Model', and completing a 'portfolio' which shows that
work has been undertaken to professional standards. The PDS will play a
major role in awarding Chartered Engineer status to computer professionals
in the future.

8.5.5 Summary

Professional status involves recognition by a legally established chartered
body, gained from passing an accredited courses and/or a period of recognized work experience. Codes of practice and conduct, promoting both
quality and standards to system development are enforced upon members and
it is these which ensure a 'professional' approach and protect public interests.

Knowledge engineering is a relatively new and immature discipline, and
does not yet have its own recognized professional status. It is, however, vital
(White and Goldsmith, 1990) that knowledge engineers act in a professional
manner if knowledge-based systems are to really take off in business and
industry in the future and if knowledge engineering is to ever gain true, legal,
professional status.

8.6 Conclusions

Knowledge engineering is an emerging new discipline which, if it is to gain
the confidence of industry and commerce, must demonstrate that it is built
upon strong foundations. This means adopting tried and tested methods, tools
and techniques for project management and software development. Standardization in these areas is a process which takes a great deal of time and
investment, but experience in software engineering has shown that it is well
worth the effort.

There is a story (perhaps apocryphal) (Ross, 1993) about a seventeenth-
century French nobleman who went to buy a new sword. Now this nobleman,
a count, was somewhat haughty and when he saw the swordmaker's wares he
picked up the nearest rapier, frowned down his nose at it and suggested that
the blades were blunt. The swordmaker, who was somewhat quick-tempered
(and no friend to noblemen), seized the rapier from the count's hands and,
quick as a flash, sliced him in two from head to toe. So sharp was the sword
that the nobleman did not feel a thing, and hardly knew what had happened
to him until he tried to move away and his two sides separated.

There are those who will detract from the work of the knowledge engineer
in the same way as the count criticized the swordmaker in the story cited

above; if knowledge engineers cannot prove that their practice is built upon a sound theoretical basis, and on the use of tried and tested methods and techniques, then such criticisms may to some extent be justified.

What the story about the nobleman and the swordmaker does suggest is that the very best argument that any artisan can make is that what he or she produces is of the highest quality. It might be a little extreme to slice one's critics in two and we do not advocate this particular approach for the knowledge engineer. It would be far better for knowledge engineers (as no doubt many already do) to adopt a professional, structured approach to KBS development and to produce working examples of KBS technology of a consistently high quality.

The current trend in KBS construction in the UK tends towards the development of systems using KBS shells such as CRYSTAL and ESTA, in conjunction with the prototyping technique. This combination has proved effective for building the small, stand-alone systems that are typical of many of the currently operational knowledge-based systems in UK commerce and industry. This allows KBS developers to produce tangible results quickly and at low cost.

At the moment, many companies with an interest in KBS are still at the stage of exploring the technology. The discipline of knowledge engineering is itself relatively new, and methods, tools and techniques are continuously appearing to improve the way in which KBS are built.

In the near future, the hybrid system which integrates conventional and knowledge-based elements will become more widespread. The construction of KBS will therefore be subject to the same commercial constraints that are now applied to the development of traditional software. Users (who may not even be aware that the system they are using has a knowledge-based element) will expect their systems to perform at the same level of efficiency, and be reliable and user-friendly. Systems should also be economical and maintainable. These are the same properties associated with traditional quality software systems. Methodologies and automated tools will therefore become increasingly important in controlling the development of quality KBS in the near future.

The knowledge engineer needs to be a multi-skilled, multi-talented individual with experience and expertise in many areas including KBS technology, computer science, analysis, human relations and interpersonal skills, programming and information gathering. This book has attempted to provide a practical introduction to these areas.

Solutions to selected exercises

Chapter 1

1. Definitions of data, information and knowledge:

- **Data** – data refers to isolated facts such as individual measurements. Items of data have no meaning on their own.
- **Information** – information consists of symbols such as text or numbers, but this time there is some meaning, or semantics, associated with the symbols. That is, information is data with added semantics.
- **Knowledge** – understanding, awareness or familiarity acquired through education or experience. Anything that has been learned, perceived, discovered, inferred or understood. The ability to use information.

2. Examples of important factors in an engineer's job:

- professionalism
- standards
- tools
- rigour
- keeping up to date
- honesty
- integrity
- quality
- documentation
- code of practice
- code of conduct

Chapter 2

1.
- monitoring
- design/prediction
- planning
- interpretation

3. Five facts:

- The TV is fitted with a built-in aerial.
- The handset has a range of approximately seven metres.
- When the power is on the indicator will glow constantly during Operation and Standby modes.
- The aerial socket is on the back of the TV.
- Operation of the handset is possible up to an angle of 30°.

Five rules:

> **If** liquid is spilled into the TV **then**
> serious damage may result
>
> **If** you do spill liquid into the TV **then**
> disconnect the mains plug **or**
> remove the car battery **and**
> consult a specialist
>
> **If** the Power Indicator doesn't glow **then**
> check the fuse **and**
> check the wall socket
>
> **If** the batteries are low **then**
> the remote control may not work
>
> **If** you don't have a suitable TV aerial **then**
> seek advice

Table A.1 *Factors for and against prototyping*

FOR	AGAINST
user involvement	may be difficult to track versions
quick to see software	unstructured
more likely to get a system which matches user requirements	encourages users to ask for more!
early test of feasibility	may not match QA procedures

Table A.2 *Factors for and against structured methodologies*

FOR	AGAINST
structured	need to learn them
documented	may be unwieldy
well-understood	may not apply to all situations/ problem domains
tried and tested	take time to apply
may have tool support	necessity for documentation
visible for project management/ control purposes	
QA may be built in	

Chapter 3

1. See Tables A.1 and A.2 for lists of factors for and against prototyping and structured methodologies respectively.

Chapter 4

1. The transcript is quite detailed and would lead to a very complex flow-chart. However, it can basically be split into two factors:

- checking the product
- checking the machine

as shown in the flowchart in Figure A.1.

2. Ten sample rules:

   If there is a problem **then**
   examine the product and check the machine.
   If there is a problem **then**
   check the rimming machine itself to see that the water is flowing correctly **and**

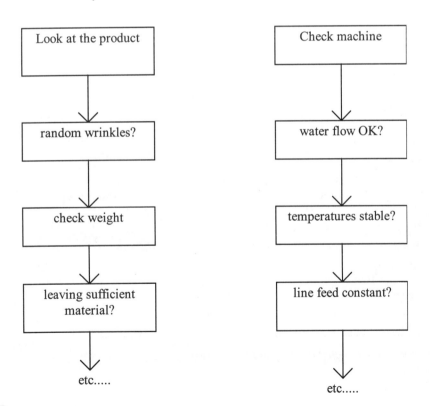

Figure A.1 *Segment of flowchart for hot wrinkle problem.*

that the temperatures look stable **and**
that the line itself is feeding cups in a constant stable manner.

If   there is nothing out of the ordinary about the rimming machine **then**
look at the cups themselves.

If   the problem is in random areas **then**
the next thing to do is to check the product weight.

If   the weight is not correct **then**
it probably means that you are not leaving sufficient material in the
cup to give you a decent curl.

If   there is a problem in the rim of the cup **then**
you have not got the correct thickness of material right round.

If   you find that you have random wrinkles across the set **then**
check the product weight.

If   you are over-heating **then**
decrease the temperature over-all.

If   you are over temperature **then**
increase contact.

If   you slow the water down **then**
it is chilled water entering the centre of these rollers **and**
it cascades both ways.

Chapter 5

A generic frame is shown in Figure A.2 and example day frames are shown
in Figures A.3 and A.4.

Chapter 6

DAY FRAME	
Day of week	From set [Mon, Tue, Wed, Thu, Fri, Sat, Sun]
Misery factor today	From set [rain, snow, sleet, frost, none]
Misery factor forecast tomorrow	From set [rain, snow, sleet, frost, none]
Wind today	From set [strong, light, none]
Wind forecast tomorrow	From set [strong, light, none]
Day type today	From set [Weekday, Sat, Sun, Bank_holiday]
Day type tomorrow	From set [Weekday, Sat, Sun, Bank_holiday]
Today's gas usage	Number
Tomorrow's gas usage estimate	Number

Figure A.2 *A generic day frame.*

Day of week	Tue
Misery factor today	none
Misery factor forecast tomorrow	rain
Wind today	none
Wind forecast tomorrow	none
Day type today	Weekday
Day type tomorrow	Weekday
Today's gas usage	X
Tomorrow's gas usage estimate	X + 5% + 10%

(Note the method for calculating gas usage in the final slot: X + 5% (day factor) + 10% (misery factor). This may also need to use information from previous frames; for example in the case of holidays)

Figure A.3 *Example 1*

DAY FRAME	
Day of week	Sun
Misery factor today	none
Misery factor forecast tomorrow	none
Wind today	none
Wind forecast tomorrow	strong
Day type today	Sun
Day type tomorrow	Bank_holiday
Today's gas usage	X
Tomorrow's gas usage estimate	Sat usage + 10% (for wind)

Figure A.4 *Example 2*

1. interview(X):-   type(X),
                     drive(X),
                     live(X,london).

2. live(john_smith,cambridge).
   drive(john_smith).
   live(charles_brown,london).
   drive(charles_brown).
   type(charles_brown).
   live(mary_jones,glasgow).

```
type(mary_jones).
live(sue_evans,london).
drive(sue_evans).
type(sue_evans).
live(alice_green,luton).
drive(alice_green).
type(alice_green).
```

3.  ```
    ?- interview(X).
    X = charles_brown? ;
    X = sue_evans? ;
    no
    ```
    ```

Glossary

AI workstation – a computer workstation designed specially for doing AI work (for example, a LISP machine).

Algorithm – a step-by-step procedure.

Artificial intelligence (AI) – a subfield of computing concerned with attempting to make computers model human intelligence.

Backward chaining – a search technique that begins with a possible goal and works 'backward' through a chain of rules in an attempt to satisfy that goal; a goal-driven procedure.

Blackboard architecture – an architecture that lets knowledge sources communicate through a central database called a blackboard.

Case-based reasoning (CBR) – reasoning based upon a set of previous case histories.

Certainty factor – a percentage supplied by a KBS to express the probability that a conclusion reached is correct.

Class – a term used in object-oriented programming for a group of objects which have the same characteristics.

Control strategy – a method for selecting the inference steps. For example, backward chaining is a control strategy.

Database – the organization of files into related units that are then viewed as a single unit. The data are then made available to a wide range of users.

Decision style – manner in which decision makers think and react to problems. This includes their perceptions and beliefs.

Declarative knowledge representation – representation of knowledge in the form of facts and assertions.

Deep knowledge – knowledge which includes understanding of the fundamental principles of a problem domain.

Default value – the value given to a symbol or variable automatically if no other value is defined.

Demon – a procedure that is automatically activated if a specific, predefined state is recognized.

Development environment – the environment for building a KBS.

Distributed AI – splitting of a problem to multiple systems for deriving a solution.

Domain – area of knowledge or expertise.

Domain expert – a person with expertise in the domain in which the KBS is being developed. The domain expert works closely with the knowledge engineer to capture the knowledge and place it in the knowledge base.

Elicitation of knowledge – the acquisition of knowledge from people. The term is frequently used interchangeably with knowledge acquisition.

Embedded systems – the inclusion of one system inside another one.

Encapsulation – the coupling of data and procedures in object-oriented programming.

Explanation facility – the component of a KBS that can explain the system's reasoning and justify its conclusions.

Expertise – a set of capabilities including extensive domain knowledge, heuristic rules and skilled problem solving.

Expert system – a computer system that applies knowledge in a specific domain in order to solve problems, give advice or recommendations, as would a human expert.

Firing a rule – obtaining information on either the IF or the THEN part of a rule, causing the rule to be executed.

Forward chaining – Data-driven search in a rule-based system. The converse to backward chaining.

Frame – Knowledge representation scheme that associates one or more features with an object in terms of slots.

Goal-directed (driven) search – Search that starts from the goal (or hypothesis); backward chaining.

GUI – graphical user interface.

Heuristics – informal, judgmental knowledge of an application area; rules of thumb.

Heuristic search – using heuristics to find a solution to a problem.

Hybrid environment – a software package that allows the construction of systems that include several knowledge-representation schemes.

Hybrid system – an integrated system. This may refer to integrating a KBS with a traditional information system.

Inference – the process of drawing a conclusion from given evidence; to reach a decision by reasoning.

Inference engine – that part of a KBS that performs the reasoning function; the driving force within a KBS.

Inheritance – the process by which one object takes on the characteristics of another object higher up in a hierarchy.

Instantiation – the process of assigning a specific value to a variable.

Interface – the portion of a computer system that interacts with the user. Also known as the user interface or HCI (human–computer interface).

Justifier – the explanation facility in a KBS.

Knowledge – understanding acquired through education and/or experience; anything that has been learned, discovered, inferred or understood; the ability to use information.

Knowledge acquisition – the extraction of knowledge from various sources, especially from experts.

Knowledge base – A collection of facts and rules; the assembly of all of the information and knowledge from a particular problem domain.

Knowledge-based system (KBS) – A computer system which encapsulates human knowledge.

Knowledge engineer – a specialist responsible for the development of a KBS. The knowledge engineer works closely with the domain expert(s) to capture the knowledge in the KBS.

Knowledge engineering – the engineering discipline whereby knowledge is integrated into a KBS.

Knowledge refining – the ability of a KBS to analyse its own performance, learn and improve itself for future consultations.

Knowledge representation – a formalism for representing knowledge in the computer.

Knowledge worker – an employee who uses knowledge as a significant input to his or her work.

LISP (LISt Processing) – an AI programming language, created by AI pioneer John McCarthy. Especially popular in the USA.

LISP machine (or 'AI workstation') – a computer designed primarily for developing KBS. Recently these machines have been extended to serve several users simultaneously.

Machine language – a language for writing instructions in a form to be executed directly by the computer. The language is usually in a binary format.

Machine learning – a computer that can learn from experience.

Multiple experts – a case in which two or more experts are used as the source of knowledge for a KBS.

Organizational culture (climate) – staff attitudes within an organization concerning a certain issue (such as technology, computers, etc.).

Pattern matching (*see* **Pattern recognition**) – matching the IF and THEN parts in a KBS.

Pattern recognition – the technique of matching an external pattern to one stored within a computer. This is used in inference engines, image processing, neural computing and speech recognition.

Procedural knowledge (in contrast to declarative knowledge) – knowledge about procedures for problem solving.

Procedural language – the language in which the programmer must define the procedures (steps) that the computer is to follow.

Production rules – a knowledge-representation method in which knowledge is formalized into 'rules' containing an IF part and a THEN part.

Prolog – a declarative programming language (PROgramming in LOGic).

Protocol analysis – a manual knowledge-acquisition technique.

Prototyping – an approach to software development in which a scaled-down version of a KBS is constructed in a short time, tested and improved in several iterations.

Rapid prototyping – the quick development of an initial version of a KBS, usually a system with 25–200 rules. This is used to test the effectiveness of the approach taken.

Ready-made KBS – a mass-produced package that may be purchased from a software company.

Real-time – when results are given rapidly enough to be useful in directly controlling a physical process or guiding a human user.

Rule – knowledge expressed as IF *premise* THEN *conclusion*.

Rule-based systems – a system in which knowledge is represented in terms of rules.

Rule induction – a process by which rules are created by a computer from examples of problems where the outcome is known.

Semantic network – a knowledge-representation method consisting of a network of nodes, representing concepts or objects, connected by arcs.

Semantics – meaning in language; the relationship between words and sentences.

Sequential processing – the traditional computer processing technique of performing actions one at a time in a sequence.

Shallow (surface) representation – a model that does not capture all of the forms of knowledge used by experts in their reasoning; contrasted with **Deep knowledge**.

Shell – A KBS stripped of its domain-specific knowledge. A kind of expert-system development tool.

Slot – a subelement of a frame of an object.

Uncertainty – a value that cannot be determined during a consultation. Many KBS can accommodate uncertainty; they allow the user to indicate if he or she does not know the answer.

User-friendly – where user interaction with a computer system is easy and comfortable.

User interface (or HCI) – *see* **Interface**.

Validation – has the right system been built?

Verification – was the system was build to specification?

VLSI (Very Large-Scale Integration) – the process of combining several hundred thousand electronic components into a single integrated circuit (chip).

What-if analysis – asking the computer what the effect will be of changing some of the input data.

Workplace (or blackboard) – *see* **Blackboard architecture**.

References

Aamodt, A. and Plaza, E. (1994) Case-based reasoning: foundational issues, methodological variations, and system approaches. *AI Communications*, **7**(1), 39–59.

Althoff, K.D. and Wess, S. (1992) *Case-Based Reasoning and Expert System Development*, Contemporary Knowledge Engineering and Cognition, First Joint Workshop Proceedings.

Awad, E. and Lindgren, J.H., Jr (1992) *Skills And Personality Attributes Of The Knowledge Engineer*, IAKE '92 Proceedings.

Bader, J., Edwards, J., Harris-Jones, C. and Hannaford, D. (1988) Practical engineering of knowledge-based systems. *Information And Software Technology*, **30**(5).

BCS (1992) *Code Of Conduct*, British Computer Society, PO Box 1454, Station Road, Swindon.

BCS (1990) *Intelligent Systems Engineering*, IEE/BCS Conference Publication No. 360.

Beynon-Davies, P. (1991) *Expert Database Systems: A Gentle Introduction*, McGraw-Hill, London.

Cavell, S. (1992) Survey of use of methods in the UK.

Chen, X., Kendal, S., Potts, I. and Smith, P. (1995) An integrated methodology for the development of hybrid information systems, in *Research and Development in Expert Systems XII*, Information Press Ltd, Oxford, England.

Cooke, N. and McDonald, J. (1986) *A Formal Methodology For Acquiring And Representing Expert Knowledge*, Proceedings Of The IEEE, 1422–30.

Davis, C.J., Gillies, A.C., Smith, P. and Thompson, J.B. (1993) Current practice in software quality and the impact of certification schemes. *Software Quality Journal*, **2**(1).

DTI (1989) *The use of KBS in Manufacturing*.

DTI (1990) *TickIT, Guide To Software Quality Management System Construction And Certification Using EN29001*.

DTI (1992) *KBS: Survey Of UK Applications*, Touche Ross And Co.

Edwards, H.M, Smith P *et al.* (1991) A prototyping approach to LIMS design, *Laboratory Information Management*, **13**(1).

Eva, M. (1992) *SSADM (Version 4) A User's Guide*, McGraw-Hill, London.

Feigenbaum, E.A. and McCorduck, P. (1984) *The Fifth Generation*, Pan.

Gillies, A. and Smith, P. (1994) *Managing Software Engineering*, Chapman & Hall, London.

Gillies, A.C., Smith, P. and Lansbury, M. (1994) The validation of KBS: current practice and agents for change. *Journal for the Integrated Study of Artificial Intelligence, Cognitive Science and Applied Epistemology*, **2**(1).

Gorney, D.J. and Coleman, K.G. (1991) Expert system development standards. *Expert Systems With Applications*, **2**(4).

Hardy, C. (1993) The development of a quality control expert system. MSc project, University of Sunderland.

Hickman, F.R. (1980) *The Pragmatic Application Of The KADS Methodology*, The Knowledge-Based Systems Centre Of Touche Ross Management Consultants UK.

Hoffman, R. (1986) Procedures for efficiently extracting the knowledge of experts. Final Report, Contract No. F49620-85-C-00013, Air Force Office Of Scientific Research, Bolling AFB, Washington, DC.

Huang, S.M., Smith, P., Tait, J.I. *et al.* (1994) The development of an expert database system by reusing existing databases. Proc. EXPERSYS 94.

Ince, D. and Hekmatpour, S. (1987) Software prototyping – progress and prospects. *Information and Software Technology*, **29**(1).

ISO (1991) ISO9000-3, British Standards Institute, UK.

Jawad, A. (1991) The development of an expert system for ventilator management. MPhil thesis, University of Humberside.

Jorgensen, A.H. (1984) *On the Psychology of Prototyping: Approaches to Prototyping*, Springer, New York.

Kawaguchi, A., Motoda, H. and Mizoguchi, R. (1991) Interview-based knowledge acquisition using dynamic analysis. *IEE Expert*, **6**(5).

Kelly, G.A. (1955) *The Psychology Of Personal Constructs*, Norton, New York.

Kingston, J (1991) Knowledge based systems in the UK financial sector, *AIAI*, University of Edinburgh.

Kolodner, J. (1993) *Case-Based Reasoning*, Morgan Kaufmann, New York, NY.

Kuo, J. (1995) Expert systems in the application of product processes by using case-based reasoning. MSc dissertation, University of Sunderland.

Lansbury, M. (1993) A survey of practices in knowledge engineering. MSc project report, University of Sunderland.

La Salle, A.J. and Medsker, L.R. (1991) Computerised conferencing for knowledge acquisition from multiple experts, *Expert Systems With Applications*, **3**(4).

Leonard, D. (1992) The development of a forecasting system for gas demand. MSc project, University of Sunderland.

Lighthill, J. (1972) *The Lighthill Report on Artificial Intelligence*, Science Research Council.

Lin, C. (1993) Development of an intelligent HRM system. MSc project, University of Sunderland.

Longworth, G. (1981) *NCC Standards in Programming*, The National Computing Centre, Manchester.

Luber, G.F. and Stubblefield, W.A. (1989) *Artificial Intelligence and the Design of Expert Systems*, Benjamin/Cummins, Redwood, CA.

Markakis, D. (1994) A comparison of knowledge representation techniques. Bsc project report, University of Sunderland.

Minsky, M. (1975) A framework for representing knowledge, in *The Psychology of Computer Vision*, (ed. P.H. Winston), McGraw-Hill, New York.

Montgomery, A. (1988) *Gemini – Government Expert Systems*. Proceedings of Expert Systems 1988, The Eighth Annual Technical Conference of the British Computer Society Specialists Group on Expert Systems, United Kingdom.

Myers, G.J. (1979) *The Art of Software Testing*, Wiley–Interscience, Chichester.

Naumann, J.D. and Jenkins, A.M. (1982) Prototyping: the new paradigm for systems development. *MIS Quarterly*, **6**(3).

Ng, S., Smith, P., Steward, A.P. and Roper, R.M.F. (1991) *Criteria for the Validation of Expert Systems*. Proceedings of The World Congress of Expert Systems, vol. 2.

O'Keefe, R.M. and Lee, S. (1990) An integrative model of expert systems verification and validation. *Expert Systems With Applications*, **1**(3), 231–6.

O'Neil, M. and Morris, A. (1989) Expert systems in the United Kingdom: an evaluation of development methodologies. *Expert Systems*, **6**(2).

Parsaye, K. and Chignell, M. (1988) *Expert Systems for Experts*, Wiley, New York, NY.

Porter, D. (1992) *Towards The CommonKads Method*, Touche Ross Management Consultants.

Preece, A.D. and Moseley, L. (1992) Empirical study of expert system development. *Knowledge-Based Systems*, **5**(2).

Ross, P. (1993) An investigation into knowledge engineering. BSc project report, University of Sunderland.

Schank, R.C. (1982) *Dynamic Memory, A Theory of Reminding and Learning in Computers and People*, Cambridge University Press, Cambridge.

Schreiber, G., Wielinga, B. and Brenker, J. (eds) (1993) KADS: A principled approach to knowledge based system development, in *Knowledge Based Systems*, vol. 11, Academic Press, London.

Smith, P. (1990) *Expert System Development In Prolog And Turbo-Prolog*, Sigma Press, Wilmslow.

Smith, P. and Rada, R. (1994) Future trends in expert systems in the UK, in *World-Wide Expert Systems Activities and Trends*, (ed. J. Liebowitz), Cognizant Communication Corporation.

Smith, P., Ross, P., Awad, E. *et al.* (1994) A survey of the skills and personality attributes of the knowledge engineer in the UK. *KnowledgeBase*, **8**(2).

Smith, R. (1990) *Collins Dictionary of Artificial Intelligence*, Collins.

Sommerville, I. (1992) *Software Engineering*, 4th edn, Addison-Wesley, Wokingham.

Suwa, M., Scott, A.C. and Shortliffe, E.H. (1982) An approach to verifying completeness and consistency in a rule-based expert system. *The Artificial Intelligence Magazine*, **3**(4).

Thompson, I. (1990) CCTA Announcement No.ll: Update on project GEMINI, CCTA.

Touche Ross (1992) *Knowledge Based Systems: Survey Of UK Applications*, Touche Ross Management Consultants For The Department Of Trade And Industry.

Tozer, A. (1987) Prototyping as a system development methodology: opportunities and pitfalls. *Information and Software Technology*, **29**(5).

VALID (1991) Esprit II 2148, *Validation Methods and Tools for Knowledge Based Systems*, Deliverable D10: The Valid Environment, Document reference: CRVD/4.3.

Vedder, R.G. (1989) PC-based expert system shells: some desirable and less desirable characteristics. *Expert Systems*, **6**(1).

Waterman, D.A. (1986) *A Guide To Expert Systems*, Addison-Wesley, Reading, MA.

Watson, I. and Marir, F. (1994) Case-based reasoning: a review. *The Knowledge Engineering Review*, **9**(4), 327–54.

Welbank, M. (1987) Perspectives on knowledge acquisition, in *Knowledge Acquisition for Engineering Applications*, (eds C.J. Pavelin and M.D. Wilson).

White, M. and Goldsmith, J. (1990) *Standards And Review Manual For Certification In Knowledge Engineering*, Systemsware Corps, Washington, DC.

Index